Distinguishing the Church

# Distinguishing the Church

*Explorations in Word, Sacrament, and Discipline*

Greg Peters
AND
Matt Jenson,
EDITORS

⁌PICKWICK *Publications* · Eugene, Oregon

DISTINGUISHING THE CHURCH
Explorations in Word, Sacrament, and Discipline

Copyright © 2019 Wipf and Stock Publishers. All rights reserved. Except for brief quotations in critical publications or reviews, no part of this book may be reproduced in any manner without prior written permission from the publisher. Write: Permissions, Wipf and Stock Publishers, 199 W. 8th Ave., Suite 3, Eugene, OR 97401.

Pickwick Publications
An Imprint of Wipf and Stock Publishers
199 W. 8th Ave., Suite 3
Eugene, OR 97401

www.wipfandstock.com

PAPERBACK ISBN: 978-1-5326-5483-1
HARDCOVER ISBN: 978-1-5326-5484-8
EBOOK ISBN: 978-1-5326-5485-5

*Cataloguing-in-Publication data:*

Names: Peters, Greg, editor. | Jenson, Matt, editor.

Title: Distinguishing the church : explorations in word, sacrament and discipline / edited by Greg Peters and Matt Jenson.

Description: Eugene, OR: Pickwick Publications, 2019. | Includes bibliographical references and indexes.

Identifiers: ISBN 978-1-5326-5483-1 (paperback). | ISBN 978-1-5326-5484-8 (hardcover). | ISBN 978-1-5326-5485-5 (ebook).

Subjects: LCSH: Church. | Evangelicalism. | Ecclesiology. | Preaching.

Classification: BR1640 D37 2019 (print). | BR1640 (ebook).

Edward W. Klink III's "Preaching and the Interpretation of Scripture: A Call for Ecclesial Exegesis" is taken from *Becoming a Pastor Theologian*, edited by Todd Wilson and Gerald L. Hiestand. Copyright (c) 2016 by Todd Wilson and Gerald Hiestand. Used by permission of InterVarsity Press, P.O. Box 1400, Downers Grove, IL 60515, USA. www.ivpress.com.

Duane Litfin's "Proclamation: A Pauline Model for Ministry" is adapted from *Paul's Theology of Preaching* by Duane Litfin. Copyright (c) 2015 by Duane Litfin. Used by permission of InterVarsity Press, P.O. Box 1400, Downers Grove, IL 60515, USA. www.ivpress.com.

J. Stephen Yuille's "A Simple Method: William Perkins and the Shaping of the Protestant Pulpit" was first published in *Puritan Reformed Journal* 9/1 (2017) 215–30. Used with permission.

Unless otherwise noted, Scripture quotations are from the ESV® Bible (The Holy Bible, English Standard Version®), copyright © 2001 by Crossway, a publishing ministry of Good News Publishers. Used by permission. All rights reserved.

Manufactured in the U.S.A. 06/26/19

*We dedicate this book to our church families at Anglican Church of the Epiphany, La Mirada, and Fountain of Life Covenant Church, Long Beach. We are thankful to these communities for not only allowing us to live out our pastoral and theological vocations but for nurturing these vocations along the way.*

# Contents

*Acknowledgments* | ix
*List of Contributors* | xi
*Introduction* | xiii

## Part 1: Preaching

1  Preaching and the Interpretation of Scripture:
   A Call for an Ecclesial Exegesis | EDWARD W. KLINK III | 3

2  Proclamation: A Pauline Model for Ministry | DUANE LITFIN | 16

3  A Simple Method: William Perkins and the Shaping of
   the Protestant Pulpit | J. STEPHEN YUILLE | 35

## Part 2: Sacraments

4  Union, Communion, and *Communio*: Elements of
   Reformed Ecclesiology | J. V. FESKO | 53

5  Visible Signs of Invisible Grace: Sacraments for the "Low Church" |
   KEITH D. STANGLIN | 69

## Part 3: Discipline

6  Persecution, Discipline, and Rewards in Ecclesiological Perspective |
   GREG COCHRAN | 95

7  Suffering in the Struggle with Sin and the Role of Church Discipline |
   JEREMY M. KIMBLE | 109

8 Suffering and Discipline in the Overlap of the Ages | GUY WATERS | 125

9 Redemptive Church Discipline and the Lord's Supper: Lessons from Herman Bavinck | JUSTIN L. MCLENDON | 138

*Bibliography* | 155

*Name Index* | 167

*Subject Index* | 169

*Scripture Index* | 171

# Acknowledgments

Having edited *Marking the Church: Essays in Ecclesiology* (Pickwick Publications, 2016) together a few years ago, we knew that editing another book together would prove to be just as enjoyable as the first and perhaps even easier. It was easier but that does not mean that we were any less dependent on others for assistance and encouragement. We remain thankful to the leadership of the Evangelical Theological Society for sponsoring the Ecclesiology Consultation/Study Group for a decade now, and to those who have given, listened to, and discussed papers at our annual meeting. Thank you to the members of the Ecclesiology Consultation/Study Group Steering Committee for their time, energy and talents. We also remain deeply grateful to the Torrey Honors Institute and Biola University, where we are surrounded, supported, and encouraged by a wonderful community of scholar-friends. Financial assistance for the publication of this book was provided by the Ressourcement Institute.

# Contributors

**Greg Cochran** is Professor and Director of Applied Theology at California Baptist University.

**J. V. Fesko** is Academic Dean and Professor of Systematic Theology and Historical Theology at Westminster Seminary California.

**Jeremy M. Kimble** is Assistant Professor of Theology at Cedarville University.

**Edward W. Klink III** is Senior Pastor at Hope Evangelical Free Church in Roscoe, Illinois.

**Duane Litfin** is President Emeritus at Wheaton College.

**Justin L. McLendon** is Instructor at Grand Canyon University

**Keith D. Stanglin** is Professor of Scripture and Historical Theology at Austin Graduate School of Theology.

**Guy Waters** is James M. Baird Jr. Professor of New Testament at Reformed Theological Seminary.

**J. Stephen Yuille** is Vice President of Academics at Heritage College and Seminary and Associate Professor of Biblical Spirituality at The Southern Baptist Theological Seminary.

# Introduction

ONE OF THE GIFTS evangelicals offer to the larger church is our relative lack of interest in the church. Let us explain: for much of our history, evangelicals have been so interested in the Bible, in Jesus, in the conversion of the lost that we have had little time for the more nuanced points of the nature and function of an institution like the church. We are happy to partner in worship and ministry with all those who love the Lord who seeks to save the lost. We are ready to call "sister" and "brother" any who share our love of Jesus. And so we are baffled at closed communions and scratch our heads over the seemingly needless worrying about procedural things, when much more pressing concerns lie all around. We are content to acknowledge the unity of all those who trust in Jesus in the invisible church.

Still, for all our theoretical disinterest in ecclesial matters, we recognize the need to discern the body, to be able to distinguish between the true and false church, the apostolic and the apostate. If, on the one hand, we are surprisingly ready to make common cause across denominational lines, we will balk quickly at the idea of softening or sidelining our central commitment to the grace of our Lord Jesus Christ as the one hope of the world. And so, even we evangelicals find ourselves in the position of needing to inquire into the nature and function of the church, thereby discerning those with whom we might labor in the Lord's vineyard.

Discernment is a tricky thing. "The wise of heart is called discerning," but Scripture is littered with foolish hearts who discern little (Prov 16:21). False prophets abound; true prophets are hard to come by. Ours is a culture of vitriol, of aspersions cast, yet strangely also one in which to be "judgmental" is to commit the unpardonable sin. One might be excused in such a culture for avoiding all appearances of judgment. But discern we must—that is, we must look closely at the churches around us, or at the very least at our own local church, and do our best to determine whether it is a true and faithful church.

The Reformers faced a similar challenge. Still reeling from the disfiguring demands of Rome, the last thing they wanted to do was set up a series of hurdles as they went about re-founding the church on the gospel. But they knew criteria for discernment were necessary. The most common such criteria come in Calvin's claim that the church "becomes visible to our eyes" wherever "we see the Word of God purely preached and heard, and the sacraments administered according to Christ's institution" (*Inst.* 4.1.9). Calvin knew that God knew his elect sons and daughters from all eternity, but Calvin also knew that *we* need to know, or at least have a good guess at, where those people are to be found—not least because Christ has promised to meet us "where two or three are gathered" in his name (Matt 18:20).

Of course, the devil's always in the details. Calvin called for more than a church of Word and sacrament. He wanted a church where God's Word was "purely preached and heard"—where the preaching was undiluted with the vain philosophies of the world, where the congregation listened and learned—and one where the sacraments were duly administered, that is, administered "according to Christ's institution," which immediately suggested to the Reformers that there were only *two* sacraments, and which launched a thousand exegetical arguments (pure preaching is not as simple as it sounds at times) about the nature of that institution.

It has not always been easy to distinguish the true church from its counterfeits. False prophets wear sheepskin; so do false churches (Matt 7:15). Perhaps this is why Luther could speak of suffering as a telltale sign of God's people and many Anabaptist and Reformed Christians include discipline among the distinguishing marks of the church. Both of these sharpen the distinction between church and world. To be among God's people is to endure persecution; it is to put oneself under the Word in such a way as to expose oneself to the possibility of discipline, being barred from the Lord's table and, eventually, excommunication. These thorny features of the church take on particular poignancy these days, as the global church continues to live in unparalleled persecution and the American church suffers from a festering open wound brought on by sins of sex and power and exponentially exacerbated by a failure of discipline. (Sin is no respecter of denominations here; we could cite megachurch pastor Bill Hybels or former-Cardinal Theodore McCarrick, who themselves are only singular examples of a much deeper wound.)

## INTRODUCTION

The essays in this volume were originally delivered at the annual meeting of the Evangelical Theological Society in the Ecclesiology Consultation from 2015–2017. The consultation itself was founded with the purpose of having more intentional discussions about ecclesiology at the largest annual gathering of evangelical theologians. Following four years dedicated to the Nicene marks of the church (unity, holiness, catholicity, and apostolicity), since collected in *Marking the Church* (Pickwick Publications, 2016), we spent three years considering the traditional Reformational marks (Word, sacrament, suffering, and discipline). The steering committee for the consultation then invited scholars to speak on these topics, giving the speakers as much latitude as possible in the content of their talks—hence the diversity represented in this volume. The essays do not present one particular methodology or approach to the marks of the church. The various approaches to the marks are, we believe, the strength of this volume; for just as the church is diverse in its form and expression, so too are these essays.

# Part 1

# Preaching

# 1

# Preaching and the Interpretation of Scripture
*A Call for Ecclesial Exegesis*

—Edward W. Klink III

## Introduction

Preaching the Word of God is one of the primary tasks of the pastor, and Scripture exhorts the pastor to handle correctly the word of truth (2 Tim 2:15). So what does it look like to handle correctly the Word? That is, what does the exegesis of the preacher look like? This question runs against the division of labor that exists between the approach to exegesis done in the academy (e.g., the university and seminary) and the approach to exegesis done in and for the church. In this chapter I would like to suggest that the preaching required of the pastoral office demands a different kind of exegesis. My concern is that for too long preaching has been directed and defined by the rules and social location of the academy and not the church. This, I believe, needs to be corrected; but first, it needs to be explained.

For example, one of the primary resources pastors use when preparing a sermon is the commentary. It is, for all intents and purposes, the guide or tutor for pastors as they perform the interpretation of Scripture. It is standard for the modern commentary to include an introduction to the text to be commented upon, almost always in relation to its historical context. The author, origin, and purpose of the document are usually explored and defended with the assumption that such data is significant for the interpretation to follow. It is unquestionable that this historical information about the text is vital to understanding correctly its meaning and application, yet it is rare for commentators to defend or even explain this implicit methodological foundation. This is unfortunate for two primary reasons.

First, it minimizes the hermeneutical issues involved in any kind of interpretation. Presumably modern commentaries take for granted that the commentary genre is an overtly historical task, and therefore feel no need to explain their method and its philosophical/theological underpinnings to the reader. But this is hardly the case. Not only does the text carry its own interpretive commands innate to its origin and nature, but the act of interpretation forces the interpreter to make a plethora of methodological assumptions regarding the text in view.

The second reason is even more important: it minimizes that the text in view is in fact part of the Christian Scriptures. The very reason why there is so much interest in this particular text is treated as unimportant to the task at hand. By definition, this text raises the interpretive stakes: its author is not merely historical but also divine, and its audience is not merely confined to the ancient world but still exists and receives this text in the modern world. Without denying that this text has an origin and purpose in a time long past, as Scripture it must also be understood to have a divine origin and eternal purpose that demands its reception in every generation—even those still to come.

The exegesis required for the task of preaching demands a particular definition of the nature of the Bible and, therefore, makes particular demands regarding the rules of its interpretation. Said another way, before we can explain what the Bible *does* we must first explain what the Bible *is*. This means that exegesis must be appropriately aligned with the object of study. And since the preacher sits under the authority of the Bible, its identity, nature, and context give direction to how it is interpreted and to its subject matter. For the pastoral theologian, the object of study is not completely defined by the categories of ancient text, literary genre, or historical document, for this particular kind of text demands to be defined according to its divine identity as Christian Scripture. Such definitions and practices can simply be described as an *ecclesial exegesis*—the manner in which the preacher correctly handles the word of truth (2 Tim 2:15).

## A Doctrine of Scripture for Exegesis

To define any part of the Bible as Christian Scripture is to place it in a much larger communicative context than simply the historical context in which it took on its literary "flesh."[1] By categorizing the Bible as Scripture we are

---

1. The following is adapted from the introduction in Klink, *John*, 4.

depicting it in light of its "origin, function, and end in divine self-communication"; yet we are also depicting the manner in which it must be read and the kinds of responses appropriate to its nature: "'Scripture' is a shorthand term for the nature and function of the biblical writings in a set of communicative acts which stretch from God's merciful self-manifestation to the obedient hearing of the community of faith."[2] While such language might not be common vernacular in an introduction in the world of biblical studies and commentaries, it should be, for the object of interpretation demands to be treated according to its true and sacred nature. Not to treat the Bible as Scripture is itself a form of eisegesis, and it is a disobedient hearing of the (canonical) text's own claim and the God by whom it was authored.

The doctrine of Scripture is necessary for the exegetical task in two ways. First, it gives *insight* to the interpretive rules demanded by the object of interpretation. In a sense, Scripture becomes its own kind of genre: "If genre is a function of communal reception and usage as well as of inherent characteristics, then the genre of the biblical texts is that of 'holy Scripture.'"[3] Functionally, then, the doctrine of Scripture explains the (theological) genre of the Bible and the generic conventions to be followed by the faithful reader.

Second, the doctrine of Scripture gives *oversight* to Scripture's constituent parts and unifies their functions. Three are immediately apparent: (1) since the Bible speaks in time and space history, a doctrinal framework is needed to make sure history remains subservient to the God of creation; (2) since the Bible speaks in literary form, a doctrinal framework is needed to make sure words stay subservient to the Word; and (3) since the Bible speaks about the things of God, a doctrinal framework is needed to make sure theology is defined by the person and work of God himself, the true subject matter of the things of God. In short, *the doctrine of Scripture gives oversight to the historical, literary, and theological components of the revelation of God, which we will refer to as "creation," "canon," and "creed" in order to match their doctrinal nature.* A brief explanation of each is in order.

---

2. Webster, *Holy Scripture*, 5.
3. Watson, *Text, Church and World*, 227.

PART 1: PREACHING

## Creation

The doctrine of Scripture provides the necessary requirements for understanding the historical content and context of the Bible. If we make interpretive judgments regarding the meaning of the Bible by comparing it to the historical (and social-cultural) setting in which it originated and occurred without the oversight or mediation of the doctrine of Scripture, we conflate the meaning of the text to its historical context. The Bible is not to be read as any other book. If we suppose texts are wholly limited and confined by their immediate circumstances of origin and that as soon as they stray from their appointed time and place they will be misread and misunderstood, we embrace a historical perception of this body of writings that is theologically foreign to them. This is not to say that Scripture is unhistorical or less historical—not at all! It is to say, rather, that it is more; that it speaks from a more comprehensive position.

The work of J. Todd Billings is helpful here. He explains that every interpreter implicitly answers two questions when they interpret the Bible: (1) Is revelation grounded in inherent, universal human capacities or in the particularity of God's action with Israel and in Jesus Christ? and (2) Is Scripture received from within a deistic hermeneutic or within a Trinitarian hermeneutic?[4] In both cases a doctrinally-defined reading of Scripture necessitates the latter option, for an interpretation that is naturalistic and/or deistic is poorly matched to the divine character of Scripture. The interpreter is given dogmatic reasons to believe that God was involved in the entire, messy process, from the historical event to the textual expression of the text of Scripture (composition, transmission, and reception). This requires a highly theological account of "history," not only as a tool of interpretation but also as a philosophical construct.

Murray A. Rae has provided a sophisticated account of a theology of history. He argues that in relation to biblical interpretation "the very idea of history requires both the biblical doctrine of creation, and a teleology, an account that is, of the directedness of history towards some goal."[5] Rae argues that theology had been excluded from the consideration of biblical texts, which ironically is itself a dogmatic presupposition.[6] The key for Rae is the logical priority of Scripture: "We simply cannot proceed to investigate

---

4. Billings, *The Word of God for the People of God*, 71–104.
5. Rae, *History and Hermeneutics*, 2.
6. Ibid., 19–20.

the Bible's witness to revelation by assuming that we know apart from revelation what history is. The order of knowing must be reversed."[7] Since all history doctrinally finds its purpose (*telos*) in the person and work of God, history only has meaning in the purposes of God. This is why the doctrine of creation is so important (and must be related) to the doctrine of Scripture. Creation implies that the world is invested with a *telos*: "There is a reason for its being, and history, in consequence, is to be understood as the space and time opened up for the world to become what it is intended to be."[8] History becomes God's own mission, under his creative, providential, and redemptive purposes, to extend himself to the world. The referentiality and meaning of Scripture, therefore, is given definition not only by its placement in the originating (historical) context, but also in the fuller context of God's communicative grace.

A doctrine of Scripture allows the biblical text, with all of its historical necessity and detail, not to bow the knee to the claims of historical naturalism. According to John Webster, "For a Christian theological account of Scripture . . . the problem . . . is not the affirmation that the biblical texts have a 'natural history,' but the denial that texts with a 'natural history' may function within the communicative divine economy, and that such a function is ontologically definitive of the text. It is this denial—rather than any purely methodological questions—which has to form the focus of dogmatic critique."[9]

The history in the Bible, therefore, cannot be understood by rational inquiry without recourse to revelation; nor can its purpose and meaning be reduced to a set of laws or by comparison to apparent analogous entities; to do so would be naturalistic and deistic. Rather, history, once understood to be framed by the Alpha and Omega (Rev 22:13), becomes a subset of creation—and therefore the Creator—and is embedded with promise and purpose that is revealed in the person and work of Jesus Christ, who is both its ground and goal.[10]

---

7. Rae, *History and Hermeneutics*, 29. Webster, *Holy Scripture*, 6, makes the identical claim: "This order is critically important because, unless their strict subservience to communicative divine activity is stated with some firmness, both text and practices of reading and reception may break loose and become matters for independent or quasi-independent investigation and explanation."

8. Rae, *History and Hermeneutics*, 51.

9. Webster, *Holy Scripture*, 19.

10. Compare Augustine, *Teaching Christianity*, 152.

## Canon

The doctrine of Scripture not only gives definition to the material nature behind the text, but also to the literary nature of the text itself. By "canon" I am referring to more than the collection of biblical books;[11] I am referring here primarily to Scripture's function and identity, both of which have implications for interpreting textual units and books in the Bible. First, according to its *function as canon*, a biblical book cannot be treated as if it were a single unit. Without denying that a biblical book took on literary "flesh" in the context of a particular historical author and audience, as the Word of God it was always intended (doctrinally) to be read as part of a collection. Though an argument could be made that a biblical book was originally created (historically) with this intention from its inception,[12] our argument is more dogmatic than historical. Since a biblical book makes up one of many parts of God's intentional communicative Word, then a book must be viewed as functioning cooperatively. This in no way denies that the book had value and meaning in its particular historical context, only that its meaning is so tied to its larger, canonical context that the latter extends and even explains the former. In the providence of God a biblical book's historical and canonical contexts function symphonically to communicate the intended fullness of the Word of God.

Second, according to its *identity as canon*, a biblical book cannot be treated as if it were a point of access to the Word of God but the very source of the Word of God. That is, the Bible is not a window to that which is inspired but is itself the inspiration. When we speak of Scripture we are speaking about the source of revelation and claiming (dogmatically) that Scripture is the locus of revelation, not merely a mediator of revelation. This issue is easily confusing and needs to be attended to carefully. This is not to deny in any way that the text is referring to real, historical people, places, and events, but to claim that the revelation, inclusive of real events, is located in the inscripturated account: God is giving divine commentary on his own actions in history. This text, as a divinely-inspired communicative act, is God's revelation *per se* (in or by itself).

The Bible cannot be read as just any other book. Its form, function, and canonical identity are not ancillary to its interpretation and meaning;

---

11. See Webster, *Word and Church*, 11–17.

12. See Smith, "When Did the Gospels Become Scripture?"; compare Klink, *The Sheep of the Fold*, 252–54.

they are determinative. Even the reality to which it points cannot be defined without recourse to revelation; nor can its meaning be determined outside of its canonical context. Rather, a biblical book, for example, once understood to be framed by the rest of Scripture, becomes a subset of the biblical canon and embedded with the full significance of the Word of God. Canon is not ultimately a historical account of the biblical collection, but "a trinitarian and soteriological account of revelation . . . in which God establishes saving fellowship with humanity and so makes himself known to us."[13] In this way, then, the Bible is addressing not merely the past but the present, and not merely an ancient audience but the contemporary church.

## Creed

The doctrine of Scripture not only gives definition to what lies behind the text (creation) and to the text itself (canon), but it also guides the reader to the goal of the text, or its true subject matter. In light of God's use of creation in Scripture and the canon of Scripture, the Bible can be described as "Jesus Christ's own self-utterance."[14] Since Scripture is God's communicative act, then its message and subject matter is about him—his person and his work.

One of the consequences of the historical-critical approach to the Bible is the loss of connection between the doctrines of the church and the text of Scripture, primarily because Scripture is expected, according to scholarly rules of interpretation, to be grounded historically in its ancient context. This excludes, by methodological necessity, eternal theological truths. The text's "literal sense" refers to subjects driven by and derived from the context of the book's origin, not "figuration or typology [which] was a natural extension of literal interpretation" in earlier eras of biblical interpretation.[15] The doctrines of the creeds, according to this approach, are entirely imposed upon the text of Scripture.

Against this understanding, David S. Yeago explains that Scripture speaks not merely with concepts (the use of explicit words/terms) but also judgments. These judgments can use a variety of concepts but in a manner that speaks beyond them, making a further, implicit referential claim.[16] A

---

13. Webster, *Word and Church*, 27.
14. Ibid., 35.
15. Frei, *The Eclipse of Biblical Narrative*, 2.
16. Yeago, "The New Testament and the Nicene Dogma."

text *uses* concepts but *makes* judgments so that the "only way to uncover the judgments made in a text is to pay close attention to what is said and implied, to the specific, contingent ways in which its conceptual resources are deployed."[17] In this way, then, the text may make judgments beyond its use of concepts so that it may (and does!) speak to subject matters not contained by any one concept. Ecclesial exegesis, for example, interprets the Gospel of John's depiction of the relation between the Father and the Son as reflective of the Trinitarian identity of God, even if the concept (Trinity) is not used. If God is Trinitarian in nature, then depictions of him, even if partial, are also reflective of the Trinity. In a sense, *without denying the logical priority and authority of Scripture, the subject matter of Scripture functions in a circular manner, not only as the result of a reading of Scripture but also as a guide for further readings.*[18]

The subject matter of Scripture has been deemed by the church to be clear, and the church has summarized this in the doctrine called the perspicuity of Scripture. However, it is not clear because the meaning of the text and its subject matter are obvious. Rather, it is because of the (doctrinal) conviction "that Scripture has the capacity to address and transform the human being, and to offer a reliable guide to human action."[19] Webster defines it well: "Scripture's clarity is neither an intrinsic element of the text as text nor simply a fruit of exegetical labour; it is that which the text becomes as it functions in the Spirit-governed encounter between the self-presenting saviour and the faithful reader. To read is to be caught up by the truth-bestowing Spirit of God."[20] The doctrine of Scripture guides the reader to look rightly at the text, that is, to look for the self-presentation of God through the work and person of Jesus Christ by the empowering Holy Spirit.

## Postures and Principles of Ecclesial Exegesis

So what does an ecclesial exegesis look like? Although there are presuppositions and stances that one must adopt from the start, a robust doctrine of Scripture is expressed methodologically not by a rigidly defined procedure, but by a posture that is sensitive to the text's own movements, pressures,

---

17. Ibid., 162.
18. Helpful on this point is Trueman, *The Creedal Imperative*.
19. Yocum, "Scripture, Clarity of," 727.
20. Webster, *Holy Scripture*, 95.

and expectations (both explicit and implicit) that are demanded by an obedient, believing reader. It is an art as much as it is a science.

This posture is especially important when interpreting biblical history. In general, ecclesial exegesis will begin with certain presuppositions that hold tightly to the necessity and meaning-deriving use of history while at the same time limiting the tenets of historical science by the doctrine of Scripture. But this does not provide a step-by-step procedure, for it is directed equally by both the text's historical concepts and context and the text's judgments and theological subject matter. In fact, the art of this kind of interpretation is the ability to allow both the text and its direction for meaning to be cooperatively active and interrelated in the exegetical process. As much as it is an art, it is only because it is a creative balance of two sciences. If there is a foundation, it is God, since by definition Scripture is his spoken word. Yet this does not distance history but embraces it, since God is the Creator of his creation. And because there is a God, there is a goal (*telos*) of interpretation: the communicative intention of God, in historical event and written expression.

Ecclesial exegesis might be described as the application to the text of what Webster calls "biblical reasoning," where the text is read and applied by both exegetical and dogmatic reasoning.[21] In this approach the words of the historical authors "are not wholly identical with the divine Word, but they are the subject of a special mission, they are 'sent from God.'" They are an embassy of God in which "Scripture is the textual settlement," extending the prophetic and apostolic speech into the church's present.[22] Ecclesial exegesis, therefore, is an intellectual engagement with the living and gracious communication and self-presentation of God. It is no less than participation in the depths of the life of God by means of his Word to the world.

The posture of ecclesial exegesis might be summarized in ten principles:

## General Interpretive Presuppositions:

- It begins with the presupposition that the Bible is living, trustworthy, and authoritative.
- It begins and ends with God—his history, his words, his ordering, intentional communication (Spirit-led, Christ-centered, God-glorifying).

21. Webster, "Biblical Reasoning."
22. Ibid., 740.

- Its subject matter is Jesus Christ/the gospel, and its purpose is for the love of God and neighbor (cf. Augustine).
- It assumes that the most fitting context for interpreting and hearing the Bible is the church and not the academy, since its message is both content and confession.
- It is willing to submit to the Bible's message: its truths and its commands.

*Principles for Interpreting Historical Narrative:*
- It is an integration of the historical and doctrinal *context*.
- It is an integration of the historical and doctrinal *content*.
- It is an interpretation of the text and not the event.
- It assumes that the details in the text, even the seeming contradictions, are purposeful and intentional in what they intend to communication.
- It assumes the text is making canonical connections and not merely historical-author connections.

## The Practice of Ecclesial Exegesis: John 3:22 and 4:2

Here is an example of how ecclesial exegesis plays out with a particular passage. In John 3:22–26 a dispute between the disciples of John (the Baptist) and an unidentified Jew connected itself to the nearby and seemingly parallel ministry of Jesus. The disciples of John (and maybe the unidentified Jew as well) come to him with concerns over Jesus' seemingly parallel ministry that is becoming more successful. The point of tension between John and Jesus is fueled by a statement in 3:22, where the narrator informs the reader that Jesus was performing baptisms.

This almost add-on statement has raised more than a few questions—most notably: *why* was Jesus baptizing and *what* did this baptism signify? Even more, just over a dozen verses later, in 4:2, the narrator explains that Jesus was not baptizing, but only his disciples were. Then why did 3:22 announce so unequivocally that Jesus was baptizing, with the third-person singular verb explicitly connecting the act of baptism to Jesus? That is, why is he named as the author of baptism (according to 3:22) although he did not physically perform the baptism (according to 4:2)? Edwyn Hoskyns explains it best: "The dilemma of modern exegesis of the Fourth Gospel is perhaps nowhere more clearly illustrated than in the divergent and opposite handling of this passage."[23]

If these two verses are used to construct an event behind the text, then 4:2 can be used to explain away any confusion or uncertainty regarding 3:22, functionally eclipsing its narrative intention. But interpreted as a text, with both verses assumed to be serving an intended and cooperative purpose, the intention of 3:22 cannot be so easily dismissed (principle 8). In fact, the dissonance created between 3:22 and 4:2 might be exactly the point, directing the reader to see a truth that extends beyond the historical action of an event to a textually-mediated theological reality regarding the actions of God (principle 9).

One thing 3:22 clearly does is make a direct connection between Jesus and the baptisms being performed. This necessary connection between baptism and Jesus gives significant direction to the reader. Regarding the larger scene, it is correct to see a similarity between the baptism of John and the kind of baptism Jesus is performing through his disciples. But in another sense, as the following verses will make clear, there is also an important difference. In fact, it might be best not to describe Jesus' baptism as being patterned by John's, even if the historical occurrence appeared as such. For John's baptism was never his own; it was always intended to be (or to become) the baptism of Jesus. And John's baptism was never cleansing in and of itself; it is no coincidence that John is never even called "the Baptist" in the Fourth Gospel, for he cannot be the true Baptist (see John 1:33). As Martin Luther explains, "For now Christ wants to take Baptism over from John, since John had been merely a servant discharging his duties of this office until now."[24]

This verse, therefore, is providing a thematic introduction to the impending scene. While supporters of John (the Baptist) might see a distinction, even competition, between the two baptisms (John's and Jesus'), there has always and only been one baptism. It is a baptism from above, involving the Spirit, and performed by Jesus, the true Baptist. In the words of Augustine: "Take away the water, it is no baptism; take away the Word, it is no baptism."[25]

---

23. Hoskyns, *The Fourth Gospel*, 226.
24. Luther, *Sermons on the Gospel of St. John*, 414.
25. Augustine, "Homilies on the Gospel of John," 100.

For this reason it is best to view the comment in 4:2 not as an attempt to separate Jesus from the act of baptism but as an attempt to show that the similarity between those who are doing the baptizing, John the Baptist and the disciples of Jesus, is founded upon Jesus, who is authorizing true baptism on both accounts.[26] This is why "he was baptizing" had to be third-person singular, for the same reason that baptism in the Church is always done in the name of Jesus (Acts 10:48; compare Matt 28:19). It becomes imperative, then, that one not understand the statement "Jesus was baptizing" to be subsumed under the already existing baptism of John, as is common when viewing the events from within linear history. While it is true in one sense that John's baptism came first, in another and more important sense Jesus/God was already well at work before John—from "the beginning" (1:1). And since John's own beginning has already been rooted in the work of God (see 1:6), it would be entirely inaccurate to view even the smallest part of John's ministry as conflicting with and not serving under the ministry of God through Jesus Christ.

In the end, the dissonance created between 3:22 and 4:2 pressures the reader to see the innate connection between Jesus and the sacrament of baptism. All baptisms originate and are empowered by the work and person of Jesus Christ. This doctrinal truth is expressed by the Fourth Gospel not in propositions, but by the dissonance created by two seemingly contrasting texts in a historical narrative (principles 6 and 7). While historical-critical exegesis is designed to resolve the conflict, an ecclesial exegesis assumes that the details in the text, even the seeming contradictions, are purposeful and intentional in what they intend to communication (principle 9). A further assumption is that this scene, with all of its historical issues and details, is part of a greater divine communication that matches the rest of Scripture's depiction of the doctrine of baptism (principle 10). Interestingly, John Calvin (against the Anabaptists) and Augustine (against the Donatists) used this text to refute those who denied the validity of a baptism because of a perceived problem with the baptizer.[27] Jesus is, and has always been, the source and substance of Christian baptism.

---

26. Aquinas, *Commentary on the Gospel of John*, 1:207–8.

27. Compare Calvin, *Gospel according to St. John 1–10*, 88: "He calls Christ's Baptism that which He administered by others, to teach us that Baptism is not to be valued from the person of the minister, but that its whole force depends on its author, in whose name and by whose command it is administered."

## Conclusion: A Call for Ecclesial Exegesis

For over two centuries the academy has made radical claims regarding the interpretation of the church's book, with professors—not pastors—serving as the interpretive magistrates, defining what the object of interpretation is and, therefore, what interpretation does. The pastoral office requires a different kind of exegesis, just as Scripture is a different kind of text. The exegesis required for the church's preaching must include not only all the categories at home in the social location of the academy, but also the categories belonging to the social location of the church. This "ecclesial exegesis," for lack of a better title, is not less than academic but more than that, for it is concerned with an ancient text that is also the living, authoritative Word of God. The office of the pastor offers its own direction and definition to the nature of the Bible and the rules by which it is interpreted for the preaching of the Word of God.

# 2

# Proclamation

*A Pauline Model for Ministry*

—Duane Litfin

To set the context for this discussion, let us begin by outlining two contrasting models for ministry—models not just for a preaching ministry but for Christian ministry in general. The first is what I will call the *natural model*. Countless individuals, including those in ministry, function unreflectively within this framework every day. This widespread use in turn reinforces this model's dominant status.

According to this model, we begin by determining what we wish to accomplish. What results are we after? Then we strategize so as to accomplish these results. We ask ourselves, what means should we employ to achieve these goals? Manipulative, unethical or dishonest means are obviously out of bounds, but within appropriate ethical boundaries, what must we do if we expect to achieve our aims? This is the question that guides our ministry planning. We build our strategies so as to achieve the goals we have set.

The utility of this approach is easily apparent. We decide what we are after and then orient our plans accordingly. What could be more obvious? The advantages of this pattern are so evident that it is difficult even to conceive an alternative—which is why we operate within its framework every day. Every businessman decides what he wants to accomplish and then builds his business plan to achieve it. Every lawyer determines what decision she wants from the jury and then organizes her case accordingly. Every advertiser decides what he wants the consumer to do and then shapes his message so as to achieve that aim. Every politician judges how she wants the voters to think and vote and then designs her communication strategy appropriately. In the same way those in ministry may strategize so as to accomplish their preset goals. The wisdom of this approach is self-evident. It is universally employed, patently effective, glaringly obvious. What could be more natural?

Yet therein lies the proverbial rub. What if the very *naturalness* of this model is the problem? This question leads us to consider an alternative model, a model I will call the *Pauline model*. This model is one that cuts painfully cross-grain to the natural model, and to our typical ways of thinking and doing. It is deeply counterintuitive, not to mention countercultural. Like so many other topsy-turvy aspects of the gospel, where the way up is down and we find ourselves precisely by losing ourselves, this very contrariness constitutes the Pauline model's greatest strength. Yet the natural model is a difficult thing to relinquish. A willingness to call it into question and a readiness to embrace a radically different, Spirit-dependent alternative, one that is foreign to most of our natural inclinations, requires considerable discernment. Indeed, the Apostle's success, or lack thereof, in making the case against the natural model with his ancient Corinthian readers should give us pause.

Yet the ministry stakes are high enough that the responsibility to explore these issues anew is always with us, in our generation no less than any other. This debate has bubbled to the surface many times and in countless places throughout church history, and it remains pertinent for twenty-first-century Christians as well. It may in fact be especially pertinent for contemporary Christians, particularly in our Western, Americanized culture where pragmatism is so prized and the natural model is so taken for granted. In such settings Christians may be uniquely susceptible to being captivated by the natural model's pragmatic approach to ministry, wooed by its promise and oblivious to its pitfalls.

## The Central Passage: 1 Corinthians 1–4

The thesis of this chapter is that the choice between these two models is precisely what informs Paul's famous defense of his preaching in 1 Cor 1–4. In these unparalleled chapters Paul is at pains to defend his approach to discourse (that is, his own preaching) against an alternative preferred by some of the Corinthians. To do so he contrasts his communication approach with their alternative and takes recourse to his theological presuppositions to explain and defend why he must practice the one and not the other. This argument is what renders 1 Corinthians 1–4 unique in Paul's writings.

But what is crucial for us to see is that, while 1 Corinthians 1–4 is indeed a defense of Paul's approach to preaching against the preferred Corinthian alternative, these dual alternatives are in fact only specific instances of the two ministry models presented above. In examining these two preaching alternatives we are thus examining two expressions of those broader ministry models, a point Paul makes clear before his argument is finished.

Studying the alternatives Paul sets out is therefore valuable for us at two levels. First, it instructs us about how we should think about the subject of preaching; and second, it more broadly instructs us about how we should approach Christian ministry in general. Let us take these two levels of instruction in order.

## A Preliminary Clarification of Terms

No sooner do we plunge into this discussion, however, than we discover that we need to clarify our terms. Our challenge relates to the equivocal nature of our English term *preaching*. The exercise Paul is addressing in 1 Corinthians 1–4 is primarily the preaching of the gospel to unbelievers. By contrast, the exercise many have in mind today when they speak of preaching is a Sunday sermon to churchgoers. In English we tend to refer to both as "preaching," but biblically and theologically the two settings require differentiation.

Without attempting a detailed exploration of the issues,[1] it is enough to observe that according to the Bible, the role of the Holy Spirit in bringing unbelievers (ψυχικὸς ἄνθρωπος, 1 Cor 2:14) to faith is distinguishable from the Spirit's role in maturing believers (ὁ πνευματικὸς, 1 Cor 2:15). Paul's argument in 1 Corinthians 1–4 is primarily addressing the first of these settings, the proclamation of the gospel to the unconverted. This is what we usually have in mind when we speak of "evangelism," an English term transliterated from the Greek word for "gospelizing" (εὐαγγελίζω). When this is the setting we have in mind, Paul's insights are directly relevant to our contemporary practice. When our focus is the second setting (addressing those who are already believers and who thus possess the Holy Spirit), a degree of extrapolation is required. Moreover, when this second setting is our focus the many biblical references to "teaching" (διδαχή) come into play (e.g., 1 Cor 4:17).

---

1. On which, see Litfin, *Paul's Theology of Preaching*, 305–6, 334–38.

So if we allow 1 Corinthians 1–4 to set the topic for us, the alternate approaches we will be addressing relate first and foremost to the business of bringing unbelievers to faith. What are these alternate approaches? The Corinthian alternative is the art of *persuasion,* as taught and practiced by the ancient rhetoricians; the Pauline alternative is the act of *proclamation,* as practiced by the ancient heralds. Let us take these in turn.

## The Persuader's Stance

The issues that lie behind Paul's argument in 1 Corinthians 1–4 relate directly to Greco-Roman rhetoric, or more particularly, the ancient (and modern) art of persuasion. Training in Greco-Roman rhetoric formed the crown of a liberal education in the ancient world. At its best, the art of rhetoric was not about composing purple prose or dishonestly manipulating one's audience. At its core lay something powerful, even noble. It was that art that replaced violence and coercion in free societies: the art of persuasion through discourse.

When we lay bare the essence of the thing, rhetoric was about the discovery, shaping, and delivery of arguments so as to engender belief in one's listeners. At its center lay the kaleidoscopic ability of the persuader to mold all of his efforts, both form and content, to the demands of the given situation, with a view to winning a particular verdict from them. Given *this* audience, *this* subject matter, on *this* occasion, how can I achieve the desired result? This was the question persuaders were trained to ask and answer, and the measure of their skill was the degree to which they could do so successfully, in whatever rhetorical situation they might be facing.

This was the approach to preaching—which Paul summarizes under the heading "wisdom of the world" (1 Cor 1:20)—that the apostle disavows in 1 Corinthians 1–4. It was the standard approach Greco-Roman audiences demanded if they were to be convinced. Working within the confines of their listeners' belief systems and psychological inclinations, persuaders strove to provide eloquently expressed and forcefully delivered arguments—logical, emotional, ethical—designed to engender belief. Upon these arguments the listeners would then sit in judgment, deciding whether the persuader's efforts were worthy of acceptance. If the arguments satisfied the audience's demands for proof or demonstration, they would embrace them; if not, they could be dismissed. This is the way the art of persuasion works.

## The Proclaimer's Stance

The role of the persuader, then and now, stands in striking contrast to Paul's preferred role: that of the ancient herald.[2] The role of the herald in the classical world is widely understood and we need only cite some standard observations to see the important distinction. It was demanded of heralds, says Gerhard Friedrich in his widely cited *Theological Dictionary of the New Testament* lexical treatment of κῆρυξ, κηρύσσω and κήρυγμα, that they

> deliver their message as it is given to them. The essential point about the report which they give is that it does not originate with them. Behind it stands a higher power. The herald does not express his own views. He is the spokesman for his master . . . Heralds adopt the mind of those who commission them, and act with the plenipotentiary authority of their masters . . . Yet there is a distinction between the herald and the envoy. In general one may say that the latter acts more independently and that he is furnished with greater authority. It is unusual for a herald to act on his own initiative and without explicit instructions. In the main the herald simply gives short messages, puts questions, and brings answers . . . He is bound by the precise instructions of the one who commissions him . . . The good herald does not become involved in lengthy negotiations [sic] but returns at once when he has delivered his message . . . In general he is simply an executive instrument. Being only the mouth of his master, he must not falsify the message entrusted to him by additions of his own. He must deliver it exactly as given to him . . . He must keep strictly to the words and orders of his master.[3]

The herald's role was thus strikingly different from the persuader's. Like the persuader, the herald could not dictate who would make up his audience; he had to work with what he received. But beyond this the two roles are a study in contrasts. Far from being an ever-malleable variable, ingeniously adapted to the audience so as to win the desired response, the herald's message was set for him by another. It was not a variable at all but

---

2. The verbs Paul uses to describe his public speaking—such as εὐαγγελίζω, κηρύσσω, καταγγέλλω, and μαρτυρέω—are decidedly non-rhetorical. No self-respecting persuader used such verbs to describe his own *modus operandi*. Thus, even though they deal with the subject of the human communication, such verbs play no significant role in the ancient rhetorical literature. This is understandable because the essential form of communication—announcing, testifying—they describe is very different from that of the orator; in fact, at its core it is the antithesis of rhetorical behavior.

3. Friedrich, "κῆρυξ, κηρύσσω, κήρυγμα," 687–88.

a constant: the herald was given a message by the one he represented and it was his assignment to deliver it faithfully.

And what of the results? Unlike the persuader, the herald could not maneuver rhetorically to achieve some particular effect; it was his calling to deliver his message and then watch the chips fall where they may. Upon completion of his assignment the herald might discover a variety of responses from his audience, but these were not his affair. Whatever he might desire for his audience, he was ever mindful that the responses of the audience were not in the end responses to himself but to the one he represented. It was not the herald's task to modulate his efforts so as to achieve this response or that, or to negotiate the message with his audience, so to speak, in order to develop a message they might find maximally palatable, or better yet, wonderfully convincing, or best of all, simply irresistible. Unlike the persuader, the herald was not results-driven; he was obedience-driven. He was a man under assignment.

According to Paul, his commission from Christ was specifically to serve as a herald—that is, to broadcast the gospel, "not in words taught by human wisdom" (οὐκ ἐν διδακτοῖς ἀνθρωπίνης σοφίας λόγοις, 1 Cor 2:13) lest the cross of Christ be emptied of its power (1 Cor 1:17). Why? Because God was pleased to save the world, not through human wisdom but "through the foolishness of the proclaimed message" (1 Cor 1:21, author's translation). Paul viewed the function of the herald as central not only to his own calling but to God's entire plan of redemption.

## God's Redemptive Plan

This point is strongly reinforced in Romans 10:12–17. The focus of Romans 10 is the salvation (10:1, 9, 10, 13) God has provided his rebellious creatures. God has graciously provided this salvation through the life, death and resurrection of his Son, Jesus Christ. To appropriate this salvation, however, one must be willing to recognize and call on Jesus as Lord and Savior (10:13). But "how . . . will they call on him in whom they have not believed? And how are they to believe in him of whom they have never heard? And how are they to hear without someone preaching [κηρύσσοντος]? And how are they to preach [κηρύξωσιν] unless they are sent [ἀποσταλῶσιν]?" In this last term can be heard Paul's conception of his own commission as one "called by the will of God to be an ἀπόστολος of Christ Jesus" (e.g., 1 Cor 1:1; cf. Rom 1:1; 2 Cor 1:1; Gal 1:1).

The critical role of the commissioned heralds in God's plan of redemption is thus made clear in Romans 10. First, God provides a way of salvation through the death and resurrection of his Son, Jesus Christ. Second, he commissions and dispatches messengers to declare this gracious provision to the world. Third, these messengers fulfill their commission by faithfully heralding (κηρύσσομεν, 10:8) this good news to all. Finally, the listeners are called upon to give this announcement the reception it deserves: that is, they must be willing to (1) open themselves to hearing it (as in Jesus's repeated invitation, "He who has ears to hear, let him hear"); (2) attend to what it says about God's salvific provision in Christ; (3) receive the message as true and welcome it as the good news it is; and consequently (4) recognize and embrace ("call on"; cf. "receive," John 1:12) as Lord and savior this Jesus who stands at the message's center. Says C. K. Barrett, "The hearer of the message accepts it, receives the word that he has heard. He repents; he puts his trust in Christ and accepts him as the redeeming and authoritative Lord."[4]

Thus did Paul view the role of the commissioned herald. The herald served as a crucial link in this chain of salvific consequences. Paul gives no indication that it was God's plan to send out into the world a team of persuaders whose assignment it was to generate faith (πίστις) in their listeners. Instead God sent out announcers, so that when faith was the outcome, that faith would be the product not of human ingenuity but of the Spirit's convicting application of the messenger's "word about Christ" (διὰ ῥήματος Χριστοῦ, Rom 10:17) within τοῖς σῳζομένοις (those being saved; 1 Cor 1:18); that is, τοῖς κλητοῖς (those who are called; 1 Cor 1:24; cf. Rom 1:6).

## The Issue of Argumentation

The issue of argumentation thus lies at the center of the difference between the persuader and the herald. Then and now, the persuader is always looking for arguments that will render his message persuasive. In their classic modern work, *The New Rhetoric*, Chaim Perelman and Luci Olbrechts-Tyteca echo the ancient writers. For the persuader,

> The desire to convince someone always implies a certain modesty on the part of the initiator of the argument; what he says is not 'Gospel truth,' he does not possess that authority which would place his words beyond question so that they would carry immediate conviction. He acknowledges that he must use persuasion,

---

4. Barrett, "Proclamation and Response," 12–13.

think of arguments capable of acting on his interlocutor, show some concern for him, and be interested in his state of mind.[5]

At first blush the role of the herald might seem a more humble one than that of the persuader. In another sense, however, Paul's determination to limit himself to the role of a herald, proclaiming a divine message that was not open to negotiation, had the opposite effect: it constituted an offence to human pride. Paul did not view it as his business to accommodate common human expectations by providing impressive arguments "capable of acting on his interlocutor[s]." He was in the business, precisely, of announcing "Gospel truth," confident that by the power of the Spirit this divine message would "carry immediate conviction" to those "who are being saved" (1 Cor 1:18); that is, to "those who are called" (1 Cor 1:24).[6]

Ernesto Grassi thus describes the first mark of "sacred language" as follows: "a purely directive, revealing, or evangelical character (never a

---

5. Perelman and Olbrechts-Tyteca, *The New Rhetoric*, 16.

6. Perelman and Olbrechts-Tyteca's distinction between the persuader's stance and that of the announcer of "Gospel truth" is echoed throughout the literature on philosophical and rhetorical argumentation. For example, in his discussion of the differences between persuasive and philosophical forms of argumentation, Henry Johnstone introduces a third option, that of the "prophet": "The man who wishes to persuade usually cannot hope to do so merely by making a statement . . . Unless he is regarded as a prophet, he must be willing to discuss it with others and defend it against their objections" (Johnstone, *Philosophy and Argument*, 46). In a similar vein philosopher Peter Schouls raises the idea of "proclamation": "The problem of philosophical communication derives from the presence of presuppositions in philosophy" (Schouls, "Communication, Argumentation, and Presupposition," 190). By definition, *pre*-suppositions cannot be "argued." Arguments supporting properly basic presuppositions are inevitably circular in that they must assume the truth of the presupposition they are attempting to support. Thus philosophers who hold common presuppositions can debate about what may follow from those presuppositions, but how is "argumentation" to proceed when their differences lie at the presuppositional level, where no non-circular "arguments" are available? This impasse prompts Schouls to introduce a form of communication different from "argumentation." Argumentation, says Nicholas Rescher, is "the project of seeking to elicit the acceptance of certain contentions by means of explicitly adduced substantiating reasons" (Rescher, *Philosophical Reasoning*, 77). When the differences lie at the level of competing presuppositions, where no such "substantiating reasons" can escape the problem of circularity, if communication is not to grind to a halt philosophical argument can only be replaced with a form of communication Schouls labels "proclamation," "advocacy," or "recommendation."

These technical discussions of philosophical communication lack the obvious spiritual dimension (the role of the Holy Spirit) that was so prominent in Paul's thinking. But the Apostle would surely have understood and identified with the notion of a fundamental impasse that rules out "argumentation" as an available strategy, leading instead to the employment of the prophetic proclamation of gospel truth.

demonstrative or proving function), and it never arises out of a process of inference in order not to give up its original character or absolute undetermined character." This type of speech stands in "explicit contradistinction" to "rational speech," which claims "to be demonstrative and to offer proof because it gives the reasons for its assertions." This latter type of speech is the currency of our own times, says Grassi, because

> today's situation is such that in our desacralized and demythologized world we believe in no annunciations, in no purely directive statements, in no evangelist, be it a God or a prophet. We turn to rational thought, to proofs and reasons in order to free ourselves from the subjectivity and relativity of appearances.[7]

Grassi is no doubt right about our modern way of thinking, but in fact, this is the way the art of persuasion has always worked. As Perelman says, "All argumentation addresses itself to a mind which has to judge, to appraise,"[8] and so it was with Greek argumentation. What Paul apparently believed this Greek mindset, whether in its philosophical or rhetorical manifestations, held in common with the Jewish was the human desire for "sight" or "proof" rather than a willingness to trust the announced word of the gospel (2 Cor 5:7).

## Paul's Epistemology

Paul's commitment to proclamation was at bedrock a product of his epistemology; that is, his theory of knowledge. Paul's problem was not with human reason per se, but rather with the sinful and idolatrous tendencies that inevitably blight the human exercise of reason, tendencies only the Spirit of God can remedy. In his extended study of "Paul's way of knowing," Ian Scott demonstrates that Paul viewed human rationality as "corrupted by endemic moral failure so that the human mind consistently resists interpreting the world in the terms which the Gospel requires." Paul's problem, Scott argues, was not with reason itself but with "reason which has been hijacked by human vices." Thus,

> The Spirit's role . . . seems to be a moral restoration of believers which allows them to move into a new system of values within which the Gospel is rational and plausible. Here too there is reason

---

7. Grassi, *Rhetoric as Philosophy*, 103, 104.
8. Perelman, "Philosophy and Rhetoric," 292.

to believe that Paul understood the Spirit to *renew* human reason, rather than to displace it . . . The apprehension of divine wisdom does not seem to suppress rational thought, but rather involves 'understanding' (εἰδέναι, [1 Cor] 2:12) and enables the mature to 'interpret' (συγκρίνειν, 2:13) and 'judge' (ἀνακρίνεσθαι, 2:14, 15). At the end of the passage the 'spiritual' believer is left with 'the mind of Christ (ἡμεῖς δὲ νοῦν Χριστοῦ ἔχομεν),' a new way of thinking and reasoning. This seems to confirm at least that the Gospel is itself comprehensible (even if some cannot accept it) and that the one who, under the Spirit's impulse, has accepted that message gains a new ability to reason about the world.[9]

According to Scott, rather than being incomprehensible, the gospel is simply unjustifiable in terms of standard human systems of evaluation and plausibility. The *kerygma* is foolishness to the perishing, not because it is unintelligible but because it is all too intelligible: it calls for a reversal of the human standard by which humans typically determine what will count as wisdom.

Paul's simple presentation of the gospel, then, was an intentional strategy geared to ensure that his preaching did not undermine God's subversion of the world's corrupt wisdom. Paul deliberately chose not to use eloquent rhetoric or sophisticated reasoning. Instead he wished to rely on a straightforward heralding of "Christ and him crucified," to be accepted or rejected. Why? Because he refused to frame his preaching within the values and standards of reasonableness that characterize other systems of thought. His proclamation of the gospel was deliberately designed to be incompatible with idolatrous human vices and the systems of value and plausibility those vices spawn. Paul therefore rejected both ordinary standards for rational verification and the rhetorical flair that was expected if those arguments were to carry force.

It was his calling, Paul believed, to *announce* the gospel, but it is the Spirit's role to perform a moral restoration that allows unbelievers to move into a new system of values within which the gospel is rational and plausible.[10] "Those who are perishing" would continue to find the placarded

---

9. Scott, *Implicit Epistemology in the Letters of Paul*, 34.

10. This analysis is echoed by J. Louis Martyn in his commentary on Galatians (*Galatians*, 22–23, 146–48, 276–77, 288–89). There Martyn provides an unusually insightful analysis of these contrasting dynamics, that of the rhetor and that of the cross. Echoing 1 Corinthians 1–4, Martyn shows the Apostle Paul in Galatians repudiating the art of persuasion for the purposes of preaching.

Savior ridiculous. As ψυχικόι (those without the Spirit) they would be unwilling to perceive in the crucified Christ the wisdom of God. But to the "called ones" (κλητοί), the Spirit of God would allow this same κήρυγμα to appear as profoundly right and true and worthy of belief (cf. Acts 13:48; 16:14; see also Luke 24:45; 1 John 5:20). Indeed, through the Spirit's illumination this κήρυγμα would appear for them to be the very power of God and the wisdom of God, reasonable not in the sense that they now understood all the ins and outs of *how* God was in Christ saving them, but rather in the sense that they now understood *that* God was in Christ saving them. As F. L. Godet put it, when Paul speaks in 1 Corinthians 2:4 of the demonstration (ἀπόδειξις) of the Spirit and of power, the term ἀπόδειξις "indicates a clearness which is produced in the hearer's mind, as by a sudden lifting of the veil; a conviction mastering him with the sovereign force of moral evidence."[11]

## The Centrality of Proclamation

For all of these reasons Paul resisted being pressed into the role of the persuader. He insisted that he was called to a ministry of proclamation, a ministry of lifting up the crucified Christ before his listeners. This was the ministry described by Jesus when he said to Nicodemus, "As Moses lifted up the serpent in the wilderness, so must the Son of Man be lifted up, that whoever believes in him may have eternal life" (John 3:14–15). This serpent reference, of course, was to Numbers 21:8–9, where Moses was instructed

---

11. Godet, *Commentary on St. Paul's First Epistle to the Corinthians*, 1.129. On this point see further Alvin Plantinga's detailed epistemological discussion in his book *Knowledge and Christian Belief*. Plantinga argues that "faith is the belief in the great things of the gospel that results from the internal instigation of the Holy Spirit" (here and following, pp. 62–64). Such belief is "basic," he says, like beliefs produced by memory or perception. "The belief-producing process involved is dual, involving both the divinely inspired Scripture (perhaps directly, or perhaps at the head of a testimonial chain), and also the internal instigation of the Holy Spirit." The resulting belief is thus epistemically warranted and constitutes a legitimate, albeit special, form of knowledge. Christian belief "in the typical case is not the conclusion of an argument or accepted on the evidential basis of other beliefs, or accepted just because it constitutes a good explanation of phenomena of one kind or another . . . Nor are [Christian beliefs] accepted as the result of historical research. Nor are they accepted as the conclusion of an argument from *religious experience*." Typically, "Christian belief is *immediate*; it is formed in the *basic* way. It does not proceed by way of an argument." It is the "sure and certain knowledge" of the truth directly instigated by the internal work of the Holy Spirit in the hearer upon his or her encounter with the "testimonial chain" of the gospel.

to lift the image of a serpent on a pole so that "everyone who is bitten, when he sees it, shall live." So it was that "Moses made a bronze serpent and set it on a pole. And if a serpent bit anyone, he would look at the bronze serpent and live." After his conversation with Nicodemus, Jesus twice more in John's Gospel speaks of his being "lifted up." To those who oppose him he says, "When you have lifted up the Son of Man, then you will know that I am he" (John 8:28). And later, to a gathered crowd Jesus says, "The hour has come for the Son of Man to be glorified ... And I, when I am lifted up from the earth, will draw all people to myself" (John 12:23, 32). To this John adds the explanatory comment: "He said this to show by what kind of death he was going to die" (John 12:33).

Christ's "lifting up" thus carried a dual reference: a literal reference to his being brutally "lifted up" on a Roman cross, but still more profoundly, a figurative reference to his being "lifted up" in exaltation, the first stage of his return to glory (John 17:5). The hour of his "lifting up" on the cross was the very hour of his revelation and glorification, and it was from that highly visible position that he would "draw all people to myself." Like the lifted serpent in the wilderness, whoever raised their eyes in faith to the crucified Jesus would live. To look on that forsaken man lifted up on a cross, and yet to see there the exalted Savior being lifted up to heaven in victory over death, is the avenue to salvation: "For this is the will of my Father, that everyone who looks on the Son and believes in him should have eternal life" (John 6:40).

The herald was not a persuader; he was a proclaimer, and Jesus's words help explain why. The herald's calling was, on each new occasion, to "lift up" the crucified Christ before his listeners so that they too might look on him in faith and live. This is, in fact, precisely how Paul described his missionary preaching to the Galatians: "It was before your eyes [οἷς κατ' ὀφθαλμοὺς] that Jesus Christ was publicly portrayed [προεγράφη] as crucified" (Gal 3:1). The verb προγράφω denotes the announcing or giving public notice of something. Paul was determined to depend on the simple proclamation of the herald, confident that the power of his message did not lie in his prowess as a speaker but in the exalted Christ's intent to use his "lifting up"—the public setting forth of "Christ and him crucified"—to draw the listeners to himself.

This business of lifting up Jesus before the eyes of one's listener is the essence of what we call "evangelism." Not for nothing has more than one pulpit had the plea, "Sir, we would see Jesus," posted conspicuously in front of the preacher. J. I. Packer helpfully explains why this point is so important in his classic book, *Evangelism and the Sovereignty of God*. Says Packer,

> To proclaim salvation, we must never forget that it is God who saves . . . Our evangelistic work is the instrument that He uses for this purpose, but the power that saves is not in the instrument: it is in the hand of the One who uses the instrument. We must not at any stage forget that. For if we forget that it is God's prerogative to give results when the gospel is preached, we shall start to think that it is our responsibility to secure them. And if we forget that only God can give faith, we shall start to think that the making of converts depends, in the last analysis, not on God, but on us, and that the decisive factor is the way in which we evangelize. And this line of thought, consistently followed through, will lead us far astray.
>
> Let us work this out. If we regarded it as our job, not simply to present Christ, but actually to produce converts—to evangelize, not only faithfully, but also successfully—our approach to evangelism would become pragmatic and calculating. We should conclude that our basic equipment, both for personal dealing and for public preaching, must be twofold. We must have, not merely a clear grasp of the meaning and application of the gospel, but also an irresistible technique for inducing a response. We should, therefore make it our business to try and develop such a technique . . . We should regard evangelism as a battle of wits between ourselves and those to whom we go, a battle in which victory depends on our firing off a heavy enough barrage of calculated effects.[12]

Packer's analysis strikes the nail on the head. In a recent *First Things* article entitled "Theology Worth Smuggling," Timothy George describes a famous painting by Matthias Grünewald. The painting depicts the crucifixion of Jesus, with John the Baptist standing alongside. John stands at the right of the cross with an open Bible in one hand while pointing with the other to the figure of Christ. In faded red letters behind John are the Latin words . . . "He must increase, while I must decrease" (John 3:30). "This image of John," says George, "of his bony finger pointing toward Christ on the cross, is precisely the perfect paradigm for every preacher, for every Christian, and consequently, for the church itself."[13]

---

12. Packer, *Evangelism and the Sovereignty of God*, 27.
13. George, "Theology Worth Smuggling."

## A Pauline Model for Ministry

I began this paper by sketching a distinction between two contrasting models for ministry: the *natural model* and the *Pauline model*. The herald's stance we have just described constitutes the centerpiece of the Pauline model. The persuader's stance, by contrast, constitutes the centerpiece of the natural model. What sets these two models apart are the engines that drive them. The natural model/persuader's stance is results-driven, while the Pauline model/herald's stance is obedience-driven.

The persuader's stance begins by determining the desired result, then selects its strategies so as to achieve that result. In this way the desired result drives the strategy: How can I achieve *this* result with *this* audience on *this* occasion? Skill in answering this question and then successfully implementing the chosen strategies constituted the genius of the rhetorical art. The persuader's stance is inherently results-oriented.

The herald's stance, by contrast, focuses on the speaker's efforts. The question it asks of those efforts is not, What must I do to achieve some predetermined result? The herald's question is, What is God calling me to be and to do? The herald then bends every effort toward being that and doing that. It is in this sense that the herald's stance is obedience-driven rather than results-driven. The herald is uniquely focused on fulfilling the calling of God, which in turn requires a willingness to leave the matter of results to the Spirit.

These two models mark the essential difference between proclamation and persuasion. Success in the former is measured by God's approval of one's faithfulness, while success in the latter is measured by the results achieved. Paul viewed himself as a herald called by God to proclaim the word of the cross. Some of his listeners would, by the power of the Spirit, recognize in this proclamation the wisdom of God and power of God (1 Cor 1:24). Others would turn away, finding that same message to be nonsense or scandalous (1 Cor 1:23). Yet these mixed results were not Paul's measure of success. He was intent on measuring his ministry by a different yardstick.

While both the persuader and the herald must set and reach for goals, their respective goals are dramatically different. The persuader determined the result he was after and then ordered his efforts accordingly. Paul's goal, by contrast, was to faithfully fulfill his calling and then leave the matter of results to God.

This dramatic paradigm shift, from results-driven to obedience-driven, is the fundamental difference between the persuader's stance and the herald's stance, between the natural model and the Pauline model. It is this difference that constitutes the centerpiece of a Pauline model for ministry. To embrace the herald's stance by implementing an obedience-driven instead of results-driven approach to ministry is to follow the Pauline model.

## From Specifics to Principle

Throughout 1 Corinthians 1–4 Paul is intent on defending his approach to preaching. To do so he places his approach in the context of a much larger and more general principle, one broad enough to encompass all Christian ministry. This broader principle thus undergirds, informs and is entailed throughout Paul's argument in chapters 1–4, but it comes to explicit expression in 4:1–5:

> This is how one should regard us, as servants [ὑπηρέτας] of Christ and stewards [οἰκονόμους] of the mysteries of God. Moreover, *it is required of stewards that they be found faithful* [πιστός]. But with me it is a very small thing that I should be judged by you or by any human court. In fact, I do not even judge myself. For I am not aware of anything against myself, but I am not thereby acquitted. It is the Lord who judges me. Therefore do not pronounce judgment before the time, before the Lord comes, who will bring to light the things now hidden in darkness and will disclose the purposes of the heart. Then each one will receive his commendation from God. (italics added)

In this passage Paul describes how he viewed his own ministry, and how he wished the Corinthians to view it. In this description his language rises to the *principial* level. He expresses the broader premise of which he considers his calling as a preacher to be a specific instance: *Faithfulness is the essential requirement of stewards.* This principle entails the following points, each of which Paul has in 1 Corinthians 1–4 applied to his calling as a proclaimer of the gospel.

1. God delights in employing humble means to accomplish his purposes.
2. Those who do God's work are to be viewed accordingly: they are simply Christ's servants fulfilling his calling.
3. Such servants are required above all to be obedient to what the risen Christ has called them to be and do; their highest priority must be the fulfillment of their divine commission.

4. Because they are Christ's servants obeying his call, only his approval matters. No other assessment is relevant, not even their own (1 Cor 4:3). Success can only be measured by faithfulness to what the Master has called the servant to be and to do.

## Implications for Ministry

A consideration of these features prompts four general observations about Christian ministry. First, it is important to appreciate how radically these features depart from the natural model. The Pauline model asks not, How can I achieve some predetermined result? but, What is Christ calling me to be, and what is he calling me to do? Its intentional focus on discovering and fulfilling the answers to these questions is what distinguishes the Pauline model. It is in this sense that the Pauline model is obedience-driven.

Grasping this contrast is the key to understanding why Paul was so unwilling to replace the herald's stance with the persuader's stance. He was focused on obeying Christ's instructions. This required that he be willing to leave the results to God: "For Christ did not send me to baptize but to proclaim the gospel [εὐαγγελίζεσθαι] . . . [Thus] we herald [κηρύσσομεν] Christ crucified, a stumbling block to Jews and folly to Gentiles, but to those who are called, both Jews and Greeks, Christ the power of God and the wisdom of God" (1 Cor 1:17, 23–24).

Second, this shift from results-driven to obedience-driven transfers a good deal of weight onto the issue of one's calling. What is Christ calling me to be? What is he calling me to do? The Pauline model is dependent on our ability to answer these questions.

How or where does one discover such answers? It would take us too far afield to address this complex issue in anything but the most summary fashion. But I do not regret that the Pauline model forces the issue upon us. I am convinced that the issue of one's calling receives too little attention in Christian circles.[14]

I do not refer here to the servant's initial call to faith (as in 1 Cor 1:26) but rather Christ's call upon his servants thereafter. This latter calling takes at least two forms. The first is the general calling of every follower of Jesus. The Scriptures and the historical teaching of the church provide extensive and profound content to this general calling. It is a calling that touches every dimension of the servant's existence: personal life, family life, life in the

---

14. But see the helpful treatment in Labberton, *Called*.

community of believers, in society at large, and in the natural world. Every legitimate aspect of this biblical and ecclesiastical instruction constitutes a calling from Christ himself: "If you love me," Jesus said, "you will keep my commandments" (John 14:15).

Then there is also the unique calling of the individual Christian. As Paul said to the Corinthians, every follower of Christ has been appointed to unique service: "For just as the body is one and has many members, and all the members of the body, though many, are one body, so it is with Christ" (1 Cor 12:12). The believer's calling may be to a profession, or a particular role, or some specific area of service, or any of a wide range of other possibilities. It may be permanent or temporary; it may be singly focused or multifaceted. The permutations are endless. Each calling is uniquely tailored to the individual. But every follower of Jesus Christ bears a calling and, as Paul instructs the Corinthians, none is insignificant.

Third, these same observations apply to churches or other Christian organizations. If the risen Christ, the Head of his church, has called that organization into existence—and if not, what, from a Christian point of view, is its warrant for considering itself a *Christian* organization?—he did so for a purpose. That organization thus bears, like the individual Christian, both the general calling inherent in serving Jesus and an individual calling unique to itself. Why are we here? Why did Christ raise up this organization? What is he calling us to be? What is he calling us to do? Prayerful answers to such complex questions are not always easy to come by, but they are crucial to the ability of the organization to fulfill its God-given calling.

Fourth, while the Pauline model's shift from a results-orientation to an obedience-orientation is both countercultural and, for most of us, counterintuitive, in the end it is wonderfully liberating. It frees us from obsessing over results and enables us to redefine what we consider success. We gain a different and much superior yardstick by which to measure our efforts: the prospect of a "Well done, good and faithful servant" assessment by the glorified Christ (Matt 25:21, 23; Luke 19:17). Such a yardstick requires a dramatic reorientation of our thinking and planning. Our focus becomes not results but the far healthier issue of faithfulness (1 Cor 4:2). If it is required of a servant to be found "faithful," what is Jesus, our exalted Head, calling us to be and do? How can we be that and do that to the fullest? These are the liberating questions that drive the Pauline model.

Paul's model is also liberating in a different way. To illustrate, the Old Testament figure of Nehemiah may be useful. Nehemiah faced a daunting task, one that appeared beyond his reach. He had to build a massive defensive wall around Jerusalem within a short period of time. It seemed impossible. Yet to everyone's surprise the wall went up. Nehemiah assigned families, clans and individuals their own sections of the wall (Neh 3). When each party fulfilled their particular assignment, the wall became a reality (Neh 6:15).

Nehemiah's approach suggests a useful analogy for Christ's servants as well. While none can do everything, all can do, and are indeed called to do, *something*. So the servant's question must be, What is the *something* Christ is calling me to do? What is my part of the wall? Only God can manage the whole and we must leave that to him; he calls us to tackle only the part he has assigned to us. Thus the servant must always ask: What part of the task is Jesus calling me to fulfill?

This approach is deeply liberating because it involves the crucial recognition that Christ does not expect his servants to respond every time they discover a need. *A need is not a call.* The needs of the world will always outstrip our ability to meet them. Thus only God can bear such a burden. Attempting to respond to every worthy need—and then inevitably experiencing guilt and disappointment when our efforts prove so inadequate—is a prescription for failure and burnout. We are trying to do what only God can do.

Far better is to make our decisions on the basis of Christ's call. We cannot do everything, but we can do *something*. Of the seemingly limitless needs in the world, which is God calling *me* to address? What is my part of the wall? Answering this question can prevent us from throwing up our hands in frustration and defeat when the world's needs vastly exceed our ability to meet them. We must let God be God, and then apply ourselves to the sacrificial tasks to which he has called us.

The term *sacrificial* here is an important one. The above is not an approach designed to relieve Christ's servants from costly service. On the contrary, as we spend ourselves and our resources in building our part of the wall, we must be willing to do so sacrificially, for Christ's sake and for the sake of those to whom he calls us. Learning to respond to call rather than need is not a technique for releasing ourselves from costly service; it's a plan for avoiding false guilt. False guilt is what we experience when we try to operate unreflectively on the unspoken premise that every need is automatically a call. This is a presumptuous idea, one that assumes we possess God-like capacities rather than creaturely limitations. Treating every need as a call is a surefire prescription for the sense of futility that arises when we inevitably fall short in our efforts to accomplish what God never expected, enabled, or called us to do.

In our day of instant worldwide communication we are constantly witness to more human need than any previous generation could have imagined. Yet we can never do everything even in one situation of need, much less in all such situations. We will quickly be overwhelmed if we try to respond to every need. We must learn, instead, to follow Paul's lead. What is Christ calling us to be? What is Christ calling us to do? Let us be that and do that to the best of our ability, and then leave the results up to him. This is a far healthier way for Christians to live, wooed by the call of Christ and driven only by our determination to fulfill it.

## Conclusion

First Corinthians 1–4 is largely a study in the Apostle Paul's theology of preaching. But in the end this theology of preaching must be viewed as an expression of something deeper; that is, Paul's underlying philosophy of ministry in general. In 1 Corinthians 1–4 Paul is challenging not simply an alternative theory of discourse but an entire way of looking at things—what we have called the *natural model*—that undergirds it. In its place Paul argues for his own contrasting view of things, the *Pauline model*. This contrast represents a fundamental shift, from a *results*-driven to an *obedience*-driven approach to ministry. For those who are willing to take Paul's argument seriously, this insight requires a profound reorientation of our focus, not only in our approach to preaching but to Christian ministry in general.[15]

---

15. This footnote adds nothing germane to the argument of this paper. I offer it as a small but delightful bonus to all who love the Apostle Paul and have profited from his ministry. During my research for *Paul's Theology of Preaching* I ran across an obscure little gem of information about a fascinating modern development. Given Paul's painful experiences with the Corinthian church, not to mention the rough treatment he received at the hands of the synagogue Jews and the Roman authorities in Corinth (Acts 18:1–17), we should not pass by the delicious irony of the following. In 2007 the city of Corinth convened an international conference on the subject of "Saint Paul and Corinth." Two years later the city published the conference's papers, in the prologue of which publication we read this: "The time came, finally, for Corinth to fulfill its great debt. A spiritual debt to Paul, the Apostle to All Nations; the Apostle that opened up the horizon of the Divine Revelation for the city and also endowed the city with so much prestige with his presence that Corinth today is known everywhere in the world mainly through Paul's work and his extremely significant epistles to the Corinthians" (Papadopolos, "Prologue," 19).

# 3

# A Simple Method
*William Perkins and the Shaping of the Protestant Pulpit*

—J. Stephen Yuille

## Introduction

IN A LETTER (DATED August 1, 1684), included as a preface to Thomas Manton's published sermons on Matthew 25, three ministers (William Bates, John Collinges, and John Howe)[1] encourage the reader to seek out sermons that are "substantial, scriptural, and practical,"[2] adding, "all other discourses are abusively called preaching, and Athens were a more proper place for them than a preacher's pulpit."[3] Interestingly, in the course of their commendation of Manton for his "solid" discourses, they provide a brief overview of the history of preaching.

They begin with the "ancient church," highlighting two famous preachers: John Chrysostom in the Greek and Augustine of Hippo in the Latin. They applaud these two for their "judicious explications of Scripture"—for their "plenty of matter, clearness of judgment, [and] orderliness of method."[4] Moving into the middle ages, the three ministers note a dramatic shift in preaching. They contend that it "turned into trifling about scholastic niceties," whereby preachers found their chief texts in Duns Scotus or Thomas

---

1. William Bates (1625–1699), John Collinges (1623–1690), and John Howe (1630–1705) were Manton's contemporaries. Like Manton, they were Presbyterian ministers, ejected for nonconformity in 1662. Each published popular works on divinity.
2. Manton, "To the Reader," 9:316.
3. Ibid.
4. Ibid.

Aquinas rather than in Scripture.[5] The Reformation, however, marked another pivotal turning point in the history of preaching. The three ministers speak glowingly of Martin Luther, Ulrich Zwingli, John Calvin, William Farel, Pierre Viret, and Theodore Beza, because of their faithful handling of Scripture in the pulpit. Yet, they lament the subsequent generation of preachers, who (for the most part) failed to follow the example of the magisterial reformers.[6] Finally, in their overview of the history of preaching, the three ministers arrive at their own day, affirming that God has "reserved it for a great blessing," for it is a "more fertile" season of preaching than "any since that of the apostles."[7]

How do these three ministers account for this unprecedented period of homiletic blessing? They point to one man—William Perkins—declaring that he was the first to restore preaching to "its true sense," and to teach "the true manner of it."[8] Equally significant, they claim that Perkins's "piety" became paradigmatic for the generation of preachers who followed him.

## The Life of William Perkins

Few men have been as influential in their lifetime as William Perkins, and few men of such fame have been so widely forgotten with the passing of time as Perkins. Who was he? Scholars have described him as "the principal architect of Elizabethan Puritanism," "the Puritan theologian of Tudor times," "the most important Puritan writer," "the prince of Puritan theologians," "the most famous of all Puritan divines," and "the father of

---

5. Ibid.
6. Ibid., 9:316.
7. Ibid.

8. Ibid., 9:316–17. The three ministers add the following remark: "The generality of good preachers have made it their business to preach Christ and the exceeding riches of his grace, and to study matter rather than words, upon Mr. Perkins's old principle *verba sequenter res*." This "old principle" seems to be taken from Cato's famous dictum: *rem tene, verba sequentur*—"Grasp the subject, the words will follow." Marcus Porcius Cato (234–149 BC) was a Roman statesman, often called "Cato the Elder" to distinguish him from "Cato the Younger" (his great-grandson).

Puritanism."[9] Some have gone so far as to include him—along with John Calvin and Theodore Beza—in "the trinity of the orthodox."[10]

Perkins's stature as an eminent theologian is all the more noteworthy given his less than auspicious start in life.[11] He was born to Thomas and Hannah Perkins in the village of Marston Jabbet (near Coventry) in Bulkington Parish of Warwickshire. Very little is known of him until, at nineteen years of age, he enrolled at Christ's College, Cambridge, where he soon made a name for himself, but not for the reasons we might expect. "Quickly the wild fire of his youth began to break out," notes one biographer.[12] Another declares that he "was profane and prodigal, and addicted to drunkenness."[13] But Perkins soon came under the godly influence of Laurence Chaderton (his tutor).[14] More importantly, God began to work in his heart, producing deep conviction for sin and ultimately faith in Christ.

With renewed enthusiasm, Perkins devoted himself to his studies, receiving his bachelor's degree in 1581 and his master's degree in 1584. He was an industrious student. According to Thomas Fuller, "[Perkins] had a rare felicity in speedy reading of books, and as it were but turning them over would give an exact account of all considerables therein . . . He took strict notice of all passages, as if he had dwelt on them particularly;

---

9. Strictly speaking, Perkins was not a Puritan in terms of his ecclesiology, for he refused to align himself with the more militant figures of his era. Nor was he a Puritan in terms of his theology, for it is anachronistic to speak of Puritanism as a theological movement prior to the Arminian renewal in theology, which occurred within the Church of England during the reign of the Stuart kings. For more on this, see Tyacke, *Anti-Calvinists*. But Perkins was a Puritan in terms of his piety. "For the pure heart is so little regarded," says he, "that the seeking after it is turned to a by-word, and a matter of reproach. Who are so much branded with vile terms of *Puritans* and *Precisians*, as those that most endeavor to get and keep the purity of heart in a good conscience?" Again, "The due obedience to the moral law is nick-named and termed preciseness, and the professors thereof called *Puritans* and *Precisians*, for this cause only, that they make conscience of walking in obedience to God's law" (Perkins, *A Godly and Learned Exposition*, 3:15, 195).

10. Eusden, *Puritans, Lawyers, and Politics*, 11; Seaver, *The Puritan Lectureships*, 114; Hill, *God's Englishman*, 38; and Packer, *An Anglican to Remember*, 1.

11. For an account of Perkins's life, see Beeke and Yuille, *William Perkins*; and Patterson, *William Perkins and the Making of Protestant England*. For brief summaries, see Lee, *The Dictionary of National Biography*; Beeke and Pederson, *Meet the Puritans*, 469–80; Beeke and Yuille, "Biographical Preface," ix–xxxii; and Breward, "Introduction," 3–131.

12. Fuller, *Abel Redevivus*, 432.

13. Cooper and Cooper, *Athenae Cantabrigiensis 1586–1609*, 2:335.

14. Beeke, "Laurence Chaderton," 321–37.

perusing books so speedily, one would think he read nothing; so accurately, one would think he read all."[15]

At some point during his studies, Perkins began to preach on Sundays to the prisoners at Cambridge castle. Apparently, he pronounced "the word *damn* with such an emphasis as left a doleful echo in his auditors' ears a good while after."[16] Moreover, he applied "the terrors of the law so directly to the consciences of his hearers that their hearts would often sink under conviction."[17] His preaching soon attracted people from the town and university. As Fuller observes, "His sermons were not so plain but that the piously learned did admire them, nor so learned but that the plain did understand them."[18] Given his growing popularity as a preacher, Perkins was appointed in 1584 as lecturer at Great St. Andrew's Church, located across from Christ's College. From this pulpit, he reached people from all social classes, being "systematic, scholarly, solid, and simple."[19]

Around the time of his appointment to Great St. Andrew's, Perkins was also elected to a fellowship at Christ's College. He held this position from 1584 to 1595, serving as Dean from 1590 to 1591. Fellows were responsible for preaching, lecturing, and tutoring students, acting as "guides to learning as well as guardians of finances, morals, and manners."[20] In this role, Perkins influenced a generation of young students, including Richard Sibbes, John Cotton, John Preston, and William Ames. In the preface to one of his own works, Ames remarks, "I gladly call to mind the time, when being young, I heard worthy Master Perkins, so preach in a great assembly of students, that he instructed them soundly in the truth, stirred them up effectually to seek after godliness, made them fit for the kingdom of God; and by his own example showed them, what things they should chiefly intend, that they might promote true religion, in the power of it, unto God's glory, and others' salvation."[21] During his time at Cambridge, Perkins's reputation as a teacher and writer was unrivalled. Cotton considered Perkins's

---

15. Fuller, *The Holy State*, 91.
16. Clark, *The Marrow of Ecclesiastical History*, 851.
17. Brook, *The Lives of the Puritans*, 2:130.
18. Fuller, *Holy State*, 89–90.
19. Packer, *An Anglican to Remember*, 3.
20. Curtis, *Oxford and Cambridge*, 80. Perkins served the university in several additional capacities. He catechized students at Corpus Christi College on Thursday afternoons. He also worked as an adviser on Sunday afternoons, counseling the spiritually distressed.
21. Ames, "To the Reader."

ministry the "one good reason why there came so many excellent preachers out of Cambridge in England, more than out of Oxford."[22]

## The Need for Preaching

The English Reformation was a drawn out process, in which the country moved back and forth on multiple occasions between Catholicism and Protestantism as monarchs came and went. In a span of twenty years, the religion of the land shifted four times. But the reign of Elizabeth I brought stability and provided the much needed climate for English Reformers to solidify the church's position. Perkins played a pivotal role in this, and his works became the standard polemic against Rome.

Despite the marked progress in reforming medieval teaching in the light of Scripture, Perkins was concerned with the spiritual condition within the Church of England and the country as a whole. He was convinced that the people still suffered the ill-effects of the Roman Catholic dogma of implicit faith. That is to say, most people still assumed that as long as they accepted "some necessary points of religion" they were good Christians. In a day (not unlike our own) in which mere assent was accepted as faith, empty profession was accepted as conversion, and dead formality was accepted as godliness, Perkins was particularly troubled by the prevalence of "civility" within the professing church. "If we look into the general state of our people," said he, "we shall see that religion is professed, but not obeyed; nay, obedience is counted as preciseness, and so reproached."[23]

22. Wright, "William Perkins," 194. Perkins's influence as a theologian continued unabated after his death in 1602. This was due in large part to the widespread popularity of his writings. Eleven posthumous editions, containing nearly fifty books, were printed by 1635. At least fifty editions of his works were printed in Germany and Switzerland. There were 185 seventeenth-century printings of his individual or collected works in Dutch. His writings were also translated into Spanish, Welsh, Irish, French, Italian, Hungarian, and Czech. According to Samuel Morison, "a typical Plymouth Colony library comprised a large and a small Bible, [Henry] Ainsworth's translation of the Psalms, and the works of William Perkins, a favorite theologian" (Morrison, *The Intellectual Life of Colonial New England*, 134). Perry Miller observes, "Anyone who reads the writings of early New England learns that Perkins was indeed a towering figure in their eyes" (Miller, *Errand into the Wilderness*, 57–59).

23. Perkins, *A Godly and Learned Exposition*, 3:261. As R. C. Lovelace explains, "The problem that confronts the Puritans as they look out on their decaying society and their lukewarm church is not simply to dislodge the faithful from the slough of mortal or venial sin, but radically to awaken those who are professing but not actual Christians, who are caught in a trap of carnal security" (Lovelace, "The Anatomy of Puritan Piety," 303).

This was one of the chief reasons why Perkins was not so concerned about the external forms of the church. Instead of focusing his attention on church polity, he was primarily concerned with addressing pastoral inadequacies, spiritual deficiencies, and widespread ignorance within the church. He understood the church's most pressing need not in terms of ecclesiastical innovation, but theological instruction. Perkins viewed the church as being sound in its official doctrine and worship, yet woefully hampered on account of inadequate teaching. Prayer Book services, homilies, and catechisms introduced Protestant teaching to the people; however, these things did not lead them to deeper devotion. The average person was content with the minimum required of religious observance.

While recognizing the sinfulness of the human heart, Perkins believed that the disconcerting state of the church was explained by the lack of capable preachers: "When we see a people without knowledge and without good guides or teachers, or when we see one stand up in the congregation unable to teach, here is a matter for mourning."[24] For Perkins, this dearth of capable preachers was explained, in large part, by a lack of adequate training. The bachelor degree was void of any formal theological education; moreover, it provided no training in how to preach or provide pastoral care. The widespread assumption was that any educated man could figure out how to preach, counsel the distressed, comfort the sick, encourage the dying, and challenge the wayward. Perkins was most certainly not opposed to the university curriculum; on the contrary, he embraced it as a vital component in pastoral preparation. He believed the study of Scripture required knowledge of the arts, because these lead pastors into a deeper understanding of Scripture. But Perkins recognized that something more was needed at the university level. He believed it was necessary to set out ministerial duties (particularly preaching) in detail.[25] Out of these concerns over the state of pastoral ministry within the Church of England arose Perkins's *The Art of Prophesying: A treatise concerning the sacred and only true manner and method of preaching.*[26]

---

24. Perkins, *Exposition of the Lord's Prayer*, 83.

25. For Perkins's insights on the qualifications of a minister, see his *Of the Calling of the Ministry, Two Treatises.*

26. Perkins, *The Art of Prophesying*. It was first published in 1592 in Latin, and then translated into English in 1606. It consists of eleven chapters, covering the principles of hermeneutics, interpretation, application, and proclamation. For a thorough treatment of Perkins's treatise, see Pipa, "William Perkins." Some scholars trace Perkins's plain style of preaching to Ramism. See, for example, McKim, *Ramism in William Perkins' Theology.*

## Experiential Preaching

When a preacher stands before his congregation, he does so "in the name and room of Christ," with the goal of calling people into a "state of grace" and preserving them therein.[27] Preaching, therefore, is the means by which people experience God's grace from conversion to glorification. This experiential focus is prevalent throughout Perkins's writings.[28] A case in point is his exposition of Matthew 5:13–16, where Christ introduces the "similitudes" of salt and light. For Perkins, these chiefly apply to preachers, and are intended to instruct them in how to "dispense" God's Word.[29] In short, they must seek to express the properties of both salt and light.

Regarding salt, Perkins explained that it displays three "properties" when applied to "raw flesh or fresh wounds": it bites, it seasons, and it preserves.[30] Preaching ought to engender the same three-fold effect in people's hearts.[31] First, it should bite, that is, "rip up men's hearts, to make them see their sins." Second, it should season through the application of the gospel whereby people are "reconciled unto God, and made savory in his sight."

---

Laurence Chaderton first introduced Peter Ramus' *Ars Logica* to Cambridge students in the 1560s. Ramus (1515–1572), a convert from Roman Catholicism, proposed a method to simplify all academic subjects—a single logic for both dialectic and rhetoric. The task of the logician was to classify concepts, in order to make them understandable and memorable. This was accomplished through method—the orderly presentation of a subject. The *Ars Logica* quickly won the support of many Puritans, including Gabriel Harvey—a lecturer who used Ramus' method to reform the arts curriculum of grammar, rhetoric, and logic. Harvey's presentation deeply impressed Perkins. In his writings, Perkins regularly employed Ramus' method by presenting his subject's partition, often by dichotomies, into progressively more heads or topics, applying each truth set forth. Pipa demonstrates that Perkins did not slavishly follow Ramus, in that he was not locked into the use of dichotomy. See Pipa, "William Perkins," 161–68.

27. Perkins, *Art of Prophesying*, 2:646. For a helpful discussion about urgency in Puritan preaching, see Kuivenhoven, "Condemning Coldness and Sleepy Dullness," 180–200.

28. The term "experiential" (or, experimental) comes from the Latin verb *experior* (to know by experience).

29. While applying these verses primarily to ministers, Perkins does not deny their broader application to all Christians, writing, "As these similitudes concern the ministers, so they may well be enlarged to every Christian in this place: for in this regard the minister is a pattern to his people" (Perkins, *A Godly and Learned Exposition*, 3:27–28).

30. Perkins, *A Godly and Learned Exposition*, 3:23.

31. Ibid.

Third, it should preserve, so that "sin and corruption" are "daily mortified and consumed both in heart and life."[32]

Regarding light, Perkins explained that Christ is the "original" light, while his ministers are the "reflected" light.[33] He believed the "similitude" of light is significant for two reasons.[34] First, it reveals the proper end of preaching. In brief, God has ordained it to be a light, whereby ignorance is expelled, so that people see their sin and the way of salvation. Second, it reveals how the Word is to be preached; namely, "so as it may be a light unto men's minds and consciences, to make them see their sins, and their great misery thereby; then, to let them see the remedy from that misery, which is Jesus Christ."[35]

By such preaching God's grace breaks through into our experience. This experience begins with humiliation.[36] God "softens" our hearts by giving us a "sight of sin" arising from our knowledge of the law and a "sorrow for sin" arising from our knowledge of His displeasure.[37] We recognize that we will never attain salvation by any "strength or goodness" of our own. Having softened our hearts, God causes faith "to breed." He leads us to "ponder most diligently" His great mercy offered in Christ, and He brings us to acknowledge our "need of Christ" whereby we pray, "O God be merciful to me a sinner." Accompanying this faith is repentance, which Perkins defined as "a work of grace, arising of a godly sorrow whereby a man turns from all his sins to God."[38] From humiliation, faith, and repentance, our experience of God's grace moves to obedience. Simply put, "new obedience" is the fruit of faith and repentance, whereby a man "endeavors to

---

32. J. I. Packer explains the modern-day significance of preaching the law: "Some will assure us that it is a waste of time preaching to modern hearers about the law and sin, for (it is said) such things mean nothing to them. Instead (it is suggested) we should just appeal to the needs which they feel already, and present Christ to them simply as One who gives peace, power and purpose to the neurotic and frustrated—a super-psychiatrist, in fact... Such preaching may soothe some, but it will help nobody; for a Christ who is not seen and sought as a Savior from sin will not be found to save from self or anything else" (Packer, *A Quest for Godliness*, 164–65).

33. Perkins, *A Godly and Learned Exposition*, 3:26.

34. Ibid.

35. Ibid.

36. For more on this, see Yuille, "Ready to Receive," 91–106.

37. Perkins, *Treatise Tending Unto a Declaration*, 1:363.

38. Perkins, *Two Treatises*, 1:453.

yield obedience to all God's commandments, from all the powers and parts both of his soul and his body."[39]

For Perkins, this experience of God's grace in humiliation, faith, repentance, and obedience is essential. We must seek "the graces of God's children who are regenerate, even true faith, true repentance, and new obedience, and not rest in other gifts though they be most excellent."[40] For Perkins, there was a clear difference between speculative (notional) knowledge and sensible (inclinational) knowledge. The first involves the head alone whereas the second involves the head and heart. With this distinction in view, he exhorted his readers:

> We must labor for the power of this knowledge in ourselves, that we may know Christ to be our Savior, and may feel the power of His death to mortify sin in us, and the virtue of His resurrection to raise and build us up to newness of life for knowledge in the brain will not save the soul. Saving knowledge in religion is experimental, and he that is truly founded upon Christ feels the power and efficacy of His death and resurrection, effectually causing the death of sin, and the life of grace which both appear by new obedience.[41]

For Perkins, this affective appropriation of God's grace, moving beyond intellectual assent to heartfelt dedication to Christ, comes through only one means—preaching.[42] It is the means by which God reveals Himself to us. It is the means by which God imparts His grace to us. It is the instrument by which the Holy Spirit effects our union with Christ. In sum, Perkins affirmed that the "only ordinary means" by which to attain faith is "the word preached." It must be "heard, remembered, practiced, and continually hid in the heart."[43] Perkins inherited this view of preaching as the most effective means of grace from John Calvin, who championed the "sacramental word."[44] Commenting on Romans 10:17,[45] Calvin wrote, "This is a remarkable passage with regard to the efficacy of preaching; for [the apostle] testifies

---

39. Perkins, *A Godly and Learned Exposition*, 3:246.
40. Ibid., 3:249.
41. Ibid., 3:259–60.
42. Experiential preaching "addresses the vital matter of how a Christian experiences the truth of biblical, Christian doctrine in his life" (Beeke, *Puritan Reformed Spirituality*, 425–43).
43. Perkins, *A Treatise Tending unto a Declaration*, 1:363.
44. Calvin, *Institutes*, 4.14.4.
45. "So then faith cometh by hearing, and hearing by the word of God."

that by it faith is produced . . . when it pleases the Lord to work, it becomes the instrument of his power."[46] Perkins adopted Calvin's view, stressing the efficacy of God's Word, preached in the power of the Holy Spirit.[47] And it is this conviction that led him to formulate a method of preaching that would (in his opinion) best achieve its experiential end.

## Methodical Preaching

In *The Art of Prophesying*, Perkins laid out "the sacred and only method of preaching" in four succinct steps. The first is "to read the text distinctly out of the canonical Scriptures." At this point, Perkins's conviction regarding the authority and sufficiency of Scripture steps to the fore. He believed in the "canonical" Scriptures, consisting of the thirty-nine books of the Old Testament and the twenty-seven books of the New Testament. These constitute the "wisdom of God concerning the truth."[48] As such, they alone form the substance of prophesying. Perkins did not employ the term "prophesying" in the sense of fore-telling but forth-telling. Viewing the apostolic period as unique in the history of the church, he was a cessationist when it comes to revelatory gifts. Perkins was adamant that the nature of the Holy Spirit's work in the authors of Scripture was unique. He now illuminates what he then inspired. That is to say, he only works upon the foundation of the Word. For Perkins, this implied that the theologian's task is simply to expound what the Holy Spirit has revealed in Scripture.

The second step in preaching is "to give the sense and understanding" of the text. This is known as interpretation: "the opening of the words and sentences of the Scripture, so that one entire and natural sense may appear."[49]

---

46. Calvin, *Commentaries on the Epistle of the Apostle Paul to the Romans*, 19.401.

47. J. I. Packer maintains that four axioms underlay all Puritan thought about preaching. The first is the primacy of the intellect. The Puritans believed that all grace enters through the understanding. The second is the importance of preaching. In Packer's words, the sermon was "the liturgical climax of public worship." The third is the life-giving power of the Scripture. In other words, the Bible does not merely contain the Word of God, but it is the Word of God. The fourth is the sovereignty of the Holy Spirit. The Puritans insisted that the ultimate effectiveness of preaching is out of man's hands. See Packer, *A Quest for Godliness*, 281–84.

48. Perkins, *Art of Prophesying*, 2:649. As Breward observes, the "discussion of inspiration and the nature of the Bible was . . . fundamental to Perkins's whole theology and to his understanding of the pastoral task of proclaiming the gospel" (Breward, "Introduction," 38).

49. Perkins, *Art of Prophesying*, 2:653. Richard Muller observed that Perkins

Perkins's process is straightforward. He encouraged preachers to consider the literary style and structure of the text, and then explain specific words and phrases.[50] He also encouraged preachers to ask questions of each text. How does it relate to the principal themes of Scripture? What is its context, author, audience, and purpose? What other passages of Scripture shed light on it? In all this, Perkins emphasized that the preacher's principal goal is to "open" Scripture, so that its meaning becomes evident to all.

The third step in preaching is "to collect a few and profitable points of doctrine." Perkins referred to this process as "the right cutting of the Word."[51] In simple terms, it involves deducing the main point of a passage: theological and practical. According to Perkins, the mind is the supreme faculty of the soul. In making this assertion, he was not suggesting that the will necessarily follows the dictates of the mind. Rather, in referring to the mind as the supreme faculty of the soul, Perkins intended to convey the reality that the knowledge of God always begins in the mind because the will cannot choose what the mind does not know. In affirming the temporal priority of the mind, he remarked, "The mind must approve and give assent, before the will can choose or will: and when the mind has not power to conceive or give assent, there the will has no power to will."[52]

The fourth and final step in preaching is "to apply the doctrines rightly collected to the life and manners of men in a simple and plain speech."[53] This is where Perkins excelled by carefully dividing his audience into six categories: (1) the ignorant and unteachable; (2) the ignorant and teachable; (3) the knowledgeable and proud; (4) the knowledgeable and humble; (5) those who believe; and (6) those who have fallen. Recognizing that a typical congregation consists of people from each of these categories,[54] Perkins encouraged preachers to know their people, so that they are equipped to

---

"evidences a preference for a close, literal/grammatical location of the meaning of the text coupled with, as was true of the work of his predecessors in the Reformed tradition, a strong sense of the direct theological address of the text to the church in the present" (Muller, "William Perkins and the Protestant Exegetical Tradition," 87). Muller explains Perkins's use of "scope" and "method" in exegesis—he divides each verse, explains the meaning of its parts, and then draws out the text's argument in terms of the grammatical and logical relations of the parts.

50. Perkins, *Art of Prophesying*, 2:653–62.
51. Ibid., 2:662.
52. Perkins, *A Reformed Catholic*, 1:553.
53. Perkins, *Art of Prophesying*, 2:664.
54. For a helpful analysis of these categories, see Hulse, "William Perkins," 177–94.

"apply the doctrines" to each one through correction, admonition, and exhortation. "Thus any place of Scripture ought to be handled," wrote Perkins, "yet so as that all the doctrines be not propounded to the people, but those only which may be fitly applied to our times and to the present condition of the church. And they must not only be choice ones, but also few, lest the hearers be overcharged with their multitude."[55]

The effectiveness of Perkins's own preaching was due in large part to this last step. He had a penchant for dealing with "cases of conscience" through careful self-examination and faithful scriptural application.[56] According to one report, each of his sermons "seemed all law and all gospel, all cordials and all corrosives, as the different necessities of people apprehended it."[57] By all accounts, he was a skilled spiritual physician, who excelled at expounding and applying God's truth to those under his pastoral care. He adapted his theological learning to the needs of his people because he was determined to preach sermons that appealed to every listener. He was committed to ensuring that his preaching was clear, simple, and direct. He believed this simple method was the best way to convince the judgment and embrace the affections, thereby bringing the mind into vital contact with the meaning of Scripture.

## Supernatural Preaching

Perkins recognized, however, that his experiential end (the "sense") and methodical approach (the "manner") to preaching were insufficient in themselves to effect lasting change in others: "We preachers may cry until our lungs fly out, or be spent within us, and men are moved no more than stones."[58] There was still a missing element—unction (the demonstration of God's power). Such power is evident when people judge that the Holy Spirit is speaking through the preacher's words and gestures. Perkins explained, "When as the minister of the Word doth in the time of preaching so behave himself, that all, even ignorant persons and unbelievers may judge, that it is not so much he that speaketh, as the Spirit of God in him and by him . . . This

---

55. Perkins, *Art of Prophesying*, 2:669.

56. Breward, "William Perkins and the Origins of Puritan Casuistry," 16–22; Mosse, *The Holy Pretence*, 48–67.

57. Fuller, *Abel Redevivus*, 434.

58. Perkins, *A Faithful and Plain Exposition*, 3:424.

makes the ministry to be lively and powerful."[59] But how is such unction achieved? While recognizing that anointed preaching ultimately resides in the sovereign will of the Holy Spirit, Perkins maintained that the Holy Spirit is more likely to bless a certain kind of preaching.

This preaching is marked by simplicity. Perkins encouraged a "plain" style, because he was convinced that "a strange word hinders the understanding of those things that are spoken . . . It draws the mind away from the purpose to some other matter."[60] Closely related to this, Perkins perceived that far too many preachers were overly concerned with the "trimmings" of their sermons and, therefore, unable to convey Christ in a living way to their people. He was deeply dissatisfied with and openly critical of the "ornate" style of preaching widespread within the Church of England.[61] He believed it was weighed down with human learning, which rendered it ineffective. A pastor's aim should not be the demonstration of his skill, but the demonstration of God's power. It was essential for Perkins, therefore, that a preacher possess not only "the knowledge of divine things flowing in his brain but engraved on his heart and printed in his soul by the spiritual finger of God."[62]

This preaching is marked, secondly, by liberty. Perkins was opposed to "memorizing" sermons because he believed it quenched freedom in preaching: "He which through fear doth stumble at one word, doth trouble the congregation, and confound the memory."[63] In addition to this, Perkins was convinced that memorization hinders "pronunciation, action, and the holy motions of the affections . . . because the mind is wholly bent on this, to wit, that the memory fainting now under her burden may not fail."[64] Perkins's method was straightforward. As he prepared each sermon, he studied and prepared until he was familiar with the content of his message. Then, he developed a clear sermon outline accompanied by arguments and

---

59. Perkins, *Art of Prophesying*, 2:670.

60. Ibid.

61. As Joseph Pipa observes, the "ornate" style was chiefly concerned about "the abundant use of rhetorical devices such as repetition, heaping of examples, gradation or word-chains and schemata . . . innumerable quotations from the church fathers and various secular sources" (Pipa, "William Perkins and the Development of Puritan Preaching," 38). For more on the styles of preaching, see Miller, *The New England Mind*; Blench, *Preaching in England*; and Davies, *The Worship of English Puritans*.

62. Perkins, *Art of Prophesying*, 2:672.

63. Ibid., 2:670.

64. Ibid., 2:2.

illustrations. He felt this approach allowed for liberty in expression. This liberty was facilitated by Perkins's use of voice and body. His voice was moderate when delivering doctrine, yet fervent when applying God's truth to the heart. His bodily gestures conveyed gravity. The trunk of his body was quiet, while the motions of his arms, hands, and eyes expressed "the godly affections of the heart."[65]

This preaching is marked, thirdly, by consistency. As far as Perkins was concerned, God's grace must be evident in a preacher's life. Such grace includes a good conscience before God and man, and an inward feeling of God's truth. It also includes fear of God, love for people, constancy in life, and temperance in conduct.[66] In Perkins's estimation, holiness in a preacher is absolutely necessary, because God "abhors the combination of godly speech and an ungodly life."[67] Equally important, Perkins realized that "people do not see the ministry but the person of the minister" and, for this reason, there must be consistency between a pastor's words and walk. Perkins's own growth in godliness was a powerful example to all. According to one biographer, "he lived his sermons, and as his preaching was a comment on his text, so his practice was a comment on his preaching."[68]

Simplicity, liberty, and consistency are no guarantee of unction, but (in Perkins's estimation) characterize the kind of preaching that is most likely to experience the Holy Spirit's blessing.

## Conclusion

Given his theology of preaching (*experiential* in end, *methodical* in approach, and *supernatural* in effect), it is no surprise that Perkins gave himself wholeheartedly to it and to imparting his simple method to others. When Thomas Goodwin enrolled at Cambridge in 1613, a full ten years after Perkins's death, he could write, "The town was then filled with the discourse of the power of Master Perkins's ministry, still fresh in most men's memories."[69] His insights became the standard for a generation of preachers, thereby shaping the pulpit and pew well into the next century, and down to the present day. The initial result was so profound that, in 1684,

---

65. Ibid, 2:672.
66. Ibid.
67. Ibid, 2:671.
68. Fuller, *Abel Redevivus*, 436.
69. Quoted in Breward, "Introduction," 9.

three ministers acclaimed him as the sole reason their day was a "more fertile" season of preaching than "any since that of the apostles."[70]

---

70. Manton, "To the Reader," 9:316.

# Part 2

# Sacraments

# 4

# Union, Communion, and *Communio*

*Elements of Reformed Ecclesiology*

—J. V. Fesko

## Introduction

Discussion about the sacraments entails questions about their nature. Are they merely memorial signs or do they in some manner communicate grace to the recipient? Such questions are valid and necessary but people are quick to run to various scriptural texts and propose metaphysical principles to address how God might, or might not, convey grace to the recipient. Rather than look at the trees of this dense forest, we must first account for the forest. To change metaphors, the sacraments are but one detail in a larger doctrinal portrait. There are intricately connected doctrinal brushstrokes that inform and create the greater context for the doctrine of the sacraments. Hence a good exploration of the sacraments in the Reformed theological matrix must take this wider context into account. Three broad headings provide a rubric to examine a Reformed view of the sacraments: union, communion, and *communio*. The sacraments proclaim the union between God and man—the incarnation—which is the foundation for our redemption and subsequent communion between the triune God and redeemed human beings. But this communion between redeemed individuals and the triune God also entails *communio*, or an ecclesial bond or fellowship among the redeemed sinners. The sacraments visibly and performatively herald these realities in terms of their function as signs and seals of the covenant of grace, as the historic Reformed tradition has denominated them. In brief, this chapter first explores the historic Reformed doctrine of the sacraments under the rubric of union, communion, and *communio* through a historical-theological reconnaissance of these concepts in classic Reformed theology. Second, it explores the dogmatic differences between Reformed and Roman Catholic views. And third, the chapter briefly offers exegetical-theological reflection in support of a Reformed view of the sacraments. The chapter concludes by presenting a summation of a Reformed view of the sacraments.

## Historical-Theological Reflection: Union, Communion, and *Communio*

John Owen's work, *Of Communion with God the Father, Son, and Holy Ghost* (1657), provides a paradigmatic statement regarding the relationship between union and communion: "Our communion, then, with God consisteth in his communication of himself unto us with our returnal unto him of that which he requireth and accepteth, flowing from that union which in Jesus Christ we have with him."[1] Following patristic and medieval categories, Owen closely associates the doctrines of union with Christ and the believer's communion with the triune God. In this respect Owen employs the *exitus-reditus* pattern common to medieval theologies of participation, such as in the *Summa Theologica* of Thomas Aquinas.[2] But important to note is that when Owen invokes the connections between union and communion, he cites a text purportedly written by Cyprian of Carthage, *De Coena Domini* ("On the Lord's Supper"). The problem with this citation is, however, that Cyprian did not write the treatise. Contemporary scholarship has identified the work as originating from medieval theologian Ernaldus Bonaevallis and his work *De Cardinalibus Christi Operibus* (1156).[3] Regardless of the text's origins, the point should not be lost: Owen draws support for his doctrines of union and communion from a treatise on the sacrament of the Lord's Supper. The sacrament of the Lord's Supper has roots that extend deep into the soil of the believer's union with Christ, but this union does not begin in the believer's regeneration but with the incarnation.

According to Owen, the union between God and humankind originates in the hypostatic union of the two natures of Christ—the divine and

---

1. Owen, *Communion*, 8–9.
2. Cf. Te Velde, *Aquinas on God*, 11–18.
3. Thompson, *Eucharistic Sacrifice and Patristic Tradition*, 76 n. 14. Cf. Bonaevallis, *De Cardinalibus Christi Operibus*, 1609–78.

the human united in one person (John 1:14; Isa 9:6; Rom 1:3, 9:5; Luke 1:35; 1 Tim 3:16). The Son of God and the Son of Man are united in one person—the God-man.[4] In this, Owen follows a common path established by a number of second-generation Reformed theologians such as Peter Martyr Vermigli and Girolamo Zanchi.[5] The incarnation is an embodied prophetic promise of God's mystical union with redeemed human beings. But the incarnation is more than the revelation of the triune God's ultimate redemptive intent—it is also the very means by which he accomplishes his intended goal. The incarnational union is the basis for the redemption, the believer's mystical union with Christ. Through the incarnation Christ accomplishes his law-obedience and suffering, which becomes the legal ground of the believer's mystical union with Christ.[6] And this mystical bond becomes the basis for the believer's communion with Christ.[7] Owen repeatedly describes this bond in terms of the "conjugal relation" between Christ and the believer, that which envelopes the legal (justification) and transformative (sanctification) elements of redemption.[8] Drawing upon an older medieval interpretive tradition of theologians like Bernard of Clairvaux and repeated by other Reformed theologians such as Theodore Beza, Owen argues that this conjugal relation and "pattern of communion," is the subject matter of the Song of Songs.[9] This interpretive understanding of the Song of Songs was common within the Reformed church and even appears in the widely distributed Geneva Bible (1560).[10] The overall point in Owen's exposition is that God's creatures go out from him in their creation and return through union, which becomes manifest in the hypostatic union, then in Christ's mystical union with the believer, and in this manner God communicates himself to human beings.

Owen explains that God communicates himself by sending his Son to become incarnate, which is a work of the Spirit. God communicates himself through the Son and Spirit, and thus embraces the believer in a

---

4. Owen, *Communion*, 51.

5. Vermigli, "Vermigli to Beza," 134–47; Zanchi, *De Religione*, 1:234–35.

6. Owen, *Communion*, 170–71.

7. Ibid., 173.

8. Ibid., 54, 155.

9. Ibid., 125; cf. Bernard of Clairvaux, *On the Song of Songs*; Beza, *Master Bezaes Sermons*.

10. See, for example, the "argument" of the book in the 1560 Geneva Bible (*The Bible and Holy Scriptures Conteyned in the Olde and Newe Testament*, 280).

holy communion—a fellowship, a mystical bond. Through this spiritual indwelling, God raises the dead to life, pours out his love, and infuses the redeemed with habitual and actual grace to the end of seeing the believer produce the fruit of obedience.[11] Owen describes the nature of the Spirit's work in an extended statement worth quoting in full:

> The Father Loves us, and 'chose us before the Foundation of the world;' but in the pursuit of that love, he 'blesseth us with all spiritual blessings in heavenly places in Christ,' Eph. i. 3, 4. From his love, he sheds, or pours out the Holy Spirit richly upon us, through Jesus Christ our Saviour, Tit. iii. 6. In the pouring out of his love, there is not one drop that falls besides the Lord Christ. The holy anointing oil, was all poured on the head of Aaron: Ps. cxxxiii. 2; and thence went down to the skirts of his clothing. Love is first poured out on Christ; and from him, it drops as the dew of Hermon upon the souls of his saints. The Father will have him to have 'in all things the pre-eminence,' Col. i. 18; 'it pleased him that in him all fulness should dwell,' verse 19; that 'of his fulness we might receive, and grace for grace,' John i. 16. Though the love of the Father's purpose and good pleasure have its rise and foundation in his mere grace and will, yet the design of its accomplishment is only in Christ. All the fruits of it are first given to him; and it is in him only that they are dispensed to us. So that though the saints may, nay, do, see an infinite ocean of love unto them in the bosom of the Father, yet they are not to look for one drop from him but what comes through Christ. He is the only means of communication. Love in the Father, is like *honey in the flower*; it must be in the comb, before it be for our use. Christ must extract and prepare this honey for us. He draws this water from the fountain through union and dispensation of fullness;—we by faith, from the wells of salvation that are in him.[12]

The Father, then, pours out his love through the Spirit upon the Son, and then the Son in turn pours out the love of the triune God through the Spirit upon his body, the elect.

The Spirit accomplishes this work by uniting the believer to Christ, which he does through the "ordinance of the word."[13]

More specifically, Owen explains that the Holy Spirit establishes a ministry in the church and designates men for the task, furnishes them with

---

11. Owen, *Communion*, 203.
12. Ibid., 27.
13. Ibid., 267.

the requisite gifts so they are properly equipped to preach the word.[14] This is the means by which believers have communion with the triune God—through word and Spirit. Owen's emphasis is not unique but is common to the Reformed tradition, as numerous theologians connect the communion that believers have with the triune God to the word, whether the audible or visible word—the word preached or the sacramental word. For example, Zacharias Ursinus, the chief commentator on the Heidelberg Catechism (1563), explains that the sacraments "are pledges of that communion which Christians have with Christ in the first place, and then with each other." They are for those who are "covenanted with Christ" and are "bonds of mutual love."[15] In contrast to Roman Catholic views, which characterize the sacraments in Augustinian Platonic terms as visible signs of invisible grace, the sacraments for the Reformed signify "the new covenant itself, i.e., Christ with all the benefits which are prepared in him for believers," according to William Ames.[16] Johannes Cocceius explains along similar lines: "Sacraments are neither the causes of justification and sanctification nor the conditions of them, but the signs of the covenant, partly inviting us by the Spirit's grace to faith whereby we flee to Christ, and working morally upon faith for communion with him."[17]

All of this is to say, believers enjoy communion with the triune God through the work of Christ and the Spirit by means of the word—word and sacrament. In Christ's absence he sends the Spirit who brings the word to nourish, strengthen, and foster the communion between the triune God and the redeemed sinner. And in this manner Christ becomes present in the midst of his people and thus fellowships and communes with them. The link between union, communion, and *communio* appears prominently in the Westminster Confession of Faith (1647), which devotes an entire chapter to the communion of the saints. The Confession states: "All saints, that are united to Jesus Christ their Head, by his Spirit, and by faith, have fellowship with him in his graces, sufferings, death, resurrection, and glory: and, being united to one another in love, they have communion in each other's gifts and graces, and are obliged to the performance of such duties, public and private, as do conduce to their mutual good, both in the inward

---

14. Ibid., 268.

15. Ursinus, *Commentary*, 345.

16. Ames, *Marrow*, 1.xxxvi.23; cf. Aquinas, *Catechism*, 254; Jordan, "Theology and Philosophy," 242.

17. Cocceius, *Summa Theologiae*, LII.17, cited in Heppe, *Reformed Dogmatics*, 601.

and outward man" (XXVI.i).¹⁸ In particular, ordained ministers who have received the requisite gifts of the Spirit, namely the ability to preach and herald the audible and visible word, nurture the bond between God and his people and among one another through the ministry of the word applied by the Spirit. God joins individual believers to the Son through the work of the Spirit; the vertical bond between God and humankind also entails a horizontal bond between the individuals as they comprise the body, the church. And Christ, the head, nourishes the body through his word, the audible and visible word.

## Dogmatic Comparison: Invisible Grace and Ascent vs. the Visible Descent of Christ and His Word

In broad brush strokes, Reformed ecclesiology and doctrine of the sacraments look very similar to Roman Catholic views, as Rome frames the sacraments in terms of union and communion.¹⁹ But there are some significant differences between the two—one rests on Dionysian concepts of participation and the other rests directly on Christ and his word. Pseudo-Dionysius was influential upon the medieval church and his understanding of participation impacted later Roman Catholic theology, especially in terms of ecclesiology and sacraments.²⁰ In a common Dionysian understanding, a Platonic conception of *exitus-reditus* marks the overall structure, but within this pattern there is a hierarchy of beings. There are three ranks of angelic beings, and proximity to the triune God determines hierarchy.²¹ The higher-ranking beings have the responsibility to pass divine knowledge down to the lower beings. To convey divine knowledge down the chain is to participate in the divine. The heavenly hierarchy has its earthly counterpart in the ecclesiastical hierarchy of the church. The closer one is to God, the higher his rank.²²

---

18. Unless otherwise noted, all confessions and catechisms are cited from Pelikan and Hotchkiss, *Creeds and Confessions*.

19. See, for example, *Catechism of the Catholic Church*, §§1369–72.

20. Aquinas, *Summa Contra Gentiles*, IV:75; Leclerq, "Influence and Noninfluence of Dionysius," 30–31.

21. Pseudo-Dionysius, *Celestial Hierarchy*, I.i and III.i–ii, in Rorem, *Pseudo-Dionysius*, 145, 153–54.

22. Ibid., VII.iii; Rorem, *Pseudo-Dionysius*, 164.

Hence, monks are naturally higher in rank than laymen because they have devoted their lives to the knowledge of God and its pursuit, but higher than monks are deacons, priests, bishops, archbishops, until one ascends to the top of the hierarchy to the office of pope.[23] Just as in the angelic hierarchy, those who are higher in rank pass knowledge of the divine down the chain. Within this ecclesiastical priestly hierarchy the seven sacraments make the invisible grace of God manifest to those who otherwise do not have the ability to contemplate upon the knowledge of God.[24] Within this context one of the regular statements that appears in discussions on the sacraments is that they are visible signs of invisible grace.[25] Through the sacraments people lay hold of the invisible grace of God and thus commence their ascent to the divine and participate in the divine nature.[26]

Owen and other Reformed theologians were not averse to the broad outline of Dionysian conceptions of participation, as is evident from his initial definition of communion, where God communicates himself to his creatures and his creatures return to him. But Protestant theologians set aside certain Dionysian elements. Martin Luther refocused the sacraments away from Dionysian concepts of invisible grace and human ascent and centered them upon Christ and his word and divine descent. Moreover, people could interact directly with Christ the only mediator rather than through a hierarchical order of priests. The sacraments were no longer visible signs of invisible grace mediated through a priestly ladder by which human beings scaled the heavens but instead were visible forms of God's promises—visible forms of God's word by which he condescends to fallen sinners.[27] Reformed theologians whole-heartedly embraced Luther's reconfiguration of the sacraments.[28] Moreover, they reduced Rome's seven sacraments (baptism, confirmation, the Lord's Supper, penance, marriage, extreme unction, and holy orders) to two—baptism and the Lord's Supper—another indicator of their rejection of Dionysian hierarchical mediated sacramental access to God.

23. Pseudo-Dionysius, *Ecclesiastical Hierarchy*, V.iii, in Rorem, *Pseudo-Dionysius*, 235.

24. Ibid., I.iv; Rorem, *Pseudo-Dionysius*, 199.

25. Aquinas, *Summa Contra Gentiles*, IV:74.

26. Ibid.; Pseudo-Dionysius, *Ecclesiastical Hierarchy*, I.iv in Rorem, *Pseudo-Dionysius*, 198.

27. Luther, "Babylonian Captivity of the Church," 124; *Apology of the Augsburg Confession*, art. XIII, in Kolb and Wengert, *The Book of Concord*, 219–20.

28. Bierma, *Theology of the Heidelberg Catechism*, 73–82.

Despite the shift in sacramental theology, both Roman Catholics and the Reformed appeal to Augustine of Hippo, but they appeal to different elements of his sacramental thought. Roman Catholics appeal to texts where Augustine characterizes the sacraments as visible signs of invisible grace, whereas the Reformed appeal to statements where the African bishop describes them as visible words.[29] If we keep in mind that the word of God is both his spoken word and his Son, then this explains how Reformed theologians can repeatedly claim that the sacraments hold forth both Christ and his word. Ursinus, for example, comments on Augustine's reflections on the sacraments and then concludes: "Without Christ, who is the thing signified in the sacraments of both testaments, no one ever has been saved, or can be saved."[30] Again, Ursinus writes, "The thing signified is Christ, with all his benefits; or, it is the communion, and participation of Christ, and his benefits."[31] But when Ursinus explains the relationship between Christ and the sacrament, he makes recourse to the word: "Briefly, a sacramental form of speech is that in which the name, or property of the sign is attributed to the thing signified."[32] Ursinus appeals directly to Augustine for this connection when he defines a sacrament as "a visible word."[33] But Ursinus does not conflate or flatten the distinction between word and sacrament. Rather, "the sacraments differ from the word in this, that they signify by actions and gestures what the word does by language."[34]

The Reformed, therefore, do use the phrase "visible signs of invisible grace," but arguably place greater emphasis on the idea that the sacraments hold forth Christ, are visible words, visible promises, or signs and seals of the covenant of grace. The Tetrapolitan Confession (1530) invokes the invisible-visible grace aphorism but also calls the sacraments "outward words" (XVI). The French Confession (1559) says the sacraments are "added to the word for more ample confirmation" (XXXIV). Similarly, the Belgic Confession (1561) states that the sacraments are "visible signs and seals of something invisible" but in a Lutheran way the Belgic states they "seal the promises in us" (XXXIII).[35] The Westminster Confession calls the

---

29. E.g., Ursinus, *Commentary*, 353.
30. Ibid., 346.
31. Ibid., 347.
32. Ibid., 349.
33. Ibid., 353.
34. Ibid., 356.
35. Cf. Bierma, *Theology of the Heidelberg Catechism*, 73–76.

sacraments, "holy signs and seals of the covenant of grace, immediately instituted by God, to represent Christ, and his benefits" (XXVII.i).

The Second Helvetic Confession (1566) draws some of the strongest links between the sacraments and the word when it states: "From the beginning God added to the preaching of his word in his church sacraments or sacramental signs . . . Sacraments are mystical symbols, or holy rites, or sacred actions, instituted by God himself, consisting of his word, of signs, and of things signified" (XIX.i). But the word of the sacraments is not indistinct or vague but the visible word by which "God promises Christ the Savior" (XIX.iv). When we combine these sacramental statements with the confession's characterization of the preached word as the "very word of God" proclaimed and received by the faithful (I.iv), the sacraments take on a performative character. That is, they are not mere rites, ceremonies, or bare memorials as in a Zwinglian view, but in the words of the Westminster Shorter Catechism, they are "effectual means of salvation."[36] As the catechism states, they are effectual means of salvation, not by any virtue in them, or because of the worthiness of the one who administers them, but only through the blessing of Christ and by the work of the Holy Spirit in the hearts of believers (q. 91).

## Exegetical-Theological Reflection

The sacraments, therefore, visibly proclaim and truly enliven the believer's participation in the divine nature, to use Peter's words (2 Pet 1:4), or in theological terms, union and communion with Christ. When the preaching of the word begets the sacraments, they visibly preach Christ and his work to our other senses. The sacrament of the Lord's Supper, for example, visibly proclaims the hypostatic union—the Son of God in the flesh—as well as the believer's mystical union with Christ. As the recipient partakes of the bread and the wine, he consumes the visible word of God and receives God's grace—the grace of the transformative gospel. The recipient is not merely reminded of Christ's incarnation and work, as in a Zwinglian memorialist view. Ceremonies and rites abound in our culture and even in the church, but their performative dimension has withered. The sacraments in many Evangelical quarters are nothing more than a personal rededication or redoubling of a waning faith, and the effect is intrapsychic or at best

---

36. Cf. Zwingli, *Exposition of the Faith*, 264–65.

social, but surely not performative.[37] Rather, within the broader context of God's covenantal dealings with his people, God's word in any form has a performative character. In the simplest of terms, God does things with words. Whether in his first words uttered in the opening pages of Scripture, "Let there be light" (Gen 1:3), which brought forth the creation of light, or in Christ's death-dispelling call to Lazarus (John 11:43), God exercises his power through his word, whether in the spoken prophetic word, through the incarnate word, the inscripturated word, or the preached word in both its audible and visible forms (cf. Heb 1:1). This means that the sacramental word is an "effectual means of salvation," and a verbal-covenantal bond of our union and communion with Christ, as well as the unifying "one baptism" (Eph 4:5) and "one bread" (1 Cor 10:17) of our *communio*. Within this context the sacraments are God's performative word.[38]

We can drill down into the substratum of the sacraments when we consider specific elements of baptism and the Lord's Supper and unearth the union-communion-*communio* connections. The broader Evangelical church characterizes baptism in individualistic terms—the only one who benefits is the one who gets wet. Moreover, in various formulations, baptism is the believer's personal pledge to serve God and nothing more. With so much emphasis upon what the believer intends to say in baptism, it begs the question, What does God intend? What does God say in baptism? And why does God use water? In brief, admission rites do not shift from circumcision to baptism, from something supposedly fleshly to something spiritual, as some theologians contend.[39] Despite claims to the contrary, water is just as physical and this worldly as circumcision—less bloody, yes, less physical, no. Circumcision gives way to baptism because Christ, the seed of the woman, has arrived, been cut off (circumcised) in his bloody circumcision crucifixion, and in the wake of his completed work he has, in the words of John the prophet, baptized the church in Spirit and fire (Luke 3:16).[40]

But Christ's outpouring of the Spirit does not originate from his own hands but from the hands of the Father. The Father first poured out the Holy Spirit upon his Son—*Christ* is not Jesus' last name but an official title, *the anointed*, which begs the question, With what was Jesus anointed? The

---

37. Taylor, *Language Animal*, 81–82.

38. Ibid., 80.

39. E.g., Piper, *Brothers*, 134.

40. For detailed exegetical and theological argumentation, see Fesko, *Word, Water, and Spirit*, 199–264.

short answer is, the Holy Spirit. The Father poured out the Spirit, the bond of love between Father and Son, in order to empower Jesus to fulfill and complete his redemptive work (cf., for example, Isa 42:1–3; Heb 9:14).[41] But Christ then poured out the Spirit upon his church, powerfully enacted in the events of Pentecost. Pentecost was not just the advent of the Spirit, but the advent of Christ's Spirit—it was the earthly echo of Christ's victory procession into the heavenly holy of holies (cf. Ps 68; Eph 4:1–16).[42] Recall Peter's words to the crowd: "Being therefore exalted at the right hand of God, and having received from the Father the promise of the Holy Spirit, he has poured out this that you yourselves are seeing and hearing" (Acts 2:33; cf. Luke 3:22; 10:38). Peter sealed this proclamation of the word of God with the sign of baptism, the visible word of God and indicator that they would "receive the gift of the Holy Spirit" (Acts 2:38). These reflections bring us full-circle to Owen's beautiful observation about the shared bond of the Spirit we receive through the work of Christ. But paramount in all of this is that we recognize the communal aspect of baptism.

If we walk away from baptism and assume only the one who got wet benefited, then we have failed to understand the nature of the sacrament. When born from the preaching of God's word, the outpouring of water visibly heralds that the *whole church* has been baptized in the Spirit, not just the one lone individual. We behold the visible proclamation of Christ's promise to send the Holy Spirit and are nourished in our union with Christ, our sacred communion with the triune God, and the *communio* we all share one with another through the Spirit.

The sacrament of the Lord's Supper holds out the same truths but in a different scriptural octave. Baptism draws the collective gaze of the church to the finished work of the crucified Christ and his outpoured baptism of Spirit and fire that sacramentally and performatively proclaims the mystical bond that exists between Christ and his body. Whereas the Lord's Supper draws our attention to Christ's crucifixion as we behold the broken body and shed blood in sacramental form. At this point Roman Catholics accuse the Reformed of emptying the Supper of its christological substance because the Reformed deny the real presence of Christ in the sacrament—they deny the doctrine of transubstantiation. In fact, the Council of Trent spent a disproportionate amount of time engaging the memorialist

---

41. For more detailed exegetical and theological argumentation, see Fesko, *The Trinity and the Covenant of Redemption*, 319–26.

42. Farrow, *Ascension and Ecclesia*, 26.

views of Zwingli even though he was not the founder of a church, no reform movement bore his name, and he was long dead once the council started. Nevertheless, the Tridentine preoccupation with Zwingli's view of the sacraments exposed the Roman Catholic Church's deepest anxieties over what it perceived as the greatest threat to the integrity of the supper. Not Luther, but Zwingli and John Calvin, read through a Zwinglian lens, was a great threat to the church in Trent's eyes.[43] While the Reformed have denied the doctrine of transubstantiation, they have not denied the idea of Christ's presence at the supper.

The Reformed have denied the *local* presence of Christ in the elements because of a desire to protect two fundamental doctrines: the doctrine of the humanity of Christ and his ascension and royal session at the right hand of the Father. Christ is the God-man and as such he possesses two distinct natures, human and divine, that each retain their own distinct properties. Christ's human nature does not possess the attribute of ubiquity—his human nature can only occupy one place at a time. To deny this doctrine, whether through the doctrine of trans- or consubstantiation, imperils the humanity of Christ because it takes on the divine attribute of ubiquity and Christ's natures are no longer fully human and fully divine—two distinct natures in one person. Christ is no longer the God-man but instead a *tertium quid*. The Reformed also wanted to preserve the doctrine of Christ's ascension—his absence from the earth.[44] Does this mean, therefore, that the supper loses its significance?[45] The short answer is, no. Rather, when Christ sends forth his word through preaching, he seals it to our external senses through the sacraments and thereby stirs up our Spirit-wrought faith more powerfully and efficaciously than through the unadorned word, and by this means unites himself evermore tightly to his confederated bride. The bare word conjoined with the sacramental word strengthens the bond of our union with Christ—the supper is Christ's physical, but nevertheless sacramental, embrace from the heavens where he sits at the right hand of the Father.[46] The elements of the bread and wine are not for our physical nourishment but preach to our other bodily senses that nothing less than Christ offers his body and blood from heaven to be

---

43. Orsi, *History and Presence*, 23; cf. *Dogmatic Degrees of the Council of Trent*, session 7 (3 March 1547), "First Decree [On the Sacraments]."

44. See, for example, Vermigli, "Epitome of the Book Against Gardiner," 156.

45. Beza, "Appendix A," in *A System of Doctrine on the Sacramental Substance*, 161.

46. Beza, *Treatise on the Lord's Supper*, 60.

received by our eyes, hands, mouth, sense of smell, and most importantly, the mouth of faith. In this manner, then, believers feed upon the body and blood of Christ.[47] Beza, for example, characterizes the sacrament of the supper as a ladder (*scalis*) by which the Spirit unites us to Christ in heaven.[48] But he also highlights the intimacy, the communion, of the supper when he writes that the supper shows how close our union with Christ is, "For nothing joins us together more than food and drink since without these no one can move through this life."[49]

But why are the Reformed so insistent upon maintaining Christ's physical location at the right hand of the Father? Not only do the Reformed churches want to maintain the integrity of Christ's humanity, but they also want to preserve an eschatological point, namely Christ's earthly absence until the consummation, when he comes to judge the world.[50] This eschatological emphasis is twofold. First, Christ's physical absence reminds us that Christ's work is all but complete save the consummation, but in the intervening time he is nevertheless present through the work of the Spirit. Christ's words in the King James translation poetically capture this idea, "Lo, I am with you alway, even to the end of the world" (Matt 28:20, KJV). Despite Christ's great distance, he nevertheless remains intimately bound to us through the work of his Spirit. Peter Martyr Vermigli wonderfully illustrates this point:

> In human affairs, a husband sometimes happens to journey to a distant land, leaving his wife at home for a time, yet continuing to be (as Scripture says) one flesh with her. Their true, proper and lawful union remains perfect, through the one is absent from the other. How much more does Christ—husband of the church, as the Apostle says—remain united with his members though gone away into heaven and departed in body?[51]

In other words, despite Christ's absence, he nevertheless through his Spirit maintains and nourishes our union with him: "Thus although there is between us and Christ's body a great distance of place, yet we depend on him and are wondrously united with him."[52] If we fail to grasp that the Spirit

---

47. Ibid., 55.
48. Ibid., 23–24.
49. Beza, *System of Doctrine on the Sacramental Substance*, 164.
50. Beza, *Treatise on the Lord's Supper*, 21.
51. Vermigli, "Address to the Strasbourg Senate," 163.
52. Ibid.

is the bond of our union and thus, as Owen has written, is the agent of our union with the triune Lord, then we might fall into one of two extremes: we either tip over into an over realized eschatology, whereby all separation between Christ and church vanishes (as in Roman Catholic or Eastern Orthodox formulations), or we resort to illegitimate means of closing the gap and fall into idolatry. Like the Israelites waiting for Moses to descend from Sinai, we grow impatient with the Lord's tarrying and illegitimately create idols to close the gap.[53]

Instead of resorting to over realized eschatology or seeking illegitimate means to close the gap, we must continue to affirm two things: Christ's ascension to his royal session at the Father's right hand and the givenness of the sacraments as sign posts to the union and communion we share with Christ and the *communio* we share with one another during the interadventual period. The sacraments are not human-originated and thus a mere memorial or profession of human faith. Rather, the sacraments are divine revelation, and revelation is entirely a divine gift.[54] The apostle Paul states that he and the apostles were stewards of the mysteries of God (1 Cor 4:1; cf., for example, Col 1:27; 2:2; 4:3; Rom 16:25–26). A mystery, recall, is something once hidden but now revealed. We would not know of Christ apart from his revelation in word and sacraments. The sacraments, therefore, highlight the grace of God—they are not part of a commercial market of exchange, a quid pro quo. They are the self-giving of Christ to his bride because what shows itself ultimately gives itself.[55] Christ reveals God and thus gives himself freely to his people.

The gift-nature of the sacraments appears powerfully in the unfolding progressive revelatory shift from Old to New Testament, from the shadows and types to the anti-typical realities. Moses, Aaron and his sons, and Israel's elders were sprinkled with the blood of the covenant, ascended Mt. Sinai, and ate and drank in the presence of the Lord unharmed (Exod 24:11). Moses and the others did not ascend by their own volition but by divine invitation—which highlights the divine origins and gift nature of God's covenantal dealings with his people—in this case, a shared covenantal meal. But now, we all have been sprinkled with the blood of Christ, "that speaks a better word than the blood of Abel" (Heb 12:24), and ascend the heavens through the outpoured Spirit and eat and drink in his presence

---

53. Horton, *People and Place*, 13, 22.
54. Marion, *The Visible and the Revealed*, 80.
55. Ibid., 94–95; Marion, *Being Given*, 5.

unharmed—a gift of God's grace. Think, conversely, of those who do not know Christ or do not recognize his body and blood—they consume the supper to their judgment (1 Cor 11:27). In this respect, the supper is a miniature anticipation of the eschatological Parousia of Christ—only those who look to Christ by faith and are united to him through the bond of the Spirit share in eschatological life.

Unlike the Old Testament saints who were prohibited from consuming the blood of the sacrificial animal, we have been given the right to consume the blood of Christ, for in it we find life (cf. Deut 12:23; John 6:54; 1 Cor 11:25). And as the Father feeds his children through the Son, the manna from heaven, through the word and Spirit, we eagerly anticipate Christ's return. The supper in this respect is anything but a memorial but actually envelopes all of history. In the present we look back and commemorate Christ's sacrificial death but we also look expectantly to the future and the consummation of the age when faith will give way to sight and we will feast with Christ at the marriage supper of the Lamb as he promised (Luke 22:16–18). The sacrament is thus life-giving and sustains our union and communion with the triune God and our *communio* with one another—this is entirely the gift of God and thus a manifestation of his grace—indeed, the visible words of Christ, the manna from heaven.

## Conclusion

One cannot fully appreciate the trees unless he first explores the scope of the forest. Only once he beholds the expanse of the many varied hues, shapes, and sizes of the various trees of the forest can he begin to appreciate the individual trees. In this case, we must always account for the broader doctrinal context of the sacraments in order to appreciate fully their nature and what they accomplish. Union, communion, and *communio* provides the proper context for a thick account of a Reformed doctrine of the sacraments. The word of God goes forth embodied in water, bread, and wine—revelatory sign posts that at the same time herald the incarnate Son of God in his life, death, and resurrection—and the bond of fellowship he shares with his redeemed people, his body. But the sacramental word is more than a heraldic proclamation of the crucified Christ and the communion we share with him—it is also the very same all-powerful creative word that brought worlds into existence, raises the dead to life, and transforms our lowly bodies into the glorious image of Christ. The triune God employs the sacraments as effectual means of salvation but only when there is a sufficient preaching of the gospel to create a sacrament. The word is the womb of the sacrament, for apart from the word the water, bread, and wine are ordinary and mundane—not the sacred signs and seals of the covenant of grace. The sacraments cannot exist apart from the preaching of the word. Nevertheless, these word-birthed signs and seals visibly proclaim the union of God with humankind, both in the incarnational and mystical unions—they nourish, strengthen, and sustain us. The sacraments are the means by which Christ binds us to himself and to one another. Even though Christ is in some sense absent and yet to come, he is nevertheless present through word, sacrament, and his Spirit. The disembodied word, or conversely a mute sacramental substance, is just as unnatural as a phantasmal or silent Messiah.[56] Word and sacrament ultimately belong together and find their meaning within the wider rubrics of union, communion, and *communio*.

---

56. Farrow, *Ascension and Ecclesia*, 4.

# 5

# Visible Signs of Invisible Grace
*Sacraments for the "Low Church"*

—Keith D. Stanglin

## Introduction

In an essay that addresses evangelical sacramental theology, I feel that full disclosure is appropriate from the outset. I am a lifelong member of the Churches of Christ, a non-denominational denomination that arose in the early nineteenth-century American Restoration Movement (now sometimes called the "Stone-Campbell Movement"). I would like to begin by summarizing briefly the traditional beliefs and practices with regard to the two sacraments in Churches of Christ (including Christian Churches and Disciples of Christ, all of which I will sometimes refer to with the increasingly outmoded but also handy term, "Restorationists"), pointing out the combination of ideas that makes these "Restorationist" churches distinct from most other denominations.

First, the doctrine and practice of baptism in these churches can be summarized in three points, corresponding to the mode, subject, and end of baptism: baptism is immersion of believers for remission of sins. As to the mode (immersion) and proper subjects (penitent believers only) of baptism, we are like Baptists and other evangelicals, but unlike the typical practice of Roman Catholicism and most magisterial and mainline Protestant churches. Eastern Orthodoxy, to my knowledge, is the only major group who still regularly immerses infants. As to the end or purpose, for Churches of Christ, baptism is sacramental in the sense of being, as G. R.

Beasley-Murray put it, "a symbol with power."[1] This belief puts Churches of Christ closer to Roman Catholic, Orthodox, and Lutheran views, but farther from the typical Reformed and evangelical beliefs.

Second, the doctrine and practice of the Lord's Supper in Churches of Christ may also be summarized in three points, corresponding roughly to points about frequency and purpose or efficacy: the Lord's Supper is a weekly, Zwinglian ordinance. The strict connection between Lord's Supper and (each and every) Lord's Day has for two centuries distinguished Churches of Christ from most of our Protestant evangelical neighbors who commune less frequently, but has put us in harmony with Roman Catholicism, Orthodoxy, and (much of) Lutheranism. The idea that the Lord's Supper is primarily and almost exclusively a memorial, and that it is simply an ordinance to be obeyed without the conveying of special grace, unites Churches of Christ with most Reformed and evangelical churches, but puts us at odds with the others. Thus, in sum, Churches of Christ have a high, sacramental view of believers' baptism and a low, Zwinglian view of weekly Lord's Supper.

My specific aim in this chapter is to articulate a view of the two sacraments that raises the bar for the typical "low church." These practices of the church are more than simply ordinances, commands to be obeyed in the sense of positive law. Rather, my thesis is that divine grace is conveyed in the sacraments by the presence of Christ mediated through the Spirit. This view will challenge the typical evangelical understanding of baptism and both the typical evangelical and Restorationist understanding of the eucharist. To get a hearing among these churches, the perspective should be faithful to Scripture, which is of prime importance to evangelicals. Therefore, my first concern in this discussion is biblical faithfulness. I am concerned, second, to hear the voice of the great tradition of the church (a concern that distinguishes me from some Restorationists, though not all). The greatest minds of church history are the common property of all Christians. A third concern of mine, in line with the early American Restoration Movement, is greater ecumenical understanding, especially in areas of agreement. The view that I articulate should bring "low church" fellowships into closer conversation with "high church" communions, which have often been scandalized by the evangelical marginalization of the sacraments. Thus, another conversation partner will be *Baptism, Eucharist and Ministry*, the World Council of Churches' Faith and Order document from Lima, 1982.

---

1. Beasley-Murray, *Baptism in the New Testament*, 263.

## Sacramental Efficacy *In Genere*

### Sacraments as Signs of Grace

Peter Lombard, channeling Augustine of Hippo, writes, "What is a sacrament? 'A sacrament is a sign of a sacred thing.' . . . Also, a sacrament is a visible form of an invisible grace . . . A sacrament bears a likeness of the thing whose sign it is . . . [T]he sacraments were not instituted only for the sake of signifying, but also to sanctify."[2] As Martin Luther observes, a sacrament must have a physical, visible sign; an internal, spiritual significance; and an intentional faith that makes it effective.[3] For Luther, a sacrament is the promise of forgiveness of sins conjoined with a sign, in which case there are properly two sacraments, baptism and eucharist.[4] In his *Institutes of the Christian Religion*, John Calvin opens his discussion of the sacraments with a definition consistent with all of the above. As did the Lombard, Calvin also quotes Augustine and, incorporating the same three elements of Luther's definition, Calvin writes that a sacrament is "a testimony of divine grace toward us, confirmed by an outward sign, with mutual attestation of our piety toward him."[5] As the form of the promise of God, the sacrament is a "visible word,"[6] accompanied by the promise itself, which is communicated through preaching.

Based on this brief sketch, I will characterize the traditional understanding of the sacraments as follows. A sacrament is not simply any of the many legitimate practices and rituals of the church. It is a visible sign of invisible grace, practiced by Christ himself and instituted by him for the church, administered by the church, joined with the word of the gospel. What the sacrament or ordinance or sign signifies is actually linked to the sign. Grace is truly conveyed at the moment of the sacrament. Both baptism and eucharist re-present the death and resurrection of Christ and convey the promised benefits to those who participate by faith. Let us call this a "high" view of the sacraments.

---

2. Lombard, *The Sentences*, IV.i.1 and 4.
3. Luther, "The Blessed Sacrament," 45.
4. Luther, "The Babylonian Captivity of the Church," 124.
5. Calvin, *Institutes*, IV.xiv.1.
6. Ibid., IV.xiv.6, quoting Augustine on the Gospel of John.

PART 2: SACRAMENTS

## From Moment of Grace to Mere Symbol

Whence came the "low" view, the shift in evangelical Protestant sacramental theology? How did it happen that the church began to think of its sacraments as mere symbols? How did the sacraments go from being necessary for salvation, to being unnecessary for salvation, to being simply unnecessary or altogether eliminated? As it goes with so much of history, this also is a story of pendulum swings. The Roman Church was perceived by Protestant reformers as having, in many ways, a superstitious doctrine and practice of sacraments. This stems, in part, from a sacramental view of the cosmos in general, namely, that the material world is infused with the divine presence, the transcendent made immanent. This infusion is reflected, in a special and unique way, in the incarnation. When God "the Word became flesh" (John 1:14), the divine nature had a new kind of direct contact and relation with the world, and, as a result, human nature was divinized. Medieval iconodules saw in the incarnation a paradigm for thinking about God's special presence and power in relics and images. From an iconoclastic perspective, the sacramental view of the cosmos, when taken to an extreme, can approach panentheism and, when it comes to individual relics and images, can look indistinguishable from idolatry.

To the mind of most reformers, this sacramental view had been taken to an extreme in the late medieval Western church, and idolatry was the result. In an effort to correct the error, the Reformation tended to remove the material from the liturgy and the sacred from the material cosmos. For many reformers, this de-sacramentalization of the cosmos meant the removal of special divine presence not only from relics and images, but even from the sacraments of baptism and holy communion.

With regard to the sacraments, there had always been a distinction between the sign (*signum*) and the thing or reality signified (*res significata*), that is, between the visible matter and form, on the one hand, and the grace to which they pointed, on the other. This common distinction, however, became a separation in the thought of Ulrich Zwingli. I will not speculate now on why this is the case. Besides exegetical reasons and a reaction to the late medieval situation that I have described, some have posited Zwingli's openness to Platonic philosophy, which in some forms results in a de-emphasis on the material world. Whatever the reason, Zwingli, more than anyone before him, separated the sacramental sign from the thing signified. We can call this the "Zwinglian separation." What Zwingli separated, the Enlightenment, for reasons of its own, attempted to divorce entirely: "symbol and reality have been broken apart."[7]

Although this separation was not persuasive to Martin Luther or ultimately to Lutheran orthodoxy, it does reflect well the anti-institutional impulse of the Protestant Reformations as a whole, including the Lutheran branch. The Protestant critique of the Roman Church's sacraments, begun in earnest in 1520 with Luther's *Babylonian Captivity of the Church*, led to the reduction from seven sacraments to two, as well as to the further demotion of the two that remained. Just as Scripture alone is sufficient without the teaching magisterium of the church, so also justification and absolution are available by personal faith alone without the need for grace dispensed through the church's sacraments. The emphasis on faith, Scripture, and the priesthood of all believers ended up marginalizing the institutional church. Relationship with God became predominantly personal and individual, not something experienced primarily in the gathered church or mediated through its sacraments.

As a result, the Sunday service was no longer centered around a Mass, mumbled by a priest in a language that the people, and perhaps even the priest himself, could not understand. The clergy, whose primary task had been to administer seven sacraments, was now given the principal task of preaching. With Reformed and radical Protestants, for the first time in the history of the church, there could be a Lord's Day service without the Lord's Supper. In the absence of holy communion, preaching became the new sacrament, the *conditio sine qua non* and central component of the worship assembly, in the words of the Westminster divines, "effectual to salvation."[8] Of course, preaching was neither intended nor did it have to supplant sacraments; the word simply could have been joined more deliberately to the sacraments. But supplant it did, at least for many Protestants, who began to focus on internals and preaching to the exclusion of externals and the sacraments. The baptistery and table (or altar) were no longer front and center, but the pulpit would soon, literally, take center stage.

Evangelicalism has been the proper heir to Zwinglianism, perpetuating the separation between the sign and the thing signified. In some fellowships—namely, Quakers and the Salvation Army—the unnecessary role of the sacraments has been taken to the logical conclusion, and so they

---

7. Byars, *The Sacraments in Biblical Perspective*, 11.

8. See questions and answers 154–55 of the Westminster Larger Catechism (1647) in Dennison, *Reformed Confessions*, 340.

are not practiced at all. Friends rejected "outward" sacraments, claiming that true communion is an "inward" communion with God and true baptism is baptism with the Spirit. After all, if the inward reality of grace is conveyed ordinarily apart from the outward sign, then the outward sign retains symbolic import, at best, and, at worst, it can be distracting and divisive. Most of these churches, though, continue to practice the sacraments of baptism and eucharist. When I say "low church," I affectionately mean the type of evangelicalism that practices the sacraments but has a very low or non-sacramental view of them, as opposed to an ecclesiology that views the church as the means of grace. Such "low" churches, which I take the majority of self-described evangelicals to belong to, generally insist that baptism has nothing whatsoever to do with the conversion process and that the eucharist, infrequently practiced, is a mere symbol of Christ's body and blood. As Ronald Byars characterizes this way of looking at the sacraments, they are, in the minds of many Christians, "justasymbol [sic]."[9] This low-church mindset tends to promote what John Webster has called "sacramental minimalism." Webster notes that such sacramental minimalism "has attached itself to some bits of the evangelical tradition."[10] At least as regards North American evangelicalism and its various exports, the suggestion that "some bits" of evangelicalism have been infiltrated with sacramental minimalism is vastly understated. As will be demonstrated, even when some evangelical theologians acknowledge the sacraments as "means of grace," they often do not intend to indicate the uniqueness of the sacraments, but instead list them alongside other Christian practices, such as prayer, discipline, spiritual gifts, and evangelism.[11]

## Efficacy of Baptism

### The Marginalization of Baptism

For most evangelicals, baptism amounts to human obedience rendered to Christ's command, sometimes for inclusion in the church, and a mere symbol of an already accomplished justification. To be sure, Millard Erickson, whose systematic theology may be taken as representative of evangelical

---

9. Byars, *Sacraments*, 10.
10. Webster, "On Evangelical Ecclesiology," 187.
11. E.g., Grudem, *Systematic Theology*, 950–61.

academia, denies that baptism is a "mere sign."[12] Yet he also adamantly denies that baptism is a "means of regeneration" or a "means of saving grace."[13] The concept of "baptismal regeneration," as he calls it, "contradicts the principle of salvation by grace."[14] Again, "The view that baptism is a means of salvific grace is untenable."[15] For Erickson, baptism is "an act of faith" and "a public indication of one's commitment to Christ," as well as "a setting forth of the truth of what Christ has done."[16] Like Erickson, Wayne Grudem, the author of the most popular evangelical theology handbook, denies that baptism is "merely symbolic."[17] Later, though, it becomes clearer what he means by this denial. As a means of grace, there is a "blessing" and "spiritual benefit" attached to baptism: "There is the blessing that comes with all obedience, as well as the joy that comes through public profession of one's faith, and the reassurance of having a clear physical picture of dying and rising with Christ and of washing away sins. Certainly the Lord gave us baptism to strengthen and encourage our faith."[18] Thus, Grudem concludes, "we should not say that baptism is *necessary* for salvation."[19]

The early church was not so reluctant to connect baptism directly with the grace of salvation, a point that should be too obvious to necessitate elaboration.[20] The same goes for the medieval church. The efficacy of baptism was unanimously held in the early and medieval church. The development of emergency provisions (baptism for sick infants, affusion for dying adults or when sufficient water was lacking)—that is, aberrations from the norm—testifies to the importance of baptism and the danger of departing this life without it. In the early modern period, both Luther and the Roman

---

12. Erickson, *Christian Theology*, 1101.
13. Ibid., 1097–98.
14. Ibid., 1099.
15. Ibid., 1100.
16. Ibid., 1101.
17. Grudem, *Systematic Theology*, 954.
18. Ibid., 980–81.
19. Ibid., 981. After noting that the thief on the cross was not baptized, Grudem offers the following statement on the same page (981): "Baptism, then, is not necessary for salvation. But it is necessary if we are to be obedient to Christ, for he commanded baptism for all who believe in him." This claim raises the question about the relation between salvation and (dis)obedience to Christ.
20. For a comprehensive survey, see Ferguson, *Baptism in the Early Church*.

Catholic Church continued to teach that baptism washes away actual sins, and for infants, original sin.[21]

Whence the evangelical reticence? How did we come to the modern de-emphasis on baptism? We must return to the Zwinglian separation. The sharp separation of the sign from the thing signified is unprecedented before Zwingli, who was the first theologian in Christian history to separate so clearly the physical event of the sacrament from the grace it had always been thought to convey. As Zwingli claims, "Christ himself did not connect salvation with baptism: it is always by faith alone . . . The baptism of the Spirit was also given without the baptism of water . . . There is no salvation in external baptism. We see, then, that water-baptism is a ceremonial sign with which salvation is not indissolubly connected."[22]

The Anabaptist leader, Menno Simons, though he rejected paedobaptism, followed the Zwinglian separation, pitting the sacrament against the reality: "For if we could be washed or cleansed by baptism, then Christ Jesus and His merits would have to abdicate."[23] "We are not cleansed by the washing of the water, but by the Word of the Lord."[24] "For we are not regenerated because we are baptized, as may be perceived in the infants who have been baptized; but we are baptized because we are regenerated by faith in God's word. For regeneration is not the result of baptism, but baptism the result of regeneration. This may not be controverted by any man on the basis of Scriptures."[25] Again, one can see how Quakers and the Salvation Army have simply taken the Zwinglian separation to its logical conclusion; if baptism is not integral to the salvation process, then physical baptism, like any physical sign, is superfluous and unnecessary. Even for those who still practice the physical sign of water baptism, it is not uncommon for them to disparage water baptism in favor of "Holy Spirit baptism," separating the two, as did Zwingli.

With the Zwinglian separation in full swing, namely, the removal of the visible sign from the invisible grace, there was a new emphasis on the subjective experience of salvation. Personal salvation became less about the church's role and the administration of external sacraments. In the

---

21. E.g., see Luther, "The Holy and Blessed Sacrament of Baptism," 29–43; and also the Council of Trent, session 6.4 (13 January 1547) in Tanner, *Decrees*, 2:672.

22. Zwingli, *Of Baptism*, 134, 136.

23. Simons, *Christian Baptism*, 244.

24. Ibid., 245.

25. Ibid., 264–65.

evangelical revivals, salvation became more and more—and, in American evangelicalism, exclusively—about the personal, subjective experience apart from any external sacrament or the church that administers it. John Wesley felt his "heart strangely warmed" at a society meeting, not at his baptism or in a Eucharistic service of the church. Charles Finney expressed his "baptism of the Holy Ghost" as the feeling of a "wave of electricity," coming in "waves and waves of liquid love."[26] Like Finney, Pentecostal theology calls this subjective experience the "baptism of the Holy Spirit." Such experiences are subjective and individualistic, and none has to happen in the context of the gathered body of Christ, much less through participation in the sacraments.

But water baptism had always been the church's initiation rite, the objective moment of salvation. New emphasis on the purely subjective, individualistic experience as the moment of salvation, apart from any external rite, left a vacuum in the conversion process. Ironically, those who removed the physical sign from the inward grace were then obliged to search for other objective responses to accompany and confirm the subjective feeling, that is, other external events or moments to accompany the inward salvation. These responses often happened in the context of the gathered church. For example, Finney, who regularly baptized infants, encouraged the use of the anxious seat as a reflection of the commitment that baptism once embodied. In response to critics of his "new measures," and in an attempt to emphasize the need for a convert to show his commitment, Finney said,

> If you say to him, 'There is the anxious seat, come out and avow your determination to be on the Lord's side,' and if he is not willing to do so small a thing as that, then he is not willing to do *anything*, and there he is, brought out before his own conscience. It uncovers the delusion of the human heart, and prevents a great many spurious conversions, by showing those who might otherwise imagine themselves willing to do anything for Christ, that in fact they are willing to do *nothing*.[27]

In other words, converts must do something objective. Finney continues:

> The church has always felt it necessary to have something of the kind to answer this very purpose. In the days of the apostles *baptism* answered this purpose. The Gospel was preached to the

26. Finney, *Memoirs*, 20.
27. Finney, *Lectures on Revivals*, 248, italics original.

people, and then all those who were willing to be on the side of Christ were called on to be *baptized*. It held the precise place that the anxious seat does now, as a public manifestation of their determination to be Christians.[28]

Here is an interesting admission about the anxious seat replacing baptism in evangelism. In evangelicalism, the historic initiation rite of the church, even in the context of believers' baptism, came to have little or no place in conversion. Then, by the early twentieth century, under the influence of former baseball player turned mass evangelist, Billy Sunday, making a "decision" for Christ transitioned into an exercise as simple as raising your hand from where you sit. And, throughout the twentieth century, especially in Baptist preaching and even viewed through television (for example, Billy Graham), the sinner's prayer that asks Jesus into one's heart became the prominent objective response, executed from the comfort of one's own living room.

## Baptism, the Sacrament of Justifying Grace

Although the American Restoration Movement developed in the context of the Second Great Awakening and has been much influenced by it, it charted a very different trajectory on the role of baptism. Churches of Christ insisted that baptism is an objective moment of salvation and assurance, especially in contrast to the revivalism that emphasized the subjective experience of the Holy Spirit apart from water baptism. Baptism was the biblical alternative to the revivalist mourner's bench. In Churches of Christ, baptism is an objective moment and sign of salvation and of God's promise to us, as opposed to waiting for a subjective feeling of the heart being "strangely warmed" (Wesley) or of "liquid love" (Finney). There is no need to wait in agony for subjective confirmation of salvation. Baptism embodies God's promise of salvation and its assurance, and, though the external sign is almost always accompanied by a feeling or affections, as an external sign, it does not fluctuate like a feeling, which can be fickle and elusive, as Wesley himself discovered about Aldersgate. As Henry Rack observed, "There is no clear evidence that Wesley ever received the kind of 'assurance' that he was looking for after his conversion in May 1738 and had still failed to find after

---

28. Ibid., italics original.

the briefly warmed heart."[29] Based on the New Testament, and distinct from their evangelical neighbors, the Churches of Christ retained the central importance of baptism in the conversion process.

When I say that, in Churches of Christ, baptism is for remission or forgiveness of sins, this is shorthand for all the things God promises at baptism, the importance of which is hard to miss in the New Testament. Baptism is directly associated with new birth from above and entrance into the kingdom (John 3:3, 5), forgiveness of sins and the gift of the Holy Spirit (Acts 2:38), the transition from confusion to joy (Acts 8:39), the washing away of sins (Acts 22:16; 1 Cor 6:11), the transition from death to new life and the grace that enables it (Rom 6:1–11), being joined to the body of Christ by the Holy Spirit (1 Cor 12:13), being clothed with Christ and participating in his sonship (Gal 3:26–27), being united with the dying and rising of Christ (Col 2:12–13), regeneration and renewal by the Holy Spirit (Titus 3:5), and salvation from the destruction that awaits the wicked world (1 Pet 3:20–21).[30]

At the risk of understating the biblical evidence for the sacramental view of baptism, but in order to leave space for other matters (there is much less in the New Testament about the Lord's Supper's sacramental efficacy, so I want to give it more attention below), I will omit exegetical summaries of these and other New Testament testimonies regarding baptism and, instead, simply point to the baptism of Jesus as the paradigm for our baptism, which incorporates us into Christ. What we learn from the baptism of Jesus is that when a person accepts the saving grace of God and comes to Christ in penitent faith and baptism, God declares that "this is my beloved daughter or son, with you I am well pleased" (cf. Matt 3:17), and the Spirit descends to indwell and empower for a life of testing in the wilderness. As in the case of Jesus, water baptism *is* Spirit baptism, inasmuch as the justifying grace that is signified accompanies the sign.

This high view of baptism, for which Churches of Christ have often been excoriated by evangelicals, is now increasingly embraced by evangelical leaders and is becoming the ecumenical consensus. As an example of this emerging consensus, note *Baptism, Eucharist and Ministry*, the document from Lima in 1982, published by the Faith and Order Commission of the World Council of Churches (WCC). Although the Churches of

---

29. See Rack, *Reasonable Enthusiast*, 545. On Wesley's lack of love, assurance, and emotional experience of God, see ibid., 544–50.

30. See a similar list in Beasley-Murray, *Baptism*, 264.

Christ are not an official member of the WCC, based on this document, it almost sounds as if the Churches of Christ infiltrated the group: "God bestows upon all baptized persons the anointing and the promise of the Holy Spirit, marks them with a seal and implants in their hearts the first instalment of their inheritance as sons and daughters of God."[31] Moreover, "Administered in obedience to our Lord, baptism is a sign and seal of our common discipleship. Through baptism, Christians are brought into union with Christ, with each other and with the Church of every time and place. Our common baptism, which unites us to Christ in faith, is thus a basic bond of unity."[32] For "In God's work of salvation, the paschal mystery of Christ's death and resurrection is inseparably linked with the pentecostal gift of the Holy Spirit. Similarly, participation in Christ's death and resurrection is inseparably linked with the receiving of the Spirit. Baptism in its full meaning signifies and effects both."[33]

## Efficacy of Eucharist

### Its Marginalization in Evangelicalism

*1. Merely symbolic (memorial)*

How exactly is Christ present with regard to the eucharistic elements? In the biblical account, Jesus simply says, "This is my body . . . This is my blood." Thus early Christians, with few exceptions, simply repeated the realist language of the New Testament without specifying any particular theory. Therefore, the ambiguity of the New Testament with regard to how Christ is present in the Lord's Supper carried over into the early church. After noting this lack of clarity in the patristic language regarding the presence of Christ at the eucharist, Jaroslav Pelikan writes,

> Yet it does seem 'express and clear' that no orthodox father of the second or third century of whom we have record either declared the presence of the body and blood of Christ in the Eucharist to be no more than symbolic (although Clement and Origen came close to doing so) or specified a process of substantial change by which the presence was effected (although Ignatius and Justin came close

---

31. *Baptism, Eucharist and Ministry*, Baptism, II.C.5.
32. Ibid., Baptism, II.D.6.
33. Ibid., Baptism, IV.B.14.

to doing so). Within the limits of those excluded extremes was the doctrine of the real presence.[34]

This ambiguity of language explains how theologians on both sides of subsequent medieval and early modern debates over the question of real presence could likewise appeal to the New Testament and patristic writings. These works simply did not resolve the controversies that later, more precise definitions raised. It was left to the later centuries to speculate either, on the one hand, that the consecrated elements become the literal body and blood of Jesus, or, on the other hand, that they are only figuratively so. And, sadly, along the way, it also became more customary for churches to choose one side and then condemn the other.

It is well known that, although both Luther and Zwingli rejected the doctrine of transubstantiation and its later medieval interpretation, nevertheless they could not agree on what to put in its place. It is the primary dispute, chronologically and otherwise, that divided the communions later known as Lutheran and Reformed. Based on the words, "This is my body . . . This is my blood," Luther insisted on the literal, bodily presence of Christ, whereas Zwingli insisted that the statements are metaphorical. It depends on what the meaning of "is" is. For Zwingli, "This is my body" means, "This represents my body." Thus, Zwinglians emphasized that there is no bodily presence of Christ in holy communion, and that the benefit that comes from partaking of the meal is primarily, or perhaps exclusively, one of remembrance. As this polemical concept has developed in evangelicalism, it has tended to emphasize what the Lord's Supper is not—namely, the literal bodily presence of Christ. When the negative point against "real presence" becomes the focus, it resembles what Erickson calls the "doctrine of the real absence."[35]

John Calvin spent much time and energy trying to articulate a eucharistic doctrine of presence that both Lutheran and Reformed believers could affirm. Although Lutherans finally would not subscribe to Calvin's views, Calvin inclined to stronger language than the Zwinglians with regard to the "spiritual presence" of Christ.[36] With this in mind, the language used by modern evangelicals Erickson and Grudem sounds more Calvin-

---

34. Pelikan, *The Christian Tradition*, 1:167.
35. Erickson, *Christian Theology*, 1123.
36. The entire issue of *Reformation and Renaissance Review* 18/1 (2016) includes helpful essays and primary sources related to Calvin's role in the so-called *Consensus Tigurinus*, including the events before and after it.

ian than Zwinglian. They both affirm the presence of Christ, that we meet him in holy communion. Erickson mentions that the Spirit makes Christ "real in our experience,"[37] and Grudem is pleased to advocate the "spiritual presence" of Christ.[38]

If the mode of Christ's presence is ambiguous in the church fathers, the efficacy of the Lord's Supper is a little clearer. The early and medieval church commonly thought about the eucharist in terms of conveying grace. Because the Lord's Supper grants "communion and union" with the divine nature, drawing God's people into "uniform theosis," (Pseudo-)Dionysius the Areopagite passes on the tradition of calling the eucharist the "sacrament of sacraments" (τελετῶν τελετή).[39]

Evangelical theologians are a little more guarded than the Areopagite. Erickson speaks much about the Lord's Supper being beneficial and effective, but he never quite defines what that efficacy is. The Supper does remind us of the death of Christ and symbolize the unity of believers.[40] Grudem speaks of the "spiritual blessing," "spiritual nourishment," and "spiritual participation in the benefits of the redemption that he [Christ] earns."[41] Both writers stop short of emphasizing the idea of grace being conveyed.

In Churches of Christ, although some have stressed the presence of Jesus at the table and the meal as a means of grace,[42] language about the Lord's Supper is usually Zwinglian. As in many Reformed churches, it is a commemorative feast.

---

37. Erickson, *Christian Theology*, 1122–23.

38. Grudem, *Systematic Theology*, 995–96.

39. Pseudo-Dionysius the Areopagite, *Ecclesiastical Hierarchy* III.i, in Rorem, *Pseudo-Dionysius*, 209. Τελετή means "perfector" or can refer to mystic rites. That Pseudo-Dionysius means it in the former sense is clear from his later discussion at *Ecclesiastical Hierarchy* IV.iii.12, in Rorem, *Pseudo-Dionysius*, 232.

40. Erickson, *Christian Theology*, 1123–24.

41. Grudem, *Systematic Theology*, 990, 996.

42. E.g., in addition to Alexander Campbell, note E. G. Sewell: "Proper attendance upon the Lord's Supper is a wonderful means of grace to strengthen the hearts and lives of Christians in all things connected with the service of God"; and E. A. Elam: "Every time the Supper is observed, Jesus is present." For these quotations, both of which come from the 1915 *Gospel Advocate*, and for further discussion of sacramental theology in Churches of Christ, see Hicks, "Stone-Campbell Sacramental Theology," 42 n. 34.

## 2. From Frequent to Infrequent

As for frequency, the New Testament provides implicit evidence that holy communion was taken when the church gathered on the first day of every week (see Luke 24:1, 13, 30–35; Acts 20:7; 1 Cor 11:20, 33; 16:2; Heb 10:24–25). The earliest Christian worship manual, the *Didache* (ca. AD 70), prescribes meeting every first day of the week for the Lord's Supper.[43] The earliest Christian description of a worship assembly, Justin Martyr's first *Apology* (ca. AD 155), describes meeting on Sunday for the Lord's Supper, a practice so central to the assembly and Christian life that the elements were taken by the deacons and distributed to those who were absent.[44] By the third century, there is some evidence of the Lord's Supper also on other days in addition to Sunday. It came to be offered daily in some places. But weekly Lord's Supper on Sunday remained the norm and continued throughout the early and medieval periods of church history. However, the laity in the West partook less and less frequently, and expectations became very low. By 1215 (Lateran Council IV), it was mandated that Christians should come to church to confess sins and take the eucharist at least once a year at Easter.[45]

Thus, by the thirteenth century, many Christians were partaking of the frequently offered Mass only once a year. By the early fifteenth century,

---

43. *Didache* 14:1; Holmes, *Apostolic Fathers*, 365: "On the Lord's own day gather together and break bread and give thanks [εὐχαριστήσατε], having first confessed your sins so that your sacrifice may be pure."

44. Justin Martyr, *1 Apology* 67, in Falls, *Saint Justin Martyr*, 106–7: "On the day which is called Sunday we have a common assembly of all who live in the cities or in the outlying districts, and the memoirs of the Apostles or the writings of the Prophets are read, as long as there is time. Then, when the reader has finished, the president of the assembly verbally admonishes and invites all to imitate such examples of virtue. Then we all stand up together and offer up our prayers, and as we said before, after we finish our prayers, bread and wine and water are presented. He who presides likewise offers up prayers and thanksgivings, to the best of his ability, and the people express their approval by saying 'Amen.' The Eucharistic elements are distributed and consumed by those present, and to those who are absent they are sent through the deacons."

45. Lateran IV (1215), Canon 21, in Tanner, *Decrees*, 1:245: "All the faithful of either sex, after they have reached the age of discernment, should individually confess all their sins in a faithful manner to their own priest at least once a year, and let them take care to do what they can to perform the penance imposed on them. Let them reverently receive the sacrament of the eucharist at least at Easter unless they think, for a good reason and on the advice of their own priest, that they should abstain in receiving it for a time. Otherwise they shall be barred from entering a church during their lifetime and they shall be denied a Christian burial at death."

the laity were allowed to take communion only in one kind, justified by the doctrine of concomitance; only the clergy could have the cup, too.[46] So, on the eve of the Reformation, even though the church celebrated Mass weekly (and even daily), most people did not partake frequently, and if they did, it was only the bread. But, the "Mass" or "divine liturgy" was still being celebrated every Sunday, even if only the clergy were partaking.

In addition to their insistence that the laity be given communion in both kinds, another obvious change introduced by Protestant reformers had to do with frequency. Recall that the sacramental nature of the Lord's Supper had been questioned by many Protestants, so they did not want people to think superstitiously about the bread and cup or to offer divine worship to the elements, and they did not want the ceremony of the sacrament to overshadow or trump the preaching of the word. In addition, former Roman Catholics were not accustomed to their own weekly participation. So the Lord's Supper was offered in the church less frequently. Yet Protestant believers generally celebrated the Lord's Supper more frequently than most Roman Catholic laity actually did—every quarter or month. But this is the first time in the history of the church that a congregation's Sunday service would go by without celebrating the Lord's Supper. Some reformers wanted it more frequently. Calvin preferred weekly Lord's Supper: "The Lord's table should have been spread at least once a week for the assembly of Christians, and the promises declared in it should feed us spiritually."[47] One point that Calvin made was that partaking only once a year reflected and encouraged spiritual laziness, the "torpor of the sluggish."[48] His assumption was that the Lord's Supper is a time for covenant renewal, confession of sin, and getting our lives right with God. One should not approach the table with unrepented sin. But the magistrates in Geneva would not have weekly communion. Indeed, for most Protestants, quarterly or every other month became the normal frequency for the Lord's Supper; at most, monthly. This move to displace the eucharist ensured that preaching would become the new sacrament and center of the Lord's Day assembly, without which no Sunday service would be complete. In one generation, much of Europe went from celebrating the

---

46. Communion in one kind was decreed at the Council of Constance, session 13 (15 June 1415), in Tanner, *Decrees*, 1:418–9. According to the doctrine of concomitance, only the bread was necessary, for the blood was also contained in the body.

47. Calvin, *Institutes*, IV.xvii.46.

48. Ibid., IV.xvii.46. This is the language of Henry Beveridge's translation, to be preferred over the McNeill/Battles edition's "inertia of indolent people."

sacrament without an intelligible proclamation of the Word to the proclamation of the Word without the sacrament.

Some evangelical theologians today seem fairly open to weekly Lord's Supper. Grudem notes that, if it is planned and executed well, the Lord's Supper could be done once a week.[49] Erickson does not specify how often the Lord's Supper should be taken, but he is concerned with the eucharist becoming "routinized" by observing it "so frequently as to make it seem trivial or so commonplace that we go through the motions without really thinking about the meaning."[50]

Perhaps actual evangelical practice is more telling than the opinions of professional theologians. Monthly or quarterly Lord's Supper is probably still the most common practice among evangelicals. The Lord's Supper, accompanied by the Word and once the center of the Lord's Day assembly, has been, in most Protestant churches, replaced by preaching, and, most weeks, without sacrament. And now, with the decline of preaching, many evangelical assemblies have, on most Lord's Days, no eucharist and very little preaching. It is now the music or concert, often reductionistically referred to as "worship" and juxtaposed to the preaching, that functions as the new center and, in effect, the new sacrament of evangelicalism. Thus, much of Western Christianity has gone from sacrament without word to word without sacrament to, now, concert without word or sacrament.

## Eucharist, the Sacrament of Sanctifying Grace

### 1. Real, Spiritual Presence

I would like to advocate for evangelical consideration of the real, spiritual presence of Christ in the eucharist. A brief glance at a couple of biblical passages will help to clarify my position.

In Luke 24, it is the first day of the week, resurrection day itself, and two disciples walking to Emmaus are joined by a third traveler, whom we know to be the risen Lord. They do not recognize him or, in that sense, see. Then they invite him to stay and eat, and the guest quickly becomes the host. He takes the bread, blesses it, breaks it, and gives it to them, all liturgical indications of eucharist. At that moment, they see or recognize him "in the breaking of the bread." And then, immediately, he disappears,

---

49. Grudem, *Systematic Theology*, 999.
50. Erickson, *Christian Theology*, 1126.

and they do not see him. As Jesus' baptism is paradigmatic, so also this very first Lord's Day holy communion is a paradigm for all Lord's Suppers to follow. Jesus has disappeared from our physical sight; though we eat, he is no longer physically present at the table. At the same time, our hearts burn within us because we do continue to recognize his presence in the breaking of the bread.

First Corinthians 10 is another passage that has much to teach about the eucharist, most of it indirectly, yet at the same time clearly. The first point is typological. In speaking of Israel, Paul says that they were all baptized. He then observes that "they all ate the same Spiritual food and they all drank the same Spiritual drink, for they were drinking from the Spiritual rock that followed them, and the rock was Christ" (1 Cor 10:3–4). The context of the whole passage indicates a comparison between Israel and the Corinthian Christians, who, though sharing in blessings from God, are in danger of falling. In the midst of the discussion, Paul clearly links the bread and cup of holy communion both with the Spirit and with Christ. As God's chosen people, while we share physical elements, it is also spiritual food and drink, and this nourishment is intimately connected with Christ, who, like the rock, is present with his people as the source of these blessings and who constantly accompanies ("follows") God's people in the wilderness period of testing.

Christ's special presence at the Lord's Supper is also evident later in the same chapter (1 Cor 10:16–20). As with many things in 1 Corinthians, we must find the positive point by listening to Paul's rebuke of the church. Their sharing in meals at the pagan temples made them "communers" (κοινωνοί) with those gods, or demons. You cannot do that, Paul says. Instead, your participation in the bread and the cup of blessing makes you communers with Christ. In this meal, you have communion, or *fellowship* (κοινωνία), with the body and blood of Christ. To be communers with Christ means that, though God is omnipresent and his Spirit is always with us, Christ is present at the table in a *special* way.

As noted, over the centuries, Christians have argued about what it means to say that Christ is present at the table. For evangelicals, the truth should be located somewhere between the two extremes. The elements are not literal flesh and blood, and so 1) participation is not cannibalism. When the Word became flesh, he took on a real human body subject to all the same physical limitations of space, and so 2) his *body* in its human nature, to this day, though transformed is not omnipresent, not on thousands of tables at once consumed by millions. 3) When the Bible says Jesus is the Lamb, this does not mean he is a literal baby sheep with wool and a tail, any more than saying this is his body, especially while he was at the table with the Twelve, means that it is a piece of his literal, physical human body. On these points, Zwingli was correct.

At the same time, the elements are neither meaningless nor for mere remembrance. In this meal, God sends his Spirit to mediate the presence of Christ to those who partake, and so it is not just ordinary bread and cup anymore. It is similar to baptism. The gracious, efficacious presence of Christ in the Lord's Supper says no more or less than the salvific efficacy of baptism. There is nothing inherently special about the water, but God chooses to convey grace at an objective moment, through the application of the physical element. And so the water, by God's grace, becomes for us the means of salvation, a channel of justifying grace, the blood that washes away sins. There is no chemical change to the water; it's still just $H_2O$. It is not that the water can have no ordinary use before or after baptism, or that it cannot be drained into the same system as other waste water. Likewise, since the meal is communion with Christ, and since he said we must eat his flesh and drink his blood, then the bread and cup become for us the body and blood of Christ. There is no chemical, substantial, or literal change in the elements themselves. But as our communion with God is real, God chooses, through his Spirit, to mediate to us the real, spiritual presence of Christ, conveying grace that sanctifies us as we eat. And so we say, with Scripture, that this is body and blood. The elements of bread and cup are holy things for the holy people of God. They are the body and blood of Christ, but not in a literal way that enables *latreia* of the elements or forbids any type of ordinary use after the eucharist.

Based on these biblical passages, we can ask, If Christ is not present in this meal, then what, after all, is the point? The main point is that, as this is communion with Christ, Christ is present—for our redemption and our sanctification. As long as this main point is affirmed, we should not condemn those groups who believe in the literal bodily presence, but we should grieve that those same groups have condemned the rest, and that, as in Corinth, the Lord's Supper has become a means of Christian division.

## 2. Sanctifying Grace

The point about whether grace is conveyed in the Lord's Supper is rather simple: if and when God is present with his people for their redemption, then grace follows. The grace that accompanies God's special presence in a liturgical context is clearly seen in Isaiah 6. The prophet, since he is "a man of unclean lips," is certain that he deserves to die, and he is certainly correct. Rather than perishing, though, he is spared, his sinful lips cleansed with a burning coal, and he is given a task in God's kingdom. This is sanctifying grace. Such grace can also be seen in meals eaten in God's presence. In Exodus 24:9–11, the leaders of Israel ascend the mountain with Moses to eat in the presence of God. They see God, but God does not "raise his hand against" them. This is grace. In John 6, the immediate context is not eucharistic, but the language clearly is. Following on the heels of the pre-eucharistic feeding of the 5,000, Jesus says, "Whoever eats my flesh and drinks my blood has eternal life" (John 6:54). If Christ is present in the eucharist, as already established, then grace follows.

The sanctifying "grace" that Christ bestows on those who come to the table in faith is a direct result of Christ's special presence. The invitation to come to God's table is an act of divine grace. The sign—the physical eating and the nourishment that it provides—coincides with the grace signified—the spiritual nourishment that makes God's people partakers of the divine nature. Because holy communion draws God's people into closer union with him, it is, as Pseudo-Dionysius recognized, the sacrament of divinization.

## 3. Frequency

As we have observed, most Protestants do not take holy communion every Lord's Day. The early American Restoration Movement emphasized the Lord's Supper as a weekly table, the center of the Lord's Day assembly. Thus, frequent communion became a hallmark of the Restoration Movement and, if not a scandal, at least a puzzle to evangelicals. And this rhythm is still the case in Churches of Christ today. The Lord's Supper is taken every Sunday and only on Sunday. At its worst, it can become *ex opere operato*; it is how you "punch your card" or "make it count." At best, however, the practice accompanies the recognition that the first day of the week, the day of resurrection, has theological significance for the church, that there is something truly special and indispensable about the Lord's Day eucharist.

Here is a thesis that should be tested: the same reason that the church gathers every first day of the week is the same reason the church eats the Lord's Supper every first day of the week. To put the point more clearly: whatever reason one would like to give for not taking the Lord's Supper every Sunday should be as good a reason for not meeting for worship every Sunday. Whatever reason one would provide for meeting for worship every Sunday should be as good a reason for taking the Lord's Supper every Sunday. For example, if "x" is no good reason for one, it is also no good reason for the other. Therefore, why would one gather to celebrate the resurrection of Christ, on resurrection day, and omit the very meal that he gave us to celebrate it with?

The most common reason given by evangelicals against the weekly eucharist is the danger of frequent communion leading to an empty ritual done by rote. This concern is mentioned by Erickson, cited above. This concern would make for a very weak argument against the regular practice of anything important. In fact, almost every Christian I talk to about this, regardless of their denominational affiliation, agrees that there is no good reason for not having the Lord's Supper every Sunday. Thus, many Protestants are coming around to more frequent, and even weekly, eucharist. Many evangelical churches that have no denominational ties are taking the Lord's Supper weekly. Moreover, many churches that are tied to denominations that historically have not practiced weekly eucharist are now reconsidering. There is no real theological point at stake in support of holy communion less than every Sunday.

Weekly Lord's Supper is, in fact, the emerging ecumenical consensus: "As the eucharist celebrates the resurrection of Christ, it is appropriate that it should take place at least every Sunday. As it is the new sacramental meal of the people of God, every Christian should be encouraged to receive communion frequently."[51] If we are concerned to elevate our thinking and language about holy communion, then perhaps the best way to begin to do this is through weekly Lord's Supper. Contrary to the old idea that frequent communion somehow cheapens it, weekly eucharist rather emphasizes the importance and centrality of this practice and opens the door to thinking about the presence of Christ and the grace conveyed in the sacrament.

---

51. *Baptism, Eucharist and Ministry*, Eucharist, III.31.

PART 2: SACRAMENTS

## Sacraments as God's Work

One of the chief evangelical concerns with a high view of the sacraments is the concern that they would be thought of in terms of *ex opere operato*, that they are simply a work and, even worse, a work done regardless of faith. It should be clear that I am not advocating participation or efficacy of the sacraments apart from personal faith. But are the sacraments works, in the sense that Paul opposed them to faith? Is grace to be conveyed as a result of human work? First, consider whether the eucharist is a work. God gave us this meal as a means of grace, to unite us with Christ's death and resurrection. It is God who takes something ordinary and works something extraordinary through it. We are even served it. Is eating, chewing, drinking, and swallowing a work?

How about baptism? That "baptism for remission of sins" is thought by some evangelicals to reflect "works salvation" may be why I remember hearing an evangelical once refer to it as a "heresy." (Whatever one thinks now of "baptism for the remission of sins," this concept was both important and undisputed enough to make it into the Nicene-Constantinopolitan Creed ["I acknowledge one baptism for the remission of sins"], quoting of course from Acts 2:38, and so cannot be heresy in any commonly recognized sense of the word, but is, rather, orthodoxy. "Baptism *not* for the remission of sins," in fact, would have greater claim to heresy on ecclesiastical-historical-dogmatic grounds.) Rather than a work of merit, baptism, as an objective moment of saving grace, is part of the response of faith. Remember, faith is not a work, but is opposed to the kind of works that Paul excludes from the causes of justification. Of all the responses of faith (not works of merit) in the conversion process—repentance, confession of faith, and baptism—baptism is the easiest and most passive of them all. The human is the active subject of the verbs to believe, repent, confess, but the passive recipient of baptism (one is baptized). That is, baptism is no more a human work than is verbal confession of faith or repentance, all integral to the conversion process.[52] It is hard to imagine something more passive than willingly being dunked under

---

52. In recognition of this logic, some evangelicals reject any objective, external moment as coinciding with or functioning as a means of salvation. Notably, the Grace Evangelical Society rejects the "sinner's prayer" because it makes a prayer into a condition for salvation, that is, a "work." See Myers, "Clarifying the Confusion of the Sinner's Prayer." See also the video at https://faithalone.org/video/the-sinners-prayer-southern-baptists-and-evangelism and other pages at faithalone.org.

water by another person. If there is work involved in baptism—and there certainly is—then it is God who does it.

This point is plain in Colossians 2:11–14. Here baptism is passive from the human side; it is "the operation of God" (2:12, KJV). God is the one doing the working in baptism, and faith is the means from the human side. "Faith" (2:12) is a believing and baptizing moment. Titus 3:5 offers a similar picture of the work that God does in baptism. Renewal by the Holy Spirit takes place at baptism. Again, God is the one working, and therefore is the one who receives all the glory for his grace.

Evangelicals and Protestants need to recover the biblical vision of a sacramental cosmos and of a God who works in, with, and through material substance. Think, for example, of the tree of life. God chose a particular tree whose fruit would impart life. The tree itself was not magic and presumably was not even a unique species, but was chosen by God to convey life in the eating of it. God, not the human eater, is the worker.

The Holy Spirit, as the bond of charity within the Trinity, is the gift of God's love to his people, through whom God's love has been poured out into our hearts (Rom 5:5). Perhaps what is needed is a more robust pneumatology in evangelical ecclesiology, one that allows and expects the Spirit to work in the church and to convey grace through the sacraments, as promised in Scripture. If, in the gathered assembly of God's people in worship, the Holy Spirit can work directly on, and Christ can be present to, the human heart through the means of a drum set and an electric guitar, then surely the Spirit can mediate Christ's direct presence for salvation and sanctification through the biblical means of water, bread, and cup, joined with the Word of gospel and grace.

As our hearts are restless until they find rest in God, the sacraments reflect the yearning of God to be present with his people. God is the one who invites us to the laver and to the table. God, through the Spirit, tabernacles with us so that Christ may dwell in our hearts through faith. As is the Holy Spirit himself, the sacraments also are a down payment and seal of God's promises and Christ's presence for our redemption. Perhaps they are not strictly necessary means, but the sacraments are ordinary means of God's justifying and sanctifying grace.

Finally, a practical-ecumenical suggestion: the criticism that comes from traditional Roman Catholic and Eastern Orthodox Churches is that Christ is not present in the sacraments or ordinances of Protestant churches. If Protestants do not accept this criticism (as I do not), then it does not help for evangelicals positively to insist that baptism has nothing whatsoever to do with the conversion process or that Christ is not present in the Lord's Supper. Instead, for Orthodox and Roman Catholics who are willing to grant that the Spirit can work outside of their episcopal succession, biblical language would go a long way.[53] For those who are open to Protestant churches as being more than simply "ecclesial communities," a higher view of sacraments can be a small step toward greater unity of thought and worship.[54] Evangelicals should be able to say, with the New Testament, that baptism is "for remission of sins" (Acts 2:38), without immediately having to qualify it as not for remission of sins. When speaking the words of institution, evangelicals ought to say, with the New Testament, that this "is" for us the body and blood of Jesus Christ, without immediately having to add the non-biblical word "represents." Simply using biblical language, without being scandalized by it, would help get evangelicals within earshot of the historic Christian tradition's and Scripture's doctrine of the efficacy of the two sacraments. It also may enable evangelicals to gaze more clearly into the divine beauty to which these physical signs ultimately point.

---

53. I grant that, for Eastern Orthodox and Roman Catholics who insist that the true sacramental presence of Christ does not obtain outside of their bishops' administration, this point may be a non-starter. In this case, a conversation about ministry is necessary first.

54. "Ecclesial communities" is the language of Vatican Council II's *Unitatis redintegratio*, which also recognizes the importance of dialogue on the sacraments. *Unitatis redintegratio* 22, in Tanner, *Decrees*, 2:920: "For these reasons dialogue should include among its subjects the Lord's supper and other sacraments, worship and the church's ministry."

# Part 3

# Discipline

# 6

# Persecution, Discipline, and Rewards in Ecclesiological Perspective

—Gregory C. Cochran

## Introduction

WHY WOULD A COLLECTION of essays on ecclesiology include a chapter on Christian persecution? Even more bewildering might be the question, "Why should a conversation about church discipline include a discussion of Christian persecution?" Not an immediately recognizable fit.

On the one hand, this chapter appears not to fit the paradigm shaping this book. On the other hand, however, this chapter has made it to print. Perhaps there is a connection between ecclesiology and Christian persecution. This chapter, in fact, hopes to demonstrate an inherent nexus between the persecuted church and ecclesiology. Furthermore, this connection anticipates questions germane both to church discipline and rewards. Before addressing such questions, consider an illustration that may help make more clear the connection between persecution and ecclesiology.

For nearly two decades, I have participated annually in the International Day of Prayer for the Persecuted Church (IDOP).[1] Most major persecution ministries—Open Doors, International Christian Concern, Voice of the Martyrs—support the annual IDOP campaign, often supplying testimonies and prayer guides for the events. After one such event, an astute member of the congregation asked me whether it is accurate to speak of the "persecuted church." His concern was not (like Candida Moss's) to expose

---

1. Typically, the International Day of Prayer for the Persecuted Church takes place either the first or the second Sunday in November.

"the myth of persecution."[2] Rather, he had a growing uneasiness toward the manner in which such language bifurcates the body of Christ. "Persecuted" is applied often to the church of the past or to present churches in the Middle East, but artificially separated from the evangelical Church of the United States to which many of us belong.

This man's question arose organically from a message on Hebrews 13:3 which argued for all Christians to identify with persecuted Christians on account of being in a body *with them*.[3] Being in a body with other believers through suffering is both a soteriological phenomenon—based on union with Christ—and an ecclesiological one. Something about persecution expects all Christians to identify with one another as a single entity under the headship and direction of Jesus Christ. The 2017 church shooting in Sutherland Springs, TX, made that point. As just one example, author and church growth specialist Thom Rainer posted a brief article on the Monday morning following the Sunday shooting, saying, "We are First Baptist Church of Sutherland Springs. We are your brothers and sisters in Christ. We pray for you. We care for you. We love you."[4] Rainer was not alone.

Christians often identify with one another in times of persecution. In that sense, then, the persecuted church is a single entity with the non-persecuted. We are one body in Christ. In confessional terms, "We believe in one holy catholic and apostolic Church" (Nicene Creed). Thus, when this man asked me about the danger of speaking of the persecuted church in "other" terms, I affirmed his instincts for unity and clarity, saying to him that we are in fact one body with persecuted Christians. As Dietrich Bonhoeffer once noted, "We should think of the Church not as an institution, but as a person, though of course a person in a unique sense."[5]

Nevertheless, our ecclesiology exceeds the terminology we use to speak about it. It is just too clumsy to say "the portion of Christ's one holy catholic and apostolic church presently suffering particularly intense forms of persecution." So we simply say "the persecuted church." Whether that explanation satisfies, I do not know. But the illustration demonstrates that an inherent, inescapable nexus exists between persecution and Christ's

---

2. Moss, *The Myth of Persecution*.

3. For a more detailed defense of interpreting Hebrews 13:3 as "being in a body with them," see Cochran, *Christians in the Crosshairs*, 108–15.

4. Rainer, "We Are First Baptist Church Sutherland Springs, TX."

5. Bonhoeffer, *Discipleship*, 241. For further consideration on the theological and eccesiological implications of this quote, see House, *Bonhoeffer's Seminary Vision*, 83. See also Godsey, *The Theology of Dietrich Bonhoeffer*, 168.

church. This nexus affirms the relation of persecution to ecclesiology. Not surprisingly, then, even a casual stroll through church history uncovers acute crises regarding persecution, church discipline, and the necessity of clarifying definitions of ecclesiology. One of the most notable instances of persecution begging for a new definition of ecclesiology occurred when Augustine of Hippo engaged in debate with the Donatists.

## Augustine of Hippo and the Donastists

The Donatist controversy demonstrates the interconnected nature of persecution and ecclesiology in at least two ways. First, the origin of the debate between the Donatists and Augustine was linked to the persecution which the tetrarch unleashed against the church in late February 303. As Moss notes, "In the East, the region controlled by Galerius and Diocletian, the persecutions continued and progressed."[6] The progression increased to the point that some Christians were burned alive.[7] But the persecution was even more severe in the West, in Maximian's territory which included North Africa. The faithful authorities under Maximian sought to burn Christian Scriptures and force emperor worship. Many *traditores* handed over Scriptures to be destroyed but later sought penance and restoration to the church. The churches which came to be called Donatists refused to admit the *traditores* without renewed baptism. Donatists also refused to recognize bishops who had been *traditores*. The Donatist controversy forced a century-long division in the Church, lasting from roughly 303 to 411. The division originated with persecution and demanded a reappraisal of ecclesiology in general and of church purity—or church discipline—in particular.

The second way in which the Donatist controversy exposed the nexus of persecution with ecclesiology occurred as violence increased between the followers of Donatus and the Roman Church authorities. Church authorities in Rome leaned on the wisdom of Augustine, who argued convincingly for the use of force to quell the violent clashes with the Donatists. In response, the Donatists claimed to be persecuted. Augustine responded,

> If any persons disobeyed this law, and justly suffered the penalty imposed, they might have said what these men say, that they were righteous because they suffered persecution through the law enacted by the king: and this they certainly would have said, had they

6. Moss, *The Myth of Persecution*, 157.
7. Ibid., 156.

been as mad as these who make divisions between the members of Christ, and spurn the sacraments of Christ, and take credit for being persecuted, because they are prevented from doing such things by the laws which the emperors have passed to preserve the unity of Christ and boast falsely of their innocence, and seek from men the glory of martyrdom, which they cannot receive from our Lord. But true martyrs are such as those of whom the Lord says, 'Blessed are they which are persecuted for righteousness' sake.' It is not, therefore, those who suffer persecution for their unrighteousness, and for the divisions which they impiously introduce into Christian unity, but those who suffer for righteousness' sake, that are truly martyrs.[8]

Without diving deeper into Augustine and Donatism, we can see clearly how the thread of persecution is interwoven into the historical fabric of ecclesiology. This thread of persecution is sometimes—as in the case of the Donatists—also intertwined with church discipline, particularly as that discipline relates to the purity of the church.

## Persecution and Church Discipline

More recently, two scholars have taken up these twin themes. The first, Craig Hovey, argues from the gospel of Mark that the church ought to be so closely aligned with persecution that her identity becomes that of a "Martyr-Church." The other scholar, Josef Ton—himself a pastor who was persecuted in Romania—argues that Christian persecution is providentially ordained to develop and train believers via persecution and rewards believers for their final reigning functions with Christ.

As mentioned, Hovey builds his ecclesiology of martyrdom from the gospel of Mark,[9] arguing that "martyrdom is a possibility for all Christians because the church of Jesus Christ is a martyr church."[10] Hovey takes some liberty with the gospel of Mark, employing terms like "martyr church," rather than the language of the text itself. In taking this approach, Hovey displays a bit of paradox. On the one hand, he believes hermeneutics embarked on a terrible journey of error when it believed that it was either

---

8. Augustine, "Letter 185," 636.
9. Hovey, *To Share in the Body*.
10. Ibid., 21.

possible or desirable to know the intent of the author.[11] Yet, on the other hand, the first assumption he holds in his interpretation is that "Mark was written for the whole church of Jesus Christ."[12] One wonders on what Hovey bases this assumption. Granted, such an assumption does not require that he know the mind of the author *per se*, but it does indicate his own belief that the purpose of a text is both discernible and determinative on the basis of its original authorship.[13]

For Hovey, Mark is intended to convey a martyrology in which "every Christian is a member of a martyr-church."[14] By "martyr-church" Hovey intends a community of self-denial. Self-denial worked out fully leads to martyrdom, though self-denial is not intrinsically good. Neither does self-denial warrant the pursuit of martyrdom. That would be suicide, according to Hovey. Rather, self-denial is a peaceful, non-coercive attempt to display non-violently the hope of a new order of reality in which the mechanisms of force no longer hold sway.[15] (Notice more than a hint of commitment to pacifist ideals.) In this way, Hovey argues that the church witnesses to the reality of the witness of Christ.

Hovey's work is a reminder that Markan studies are heavily burdened by contextual reconstructions. Many commentary writers interpret the gospel of Mark by way of reconstructing the background of persecution out of which it probably first arose.[16] Ironically, Hovey does much the same thing, only his work seeks to reconstruct the foreground into which Mark's gospel will always land. Such a focus on the recipients of the gospel has the tendency to diminish substantial themes of the gospel such as righteousness persecution.

---

11. Ibid.

12. Ibid., 21.

13. Hovey seems to conflate the intent of the author with the mind of the author. Cf. Stein, *A Basic Guide to Interpreting the Bible*, as well as C. S. Lewis's essay, "On Fern-seed and Elephants."

14. Hovey, *To Share in the Body*, 60.

15. Hovey is an avowed pacifist, serving as the Executive Director of the Ashland Center for Nonviolence at Ashland University, Ashland, Ohio.

16. For an overview of various theories regarding a persecution *Sitz im Leben* for Mark's gospel, see Marcus, *Mark 1–8*, 28–39.

PART 3: DISCIPLINE

Further, Hovey's approach is martyrological—based on imitation—rather than diokological[17] and based on the persecution of righteousness.[18] Essential to martyrology is an idealized form of sacrifice, a perpetual "dying" to oneself. The Christian who successfully dies to himself or herself all the way through physical death proves to be a martyr (in the technical sense). This martyrological orientation can be helpful but can also be difficult to sustain as a Christian ethic because of the now prevalent technical use of the term "martyr." For instance, consider the difficulty which arises on account of the fact that martyrdom is recognized by the church only after death. An idealized ethic based on the death of its participants is difficult to govern and impossible to assess while the individual Christian remains alive. As a result of the difficulty the church has in assessing who is upholding the martyr ideal, Hovey imports pacifistic ideals (which *can* enjoy immediate, concrete affirmation). Hovey's martyrology extols non-resistance. Others extol sacrificial death.[19] None of the attempts to define ecclesiology by way of martyrology get to the heart of either the sacrifice of Christ or the triumph of the kingdom of God which are aspects of the persecution dynamic found in Matthew and Mark. Better than martyrological constructions are those constructs which equate persecution (diokology) with ecclesiology—uniting them more or less essentially. Those who are being persecuted are the ones promised rewards now *and* in the life to come (Mark 10:29–30; 13:13). Persecution for the sake of righteousness (diokology) provides a more concrete and livable Christian ethic, without the need of importing a living idealism like pacifism.[20]

In contrast, Ton's approach is more diokological than Hovey's concept of the Martyr-Church.[21] Ton fastens persecution to ecclesiology through his use of discipline and reward. For Ton, the study of persecution is per-

17. *Diokological* references the study of the question from the perspective of persecution (presently suffered) as opposed to *martyrological*, which is the study of persecution having been endured to the end (after death).

18. For a full defense of *diokology* over *martyrology*, see Cochran, "Diokology and the Inception of the Regnal Righteousness Dynamic in Christian Persecution."

19. So Craig Slane in his defense of Dietrich Bonhoeffer as martyr. Others have argued for Christians borrowing the Noble Death ideal from the Romans. Focusing on martyrological ideals leads to idealistic ethics.

20. So, Christ in Matthew 5 is quoted as speaking to his followers, "Blessed are you when . . ."

21. Ton, *Suffering*. The material found in this discussion of Ton was first published in dissertation form (see Cochran, "Diokology") and has been adapted to the subject of this chapter.

sonal and experiential as well as ecclesiological. Ton is familiar with persecution through the experience of preaching and teaching as a Christian in communist Romania. Of his experience, Ton writes that he "preached, lectured, and wrote for nearly a decade, ready to be martyred for what I was doing, yet knowing that death would be my supreme weapon of conquest and my road to the highest glory in heaven."[22] Eventually, Ton, along with his wife and daughter, was exiled from Romania. In exile (in Wheaton, IL), Ton turned again to his studies of persecution, fleshing out how the Christian road to "the highest glory in heaven" might pass through persecution.

The conclusion of Ton's research is that persecution displays an aspect of God's discipline. He says, "Throughout the course of earthly history, God has been at work shaping His children, forming their character, preparing them for ruling, and testing their faithfulness and reliability."[23] Ton constructs his ecclesiology of persecution and rewards on three premises. First, he argues that suffering and martyrdom "should be perceived as two of the best means by which God achieves his purposes with man."[24] Ton is saying that God accomplishes his purposes in his people by means of their suffering and martyrdom. God's purpose is accomplished via the disciplinary process of testing and purifying. Through the testing and purifying of persecution, the people of God become conformed more to the image of Christ. Here is a kind of teleological, virtue ethics—a shaping of character through suffering. The people of God learn to trust God's purposes for them as they remain faithful to him through their trials. Thus, as Ton sees it, "We learn that God, the sovereign Ruler of history, has the purpose of raising and forming a people whom He plans to entrust dominion and authority and glory in His eternal kingdom."[25] This raising and forming of his people is one of the means by which God achieves his purposes with humankind.

Second, Ton's ecclesiology of persecution and rewards depends on the foundation of personal, eternal endurance. Ton connects the suffering of persecution to rewards by arguing that whatever a person achieves in this life will abide with that person in the next life. Indeed, achievements play a major role in determining whether one is counted worthy in the kingdom. Ton understands texts like 1 Corinthians 3:10–15 to teach that there is a judgment which even the people of God must face. Thus, Christian progress

---

22. Ton, *Suffering*, xii.
23. Ibid., 422.
24. Ibid.
25. Ibid., 36.

in this life is of utmost importance because "in the end, our works and our character will both determine the verdict of the judge: the place and rank He will assign to us in the kingdom of heaven."[26] Logically, one might be led to conclude from Ton's statement here that rewards are meritorious, considering that works and character will be judged in relation to place in the kingdom. Ton's third point with regard to persecution and rewards hopes to alleviate such concerns.

Third, Ton argues that this system of rewards is not meritorious. Though the believer is called to develop a character which will be judged blameless and worthy, he is not able to earn anything from God, according to Ton. The reason these efforts are non-meritorious is that God, in his sovereign rule over all things, has predestined whatsoever comes to pass, including what rank and honor each believer has in the kingdom of heaven. The root of each person's faith is the regenerative work of the Holy Spirit of God. That same Holy Spirit works out the fruit of good works and faithfulness over time. In addition, God is the one whose plan is being enacted, and it is the plan and foreordination of God which has established that there might be such kingdom rewards in heaven. In speaking this way of rewards, Ton's voice sounds in harmony with the chorus of Protestant doctrine since the time of John Calvin, Martin Luther and William Tyndale, each of whom wrote on the topic of heavenly rewards (and suffered persecution). Ton sounds quite Protestant in establishing rewards on the foundation of God's plan and foreordination.

Hugh Latimer, in a 1552 sermon, popularized this doctrinal position of predestination for eternal rewards with an oft-repeated phrase:

> Every man shall be rewarded for his good works in everlasting life, but not with everlasting life: For it is written, *Vita aeterna donum Dei*, 'The everlasting life is a gift of God.' Therefore we should not esteem our works so perfect as though we should merit heaven by them: yet God hath such pleasure in such works which we do with a faithful heart, that he promiseth to reward them in everlasting life.[27]

Emma Disley offers the following summary of the generally held Protestant doctrine of rewards:

> For the majority of Protestant writers who addressed the issue, belief in degrees of reward in heaven thus did not conflict with the

26. Ibid.
27. Latimer, "The Second Sermon," 156.

Protestant insight of justification freely attained through the merits of Christ, since rewards resulted naturally or automatically from good works, which were part of the elect's sanctification. Neither did heavenly rewards imply a recurrence of the medieval doctrine of condign merit, since Protestant writers who admitted the concept of degrees of glory hereafter were careful to attribute them not to the merit of works, but rather to the bountiful mercy of God.[28]

Ton further asserts, though, that "Protestants have been deficient in putting together a reasonable and well-integrated theology of good works, of character development, and of the momentous judgment of every Christian according to his works."[29] One should note Ton's inconsistent language. Earlier in his book, he said the judgment was *on the basis of* works.[30] Here, he alters the phrase to the less problematic rendering, *according to his works*. (*On the basis* and *in accordance* are distinct concepts, the latter being much better adapted to evangelical doctrine.) Ton expects his book to supply at least a portion of what is lacking in a Protestant theology of suffering, martyrdom, and rewards.

As Ton sees it, God works the events of suffering and martyrdom to fulfill his own grand, universal design. Suffering and martyrdom are employed by God, on the one hand, to accomplish victory and establish the final eternal kingdom of Christ, while, on the other hand, developing kingdom characteristics in the chosen people of God so that they will be worthy of honor and well-suited for reigning with Christ, each according to his own predetermined rank and place. Many questions are provoked by this understanding of suffering, martyrdom, and rewards in heaven. We shall consider further two questions narrowly related to the discussion of persecution and ecclesiology.

### Does Persecution Fit Believers for Ruling?

First, the question might be asked of Ton's thesis, How does faithfulness through persecution fit one for ruling over others in the glory of an eternal kingdom? Using texts like Daniel 12:3, 13, Ton argues that the Old and New Testaments promise regnal rewards for those who prove faithful through persecution. Leaving aside the question of whether the "allotted

---

28. Disley, "Degrees of Glory," 105.
29. Ton, *Suffering*, 321.
30. See for example ibid., 237, especially the heading and afterward.

portion" of Daniel 12:13 refers to regnal rewards in the eternal kingdom, one still wonders what exactly is the connection between suffering well on earth and ruling well in heaven?

Is Ton arguing that one who suffers is suited for ruling because he has been trained by his suffering under an abusive ruler how to rule over others justly? This argument could be put forward as a kind of Marxist-Socialist notion of the underclass learning from their oppressors how to rule more equitably. Of course, history is opposed to offering this argument any support, considering the atrocities of the Killing Fields of Cambodia and the failures of Joseph Stalin, Vladimir Lenin, and other such revolutionaries. These egregious examples of people feeling victimized and consequently rising to rule offer no sure hope that suffering leads to the ability to rule equitably. The promise of this argument breaks on the perpetual cycle of tyrannical dictators in revolutionist countries. Just because one has suffered does not mean he is also fit to rule. Victims of crimes may not prove to be good prison wardens.

Ton, of course, is not actually arguing that victims make good rulers. His position is more nuanced. He is arguing that it is *faithfulness* displayed through suffering persecution that fits one for regnal rewards. Enduring faithfulness is the quality suitable for regnal rewards. So, Ton views suffering persecution as demonstrating (or proving) allegiance to the ultimate Sovereign. As Ton argues, the one who remains faithful to the ultimate Sovereign while being threatened—even with death—by a lesser sovereign is demonstrating that he, in fact, understands authority and, thus, will rule rightly. This faithful one is learning through suffering that he has made the right determination in his allegiance (as well as in his trusting the more reliable authority). As he learns this, he further submits to God's authority and is shaped further by such submission. Thus, the faithful follower is demonstrating that he is worthy of (in the sense of being prepared for) the regnal rewards of kingdom reign.

### Can Obedience Establish Just Authority?

Following this line of reasoning, however, leads to a second question: whether obedient allegiance is sufficient to fit one for exercising authority. Allegiance to authority and a disposition toward obedient action are admirable qualities indeed, but are they also somehow related to exercising dominion? Might they not better be classified as necessary qualities for a follower than for a leader—better for a subject than for a king? Ton argues that there is a connection between the obedient spirit and regnal rewards, saying, "A person's poverty in spirit *produces* the inner qualities required for obtaining the inheritance, or for being put in charge over God's possessions."[31] But there are two very different rewards here: inheritance and being put in charge. On inheritance, post-Reformation scholars have disavowed themselves of any hint of condign merit in their soteriology.[32] The inheritance is the reward of faith which itself is a gift.

The second reward—being put in charge—again opens more lines of question. How does poverty in spirit produce the inner qualities required for being put in charge of God's possessions? Is the position of authority earned or a gift? For Ton, this production of abilities comes about as the faithful are trained by their suffering, "thereby proving them reliable."[33] To whom are the children proved reliable—God, themselves, or others? If God, then a problem arises with the notion that human suffering is necessary for God to know future suitability of his children for His work. Must God see his children endure torture in order to prove they deserve to reign with Christ? Indeed, must God see Stephen stoned to death by a mob in order to validate his reliability for future service in kingdom labors? Ton likely means the persecuted believers are proved reliable to others.

Finally, there is concern as to whether Ton's ecclesiology would lead to a diminished Christ and diminished church. The typical evangelical vision of the saints' final authority and rule sounds something like this:

> The city of God has become one massive Holy of Holies (cf. Jer 3:16–17). Consequently, human beings have been finally restored to their lost royal dignity and majesty, and, having God's name written on their foreheads, 'they will reign for ever and ever' (Rev. 22:5). 'Yahweh and his people are together and are one flesh.'[34]

Ton's vision may challenge this understanding of Revelation 22:5. For Ton, God created humans to have dominion, ruling over the earth. The Fall thwarted humankind's ability and perverted our desires in relation to regnal responsibilities. Nevertheless, the Fall did not thwart God's design

---

31. Ton, *Suffering*, 417, emphasis original.

32. See Disley, "Degrees of Glory" for an historical, theological consideration of reward.

33. Ton, *Suffering*, 419.

34. Dempster, *Dominion and Dynasty*, 234, quoting, in the last line, Karl Barth's *Church Dogmatics*.

for humans to exercise regnal authority. In redemption, then, God works to re-establish for humankind the exercise of regnal authority. Through testing his people with persecution and martyrdom, God, in effect, puts them through a training program. Ton says, "The training process is meant to produce in His children the ability to handle authority and the capacity to administrate wisely, thereby proving them reliable."[35]

Is the kingdom rule of Christ such that God depends on trained sufferers to accomplish it? Consider an observation by Grant Osborne from Revelation 2:26ff., a passage which connects suffering persecution with "authority" over the nations. Osborne asserts that those interpreters are simply wrong who interpret Revelation 2:26 as saying that Christ will give his faithful saints the authority "to rule" over the nations. The authority is not authority "to rule." Instead, "The violence connoted in the 'rod of iron' and the 'shattering' of the pottery are simply too strong for 'rule.' The 'rod of iron' in this context is probably not so much the king's scepter as the shepherd's club, a large wooden club capped with iron for killing animals that endangered the sheep."[36] The saints who overcome will indeed overcome the nations, having vanquished them in Christ and now sitting in authority over them. The overcoming (and thus reigning) is contingent upon one having already overcome the nations with the sharp sword protruding from Christ's mouth (Rev. 19:15).

Ton's understanding of regnal rewards potentially diminishes this aspect of the glory of Christ. In speaking of what he perceives as a problem in Protestant theology, Ton writes, "The redemption of man through the cross of Christ has been made so central that for many, it has become the primary purpose of human history. This is equal to saying that God created man in order to save him. The simple reformulation shows us by just how far our theology has missed the mark."[37] Against making Christ "so central," Ton argues for a sort of reverting back to the order of creation, holding that, although the Fall did cause problems, the regnal purposes for humans still exist. Ton speaks easily of the training exercises between God and his people, as though such exercises began at the Fall, have continued until now, and will continue until earth and heaven meet. He

---

35. Ton, *Suffering*, 419.

36. Osborne, *Revelation*, 166–67. Osborne cites agreement with Henry Barclay Swete; contra Robert Mounce, John Walvoord, David Chilton, and Colin Hemer. Osborne also notes that the connection to David does not allow too harsh a distinction between ruling and "destroying."

37. Ton, *Suffering*, 421.

speaks in his concluding section as though the relationship between God and humankind has not changed since the advent of Christ.[38] He says, "Throughout the course of earthly history, God has been at work shaping His children, forming their character, preparing them for ruling, and testing their faithfulness and reliability . . . Moreover, God will continue this work until the end of history."[39]

The danger of such talk is a diminishing of Christ as the one mediator between God and humans, of Christ as the ruling head and authority over the church, of Christ as the New Covenant keeper, Christ as the vindicated sovereign Lord, and Christ Himself as the saint's reward. Is it not the case that the arrival of Christ fundamentally changed the shaping of God's people?

Ton is not keen on the notion of Christ himself being the reward. He views such a position with the suspicion that it reflects a "reluctance to accept the notion of rewards and the consequent refusal to see them as a motivation for working for Christ and His gospel."[40] He cites Leon Morris as being guilty of such reluctance, but he does not interact with Morris's point that the rewards in question might be rewards related to intimacy with Christ. Millard Erickson makes a similar point in contemplating the rewards promised to the faithful. Against views like Ton's—views which rely on different ranks and levels of rewards—Erickson asks, "If this is the case, would not the joy of heaven be reduced by one's awareness of the differences and the constant reminder that one might have been more faithful?"[41] Instead, Erickson proposes that the case with rewards might be "that the difference in the rewards lies not in the external or objective circumstances, but in the subjective awareness or appreciation of those circumstances."[42] Given the centrality of Christ and the reality that everyone will bow down and confess before him (Phil 2:10–11), and given the fact that every eye will see Him, even those who pierced him (Rev 1:7); given the fact that to Christ belongs the glory and the dominion forever and ever, Erickson's point is worth considering. If Christ is all in all, then how could the people who have grown to love Him so deeply be distracted by human ranks and

---

38. Ibid.
39. Ibid., 422.
40. Ibid., 239.
41. Erickson, *Christian Theology*, 1234.
42. Ibid.

places? What Ton asserts is a turning of attention away from the works and the rule of Christ toward the works of His followers.

When the disciples in Jesus' day became motivated by ranks in the kingdom, they caused division and had to be corrected by Christ (Matt 20:24ff.). Granted, Jesus taught that there may be positions in the kingdom, but he discouraged the disciples from dwelling on such things as a motive for action. Rewards—like most anything else—can deter the faithful from keeping their eyes fixed on Jesus. Indeed, the very disciples who divided over rewards in the kingdom also proved unfaithful. In fact, all the disciples proved unfaithful in the hour of their opportunity for faithfulness (Matt 26:40)! And yet, Christ promised them that they would sit with him on thrones in the kingdom (Matt 19:28). The real tension in the biblical text is how could it be that these unfaithful followers might sit anywhere in heaven with a holy God. Is it possible that they might be justified by faith and then exalted by works? What works made Peter a rock on which to build—his thrice-repeated denial of Christ?

Ton's discussion of regnal rewards is undoubtedly provocative, and it underscores the need for continued diokological study on rewards. Nonetheless, many will remain reticent of his effort to focus more attention toward faithfulness and less on the Christ of faith. As a biblical theology of persecution and suffering, Ton's work remains too narrowly focused on rewards for martyrs and not focused enough on the righteousness of Christ and the persecution of his saints on account of him.

What Ton, Hovey, and Augustine have in common, however, is the clear sense that speaking of persecution links organically with clarifying ecclesiology. Often, persecution study attaches inexorably with issues of church discipline. Indeed, Augustine and the Donatists demonstrate from the *past* that this ecclesiological connection has been evident. Hovey attempts to link martyrdom with ecclesiology for the *present* church. And Ton points from present persecution toward the *future* church when heaven and earth meet. Ecclesiology past, present, and future can be altered by understanding persecution. Perhaps it is wise after all to have a chapter on persecution in a book on ecclesiology and church discipline.

# 7

# Suffering in the Struggle with Sin and the Role of Church Discipline

—Jeremy M. Kimble

## Introduction

In his *On the Mortification of Sin in Believers*, John Owen asserts that putting sin to death involves "constant warfare," a "laying load on sins at all times."[1] Owen further asserts, "When sin is strong and vigorous, the soul is scarce able to make any head against it; it sighs and groans and mourns and is troubled."[2] Warfare rages in the lives of believers. There is a call to not let sin reign in our mortal body (Rom 6:12), and to not present our members to sin as instruments of unrighteousness (Rom 6:13), but in fact to put the deeds of the body to death by the Spirit (Rom 8:13). These calls are made in the New Testament, recognizing the tension that we are already saints in Christ (1 Cor 1:2) who are not yet fully formed into Christ's likeness as we await glorification (Rom 8:28–30).[3] We struggle as we seek to become who we already are in Christ. Thus, while we often relate persecution and ostracization to the topic of suffering (and rightly so), in the struggle against sin there is poignant struggle, a battle against the world, the flesh, and the devil, and, in a sense, suffering.

As the church, we are to battle against these elements (world, flesh, devil) and work alongside one another in pursuing righteousness, using both formative and corrective discipline. We recognize the call to formative

---

1. Owen, "Of the Mortification of Sin in Believers," 52, 76.
2. Ibid., 76.
3. See Moo, *Epistle to the Romans*, 494–95; Schreiner, *Romans*, 421–22.

discipline as we continue to exhort each other to persevere in godliness, even in the midst of the struggle against sin (Heb 3:12–13; 10:23–25). Fellow members also struggle and suffer alongside of their brothers and sisters as they are called to bear one another's burdens (Gal 6:1–2). There is also a call to corrective discipline when the personal struggle against sin ceases and people are living in unrepentant sin (Matt 18:15–20; 1 Cor 5:1–13). If the process goes all the way through excommunication the person is subjected to a different kind of suffering in the world (1 Cor 5:5; 1 Tim 1:18). However, this corrective discipline is enjoined with humility and sorrow in the members, and always aimed at the instruction, repentance, and restoration of the sinner (2 Cor 2:5–11). All of this comes under the sovereign God who disciplines those whom he loves, which is painful, but yields the peaceful fruit of righteousness (Heb 12:3–11).

This chapter, therefore, will demonstrate that the church embodies suffering and struggle as a distinctive quality (some would even say "mark") of the Christian life, and church discipline plays a distinct role in this struggle. The first section of this chapter, then, will look briefly at four historical figures and their thoughts on the Christian life as suffering/struggle from a biblical perspective. Second, we will look more specifically into the concept of spiritual warfare, noting how, as believers, we war against the flesh and seek to walk in the Spirit. This war occurs at an individual level, but also, as we will see in the third section, ecclesially. Part of the "weapons of our warfare" (2 Cor 10:4) include formative discipline and corrective discipline, as well as divine discipline. Finally, within these spheres of discipline, warrant will be given for understanding how struggle and suffering in and through "discipline" permeates the Christian life and is a way in which God works throughout our lives to see that we persevere in the faith.

## Biblical and Historical Context

Often we do not consider that we wake up each day in a war zone (Eph 6:10–18), but we have several historical figures that remind us of the battle and struggle we are in as Christians. For Martin Luther, the Christian life in large measure consisted of *oratio* (the Word spoken in prayer), *meditatio* (active meditation on the Word), and *tentatio*, or *Anfechtung* (existential feelings of dread, tension, suffering).[4] In dealing with *Anfechtung* as one of the marks of the church, according to Luther, Christians must endure "ev-

---

4. Luther, "First Lectures on the Psalms," 414.

ery misfortune and persecution, all kinds of trials and evil from the devil, the world, and the flesh (as the Lord's Prayer indicates) by inward sadness, timidity, fear, outward poverty, contempt, illness, and weakness, in order to become like their head, Christ."[5]

He speaks to this most poignantly in his commentary on Psalm 119. Here he states that *Anfechtung* is that which teaches us "not only to know and understand, but also to experience how right, how true, how sweet, how lovely, how mighty, how comforting God's Word is, wisdom beyond all wisdom."[6] In this Psalm, David bemoans all kinds of enemies, trials, false spirits and factions, whom he must tolerate because he meditates and is occupied with God's Word (Ps 119:22, 23, 28, 50, 53, 71, 84, 115, 136, 153, 157, 161, 176). He continues, "For as soon as God's Word takes root and grows in you, the devil will harry you, and will make a real doctor of you, and by his assaults will teach you to seek and love God's Word."[7] For Luther, the life of the believer was to be understood as one marked by continual struggle, a back and forth journey between despair and hope.[8] In our journey through the Christian life, battling the world, the flesh, and the devil, God works to shape us into his image (Rom 8:1–5; 8:28–29; Jas 1:3–5). Moreover, as "theologians of the cross," we come to Christ in weakness and dependence as he offers us sufficient grace, perfecting his power in our weakness (2 Cor 12:8–10).

Dietrich Bonhoeffer, like Luther, thought a great deal about the struggle with sin and temptation in the Christian life. As he begins to comment on the Beatitudes, contained in the Sermon on the Mount, Bonhoeffer claims, "Jesus has called each individual [disciple]. They have given up everything in response to his call. Now they are living in renunciation and want; they are the poorest of the poor, the most tempted of the tempted, the hungriest of the hungry. They have only him."[9] Bonhoeffer states with utter clarity that Christian disciples have nothing in this world but hardship, but they have everything eternally with God. We follow the way of our master in denying ourselves (temptation) and taking up our crosses (suffering; Mark 8:31–38).[10] We are called to self-denial, no longer seeing ourselves,

---

5. Luther, "On the Councils and the Church," 165.
6. Luther, "Preface to the Wittenberg Edition of Luther's Writings," 287.
7. Ibid.
8. See Trueman, *Luther on the Christian Life*, 122–26.
9. Bonhoeffer, *Discipleship*, 101.
10. Bonhoeffer states, concerning this passage, "Just as Christ is only Christ as one

only the one who is ahead of us that we are following.[11] Bonhoeffer further asserts, from Romans 6:1–14 and Hebrews 13:12–13, "The call to follow Jesus is death and life. The call of Christ leads Christians into a daily struggle against sin and Satan. Thus each day, with its temptations by the flesh and the world, brings Jesus Christ's suffering anew to his disciples."[12] Indeed the Christian life is a journey of struggle and suffering as we face the world, flesh, and devil, but with the beautiful prospect of hope and endurance because of Christ's work.

Two other historical figures that speak of the Christian life in terms of warfare include John Bunyan and William Gurnall. Bunyan is likely best known for his *Pilgrim's Progress*, but just as important for this particular topic is his work entitled *The Holy War*. A well-known and popular book in the English language, *Pilgrim's Progress* depicts a man named Christian and his journey from spiritual darkness to salvation and his subsequent journey through the Christian life. Whether speaking of the slough of despond, the town of Vanity Fair, battling Apollyon, or being taken captive by the giant Despair, Bunyan depicts the Christian life as one of struggle and suffering in the fight against the world, flesh, and devil. Commenting on Psalm 23, as Christian passes through the valley of the shadow of death, seeing there "Dangers in darkness, devils, hell, and sin," as well as "snares, and pits, and traps," Christian recognizes that Jesus "preserved him in that distress."[13]

Bunyan's *The Holy War* has a similar feel to *Pilgrim's Progress* in its allegorical structure, but gets into more of the specifics of conversion, mortification, and sanctification.[14] This work depicts the battle for Mansoul, which at first is ruled by the Diabolonians and their cast of characters, but is eventually, through the impact of gospel word and Spirit, overtaken by the prince and established as territory of God. But this is not where the story ends. Battle continues to ensue as the enemy seeks to take back territory that now belongs to the prince. Bunyan reminds us that in conversion we are new creations (2 Cor 5:17) and Christ leads us in triumphal procession (2 Cor 2:14), but the struggle against sin continues until glorification.

---

who suffers and is rejected, so a disciple is a disciple only in suffering and being rejected, thereby participating in crucifixion" (ibid., 85).

11. Ibid., 86.
12. Ibid., 88.
13. Bunyan, *The Pilgrim's Progress*, 71.
14. Bunyan, *The Holy War*.

Our sins struggle much and die hard, therefore, we wage war to continually destroy sinful strongholds (2 Cor 10:1–6).

Finally, William Gurnall, Puritan pastor, conceives of the struggle against sin in the Christian life in his work *The Christian in Complete Armor*. He asserts that the continual calling of the Christian, based on Ephesians 6:10–18, is "a continued warfare with the world, and the prince of this world."[15] Piece by piece, Gurnall describes what the Christian armor is and how it is of benefit to the Christian sojourner, battling against the passions of the flesh, which wage war against our soul (1 Pet 2:11). He tells us what we can expect if we utilize them, and the consequences we will see if we do not. Gurnall is clear to state that the believer is to persevere in his "Christian course" to the end of his life.[16] He maintains that persevering is hard, many will come and peruse, but few will remain faithful. It is a "hard word! This taking up the cross daily, this praying always, this watching night and day and never laying aside our clothes and armor, unbent in our holy waiting on God, and walking with God."[17] Many come, but many depart sorrowfully like the rich young ruler. However, this is the saint's duty, "to make religion his everyday work, without any vacation from one end of the year to the other."[18] This grueling perseverance and struggle, Gurnall insists, is why so few come out conquerors: "Because all have a desire to be happy, but few have courage and resolution to grapple with the difficulties [of battling sin, Satan, and the world] that meet them in the way to their happiness."[19] Gurnall, like others in church history, understood the Christian life is filled with suffering and struggle, not just in physical persecution, but also in the spiritual battle against sin and the evil one.

---

15. Gurnall, *The Christian in Complete Armor*, 11.
16. Ibid., 15.
17. Ibid.
18. Ibid.
19. Ibid. Soon after Gurnall states, "The fearful are in the forlorn of those that march for hell, Rev 21; the violent and valiant are they which take heaven by force: cowards never won heaven. Say not that thou hast royal blood running in thy veins, and art begotten of God, except thou canst prove thy pedigree by this heroic spirit, to dare to be holy despite men and devils" (16).

PART 3: DISCIPLINE

## Warring against the World, the Flesh, and the Devil

While it has been termed in different ways throughout church history, a way to refer to the struggle of the Christian life against the world, sin, and Satan is spiritual warfare.[20] John Gilhooly notes, regarding Ephesians 6:12, "Spiritual warfare is a theological term used to describe the ongoing battle between the church and the devil and his angels. The term is not used in the Bible but is derived from a conception of the struggle of the Christian life."[21] While the topic of spiritual warfare is expansive, here the focus will be on the struggle in the Christian life with the world, the flesh, and the devil as it relates to living in obedience to God.

In its most common form, it can be argued, spiritual warfare focuses on the internal struggle between the flesh and the Spirit. The focus is remembering one's new identity in Christ and using the power of the Holy Spirit to evade temptations to sin. We do not deny the influence of the devil and his angels or the need to resist the devil, but the focus is on internal struggles primarily, rather than external, sensational struggles against spiritual powers. As Gilhooly, as well as David Powlison, claims, "Whatever else spiritual warfare entails, if it is not at root centered on believing the truths of the gospel, clinging to one's identity in Christ, and resisting sin, then it will be a failed project."[22]

Thus, we do not love the world nor the things of the world, knowing that the world, and its desires, and all it provides is temporary, it is passing away. However, those who do the will of God will live forever (1 John 2:15–17). We war with the flesh (Rom 7:7–25; Gal 5:11–22; Jas 1:13), those vestiges of our fallen human nature, in particular our sinful desires and temptations. And we battle against Satan, continually resisting him and standing firm in the Lord (Jas 4:7; 1 Pet 5:8–9). This is an ongoing struggle, all through the Christian life, knowing that we are called to put on the armor of God (Eph 6:10–20), and tear down strongholds and take every thought captive to Christ (2 Cor 10:3–5). We do this by prayer, studying Scripture and noting the truths of who we are in Christ as new creations in the gospel. And we also fight, not merely alone, but in community. It

---

20. The literature available on spiritual warfare is legion, as well as viewpoints adopted on the topic. For an introduction to the various approaches, see Beilby and Eddy, *Understanding Spiritual Warfare*.

21. Gilhooly, *40 Questions About Spiritual Warfare*, 23.

22. Ibid., 155. A recent defense of this model dubs it the "Classical Model" (see Powlison, "The Classical Model").

is in the context of local gathered bodies of believers that we are encouraged and strengthened in the faith (1 Cor 12:27; Rom 12:4; Heb 10:24–25). Therefore, spiritual warfare is also a corporate endeavor and not merely an individual one (though it is most often thought of in the latter category). As such, we can perceive of Scripture's admonitions regarding church discipline—in all of its forms—to be avenues of warfare and struggle against sin to the extent that they remind us about the deceitfulness of sin and encourage the body in the doctrine of our Lord.

## Formative Discipline

This depiction of church discipline may seem ironic. When you utter the phrase "church discipline" in most ecclesial contexts, the first thing that often comes to mind is kicking someone unceremoniously out of the church. It seems that church discipline enlarges suffering and struggle in life, only adding to the pain we already experience in the Christian life. However, that is not the way the Bible conceives of discipline.[23] The concept of church discipline can rightly be understood as divine authority delegated to the church by Jesus Christ to maintain order through mutual exhortation and the correction of persistently sinning church members for the good of those caught in sin, the purity of the church, and the glory of God.[24] Habitual, known, unrepentant sin within the church must be dealt with accordingly, but the goal is always to bring about repentance, restoration, and persevering faith for long-term peace with God (Rom 5:1).[25]

People may still tend to view discipline with a negative lens, but this ecclesial practice must be seen with the long view in mind. As fellow church members, we oversee and are overseen in our discipleship, which means we will deal with one another's sin, and this can be a painful process, joining

---

23. Portions of the sections dealing with formative and corrective discipline are derived from Kimble, *That His Spirit May Be Saved*, 6–9. Used by permission of Wipf and Stock Publishers. www.wipfandstock.com.

24. This definition is derived from a number of sources dealing with the topic of church discipline. Notable contributions to this doctrine include Adams, *Handbook of Church Discipline*; Blue and White, *Church Discipline that Heals*; Dever, *Polity: Biblical Arguments on How to Conduct Church Life*; Jeschke, *Discipling the Brother*; Knuteson, *Calling the Church to Discipline*; Laney, *A Guide to Church Discipline*; Lauterbach, *The Transforming Community*; Leeman, *Church Disciplines*; Oden, *Corrective Love*; South, *Disciplinary Practices in Pauline Texts*; Wray, *Biblical Church Discipline*.

25. See Kingdon, "Discipline," 450.

in the struggle with and for one another (Gal 6:1–2). Church discipline is not something to be feared; rather it should be embraced as we suffer in the struggle against sin, knowing we cannot shoulder this load on our own.

The concept of church discipline can be understood historically as both "formative" and "corrective." Jonathan Leeman notes, "In broad terms, church discipline is one part of the discipleship process, the part where we correct sin and point the disciple toward the better path . . . And a Christian is disciplined through instruction and correction."[26] He continues and states that the idea of both instruction and correction is why "there's a centuries-old practice of referring to both formative discipline and corrective discipline."[27] As such, churches do well in not separating discipline a great distance from their pursuit of discipleship, recognizing that the former is a crucial aspect of the latter.[28]

Formative discipline means order is maintained in the church through measures such as regenerate church membership, the right preaching and teaching of Scripture, proper administration of the ordinances, mutual exhortation, and observing the many "one another" commands contained in the New Testament.[29] Formative church discipline, according to Don Cox, "is broader than corrective discipline and refers to the nurture of believers through instruction and their shared life in the body."[30] Formative discipline—while not always called by that name—helps to give a particular mindset to the life of the church. This type of discipline is exercised in the Christian community as the members express genuine concern for each other and become dynamically involved with one another in deep interpersonal relationships, recognizing that God holds all accountable for their stewardship of life.[31] Thus, the purpose of formative discipline is to enlighten, encourage, support, and sustain one another in Christian living and in the fulfillment of the divine mission.

---

26. Leeman, *Church Discipline*, 27.

27. Ibid.

28. See Schreiner, "The Biblical Basis for Church Discipline," 105.

29. For a more thorough study of this type of discipline see Cox, "The Forgotten Side of Church Discipline," 44–58.

30. Ibid., 44.

31. See ibid., 44–45.

## Corrective Discipline

Corrective church discipline deals with the direct confrontation of sin. A forthright approach to the process of discipline is elucidated by Jesus, which helps to form a pattern for how one should approach these kinds of situations (Matt 18:15–20).[32] Jesus states that one should go directly to the person who sinned against them to see if they can restore the relationship. If reconciliation does not take place, one or two witnesses are to be brought along in order to restore fellowship. If there is no reconciliation at this point the matter is brought before the church so that the sinner can be confronted corporately. If this does not achieve the goal of reconciliation the person is to be removed from the membership of the church and treated as a "Gentile or tax collector."[33] In each of these steps, love and forgiveness are to be extended, since the goal of discipline is ultimately reconciliation.

This last step of the discipline, known as excommunication, is more rare in church settings, since issues typically are dealt with in the first or second step. Nevertheless, this area of discipline demands our attention.[34] This step of discipline does not mean that a person cannot attend a church service; rather it involves a removal of that person from the membership rolls and the exclusion of the person from partaking of the Lord's Supper due to their unrepentance. Church members must also know that they are

---

32. It should be noted that this pattern may not necessarily apply in all cases. One can see this as evidenced in 1 Corinthians 5 where Paul calls for the immediate excommunication of the sinning member without going through the other steps as seen in Matthew 18.

33. More detail will be given later regarding this phrase from Matthew 18. At this point it is sufficient to say that Jesus appears to be saying that a congregation should treat one who is excommunicated as if they were an unbeliever. As such, it is crucial to note Marlin Jeschke's exhortation and note that church discipline is nothing less than a "renewed presentation of the gospel message to the impenitent persons in that it confronts them with the truth" (Jeschke, *Discipling in the Church*, 88). As such, church discipline has both ecclesiological and soteriological concerns.

34. F. S. Piggin astutely defines this aspect of discipline: "The most extreme disciplinary measure of the church, excommunication is the exclusion of an irrevocably rebellious sinner from the communion of the faithful. In most periods of the church's history, excommunication has been understood primarily as a medicinal measure, to recall to repentance and obedience. A secondary purpose is to safeguard the community's purity. When excommunication is rightly understood, punishment has never been the object" (Piggin, "Excommunication," 422–23).

to treat the excommunicant as if that person were an unbeliever, based on an unwillingness to deal with their sin (Matt 18:17).[35]

This understanding of excommunication is needful in embracing both the love as well as the holiness of God, noting that both attributes are exercised in this practice. It is also crucial to note that this practice is done (ideally and biblically) out of love for the person under discipline. This may seem counterintuitive, but in reality the person is suffering the natural consequences of their sin, and, as we will see, likely undergoing divine discipline. Ecclesial corrective discipline aims to join this person in their struggle with sin to assist them as they continue the journey of the Christian life.

## Divine Discipline

God also disciplines his children as a Father in order that they might share in his holiness (Deut 8:5–6; Prov 3:11–12; Heb 12:3–11; Rev 3:19). That is, as a parent God reproves, corrects, and trains disobedient children in order to keep them from ever leaving his family and falling under the ultimate curse of the covenant. N. Clayton Croy contends, regarding Hebrews 12:3–11, that in its development of the themes of sonship, suffering, and perseverance, this section articulates "supremely the letter's paraenetic aim: to reinvigorate the flagging faith of the readers."[36] In regards to the discipline meted out by God in this text, there is scholarly debate over whether the discipline in mind is punitive or educative (*paideia* can connote either meaning depending on context). Ched Spellman has served readers well by observing that "By drawing on the two OT contexts of Deuteronomy 8 and Proverbs 3:11–12, Hebrews 12:3–11 is able to employ the concept of discipline both as a means of correction for disobedience and also as a means of training in obedience (or at least in a way that allows both ideas to remain active)."[37] Either way, this discipline can prove difficult, but will be to our benefit as we journey through the Christian life.

---

35. Dever and Alexander, *The Deliberate Church*, 71. Again, this statement does not infer that the church is the final authority regarding one's salvation; however one must take seriously removal from a local church, since this serves as a warning of potential final judgment and serves as a means by which the saints are called to persevere in their faith.

36. Croy, *Endurance in Suffering*, 5.

37. Spellman, "The Drama of Discipline," 490. Spellman's article deftly defends this concept: "In Heb 12:3–11, the writer seems to draw on both Proverbs 3 and Deuteronomy 8. In intertextual terms, the writer directly quotes Prov 3:11–2 and his exposition

Tracing out the statements of Hebrews 12, we observe that those united to Christ by faith must expect to experience the discipline of God. We are not to lose heart (12:3), but to take heart (12:5), since the Lord is extending his faithfulness toward those whom he loves (12:6). The discipline flows from the love of God, is proof that we are his children (12:8–10), and is for our good, to share in his holiness. To this end, D. P. Kingdon notes, "To view suffering for the sake of Christ as evidence of God's fatherly work of perfecting us is a needful corrective to the all too common idea that our happiness, *as defined by us*, is his chief concern. God would have us holy rather than happy."[38] Endurance, training, and discipline are the "interconnected concepts that the writer uses to spur his readers onward."[39] Faithfully God disciplines his own, painful though it may be, through various means—including the church—seeking to produce in them "the peaceful fruit of righteousness" (Heb 12:11).

## Perseverance of the Saints

Through the struggle and suffering experienced in the Christian life, discipline serves not as mere additional suffering, but as a means of our persevering in the faith. Believers are called to persevere in a faith that works itself out in love (Gal 5:6), for it is this kind of life that demonstrates true faith (Jas 2:14–26). Conversely, if a church member is not persevering in this kind of faith, and it manifests itself in ongoing, unrepentant sin, the disciplinary process should be applied.[40] Discipline is adjudicated so that

---

of this text echoes the drama of discipline in Deuteronomy. The wilderness generation is seen by the writer in both positive and negative terms. This makes *paideia* a particularly strategic and fitting concept to employ in some of the writer's final words of exhortation. The book of Hebrews is a written sermon sent to a group of believers undergoing persecution and the temptation to waver in their faith. They were a people experiencing spiritual exhaustion from external and internal factors. Noting the multifaceted and intertextually informed matrix of meaning within which the writer sets the concept of discipline enables this concept to become a perfect description of the intended audience of the letter: those who experience divine discipline, those with whom God is dealing with as sons" (Spellman, "The Drama of Discipline," 505). See also Peeler, *You Are My Son*, 156–61.

38. Kingdon, "Discipline," 450.
39. Spellman, "The Drama of Discipline," 506.
40. George Davis notes that in both the OT (Deut 17:8–11; 19:19–20) and the NT (1 Tim 5:19–20), church discipline was meant to serve as a deterrent to others in sinning. Recognizing that even church leaders are not exempt from discipline, a local

the church will not be contaminated and led astray by the sinning member, and also that the individual under discipline may repent, be restored, and persevere in their faith along with the rest of the church.[41]

As such, first, one should observe the connection between perseverance and church discipline as it relates to the congregation as a whole.[42] Citing passages such as Hebrews 12:15, 1 Corinthians 5:2–7, and 1 Timothy 5:20, Wayne Grudem maintains that one reason discipline is exacted is so that the sin will be kept from spreading to others and, as a result, they can effectively walk in holiness. Paul wants believers to understand that sin will not be tolerated and is dealt with as the person receives discipline from the church, and, potentially, God himself.[43] Lyle Vander Broek concurs and maintains that in 1 Corinthians 5 Paul's primary concern is for the community as a whole, and how the lack of discipline will affect them. He asserts, "The apostle feels that the sinner in their midst is a danger to the life of the community. This leaven, as we have seen, might be interpreted as a compromise to the community's holiness, as an indication that all are responsible for the sin of the one member, or as the threat of further contamination."[44] If the leaven of sin is allowed to permeate the church, as 1 Corinthians 5:6–7 suggests, the Christian community and its distinctive holiness is seriously

---

congregation would be restrained from evil and encouraged to persevere in the faith. See Davis, "Whatever Happened to Church Discipline?," 358–59. For further commentary on the discipline of church leaders, see Marshall, "Congregation and Ministry," 111.

41. See Thomas Oden, who claims, "Discipline is a part of Christ's ordering of the church, not only for fostering the proximate holiness of the church, but also for the spiritual benefit of the offender" (Oden, *Corrective Love*, 83). See also Stanton, "Reestablishment of Proper Church Discipline," 207–8.

42. Commenting on 1 Cor 5:6–8, John Calvin maintains, "The second purpose [of corrective discipline] is that the good may not be corrupted by the constant company of the wicked, as commonly happens. For there is nothing easier than to be led away by bad examples from moral living" (Calvin, *Institutes of the Christian Religion*, 4.12.5). See also Oden, *Corrective Love*, 84; and Wray, *Biblical Church Discipline*, 4.

43. Grudem, *Systematic Theology*, 895. See also Davis, "Whatever Happened to Church Discipline?" 355, who asserts, "Paul exhorted the church to exercise discipline in order to prevent the sin from 'spreading through the camp.' Paul demonstrated his recognition of the fact that every local church has a twofold responsibility: (1) to do everything within its power and ability to bring the wayward brother back to God, and (2) to exercise every precaution to make sure that the rest of the church is properly protected. This protective aspect of church discipline involves at least three areas. Every congregation is responsible for protecting the church: (1) from doctrinal error, (2) from moral impurity, and (3) from divisiveness."

44. Vander Broek, "Discipline and Community," 11; See also Thompson, *Moral Formation According to Paul*, 48.

threatened.[45] Discipline is, therefore, a necessary means in the ongoing struggle with sin in light of the final judgment.[46]

Secondly, discipline is undertaken for the sake of sinning individuals, that they might repent and subsequently persevere in their faith, enduring in the struggle of the Christian life against the world, flesh, and the devil.[47] The reason believers are excommunicated from the community of faith is because their sinful actions are not correlating with their profession of faith. Since they have been washed, sanctified, and justified by Christ (1 Cor 6:11), and since they are new creations in Christ (2 Cor 5:17), they are to walk in a manner worthy of the gospel (Eph 4:1), struggling against sin. If they refuse to repent, they are demonstrating that they were never truly believers in the first place, in that they are not enduring in faith and holiness. However, the point of excommunication is to turn sinners from the error of their ways back to an ongoing sanctification, the journey of the Christian.

Thus, Thomas Schreiner rightly notes that warnings and admonitions in the Bible have a particular function: "Warnings are one of the means God uses to keep believers running in the race, so that they keep trusting in Christ . . . By them believers are warned against departing from Christ and

---

45. In describing the identity of the church Henry Poettecker claims, "Theologically, it is God's community of grace and discipleship, the fellowship of 'sinners saved by grace' but also the community of 'the saints striving after holiness.' It is Christ's 'imperfect body' yet it is also to be His 'holy Bride.' Thus it is the disciplined church earnestly seeking to be the holy church" (Poettecker, "The New Testament Community," 18). A. E. Kreider likewise maintains, "Paul in his letter to the church at Corinth has made it clear that a church to be the church of Christ must indeed have standards. There are spiritual and moral standards of life in the church. The church must possess a distinctive Christian quality. It must manifest Christ to men and radiate His Spirit . . . The witness of the church, the spirit of its members, and the purity of its teachings are real concerns. To this end discipline is needed to restrain us from evil when tempted and to strengthen us for effective service" (Kreider, "Standards with Love," 108).

46. For more on the connection between the perseverance of the saints and the final judgment as it relates to church discipline, see Kimble, *That His Spirit May Be Saved*, 112–45.

47. James Leo Garrett asserts, "Paul's ethical admonitions show the relationship of the Christian life to church discipline. Sanctification is defined in terms of abstaining from fornication (1 Thess 4:1–8; 1 Cor 6:9–11, 18–20). Christians as sons of light are to walk in the light rather than in the darkness (1 Thess 5:4–8; Rom 13:12ff.; Eph 5:7–14) . . . A Christian is one who had 'put off the old man' and 'put on the new man' (Col 3:9; Eph 4:22–24). Yet Paul regretfully reported that many live 'as enemies of the cross of Christ,' but the 'manner of life' of Christians ought to be 'worthy of the gospel of Christ' (Phil 3:18; 1:27)" (Garrett, *Baptist Church Discipline*, 8).

the gospel."[48] Ecclesial discipline, particularly excommunication, serves as a warning of potential eschatological judgment.[49] As such, this action undertaken by the church is aimed, not at compounding suffering and struggle unnecessarily, but at moving the sinner back in the direction of repentance, trusting in Christ, and perseverance in the faith.

Discipline, therefore, is both for the community as a whole as well as unrepentant individuals, to serve as a means by which they persevere in the faith.[50] While there are other means to persevere in the faith,[51] it must be affirmed that church discipline may have been overlooked as such a means in our day. It is, however, a crucial dimension of church life aimed at running the race well.

James Thompson concurs and labors to demonstrate that there should be an eschatological dimension to church life and pastoral ministry, knowing that the goal of church leaders is to present the bride of Christ blameless before the Lord at his return (Eph 5:25–27). As such, Thompson asserts, true church ministry should constantly be leading others into ethical transformation. He maintains, "This ethical transformation means that the task of ministry is not only to communicate God's acceptance of the sinner but also to challenge converts toward transformation."[52] This at times could be a

---

48. Schreiner, *Run to Win the Prize*, 113.

49. Explicating both 1 Corinthians 5:5 and 1 Timothy 1:20—passages that demonstrate how discipline functions as a warning and a call for repentance and perseverance—Eric Bargerhuff asserts that in both contexts this process of handing a person over to Satan is remedial, correctional, and restorative so that a person can be saved in the end. Handing someone over to Satan seems to entail placing someone outside the covenant community, and, therefore, outside of the sphere of God's blessing and protection. This is done in order to destroy the flesh, which is the self-sufficient, carnal attitude of the unrepentant sinner. See Bargerhuff, *Love that Rescues*, 156. This attitude of unrepentance must be done away with in order that the sinning individual may continually bear fruit in keeping with repentance, and in so doing demonstrate their living faith in Christ.

50. Kenneth Hein reiterates this point: "Consequently, the early Church's discipline in the New Testament is to be viewed as pastoral rather than penal since it was meant to lead the offender back into the Church as an effective and living member . . . The expulsion of a serious offender was also intended to protect the rest of the community from the sinner and his faults" (Hein, *Eucharist and Excommunication*, 417).

51. These measures of growing in one's faith are typically referred to as the means of grace. They are intentional habits utilized by believers to grow as Christians, knowing all the while that it is God who works through such means to to continue the good work he began in them (Phil 1:6; 2:12–13). Such means include meditation on Scripture, prayer, confession of sins, Christian fellowship, silence, and solitude. For further details on the means of grace see Brett, *Growing up in Grace*; and Bridges, *The Discipline of Grace*.

52. Thompson, *Pastoral Ministry According to Paul*, 157.

painful process as we battle against the forces arrayed against us. However, the church must be dedicated to assisting others to persevere in their faith, and this include discipline that is for their everlasting good.

## Conclusion

The church embodies suffering and struggle in the Christian life as a distinctive quality of the Christian life, and church discipline plays a distinct role in this struggle. We walk as sojourners and strangers in this life, abstaining from the passions of the flesh, which wage war against our soul (1 Pet 2:11). Brian Tabb is right to note that ancient authors, including biblical ones, "*expect* and *accept* suffering as a present reality governed by God's sovereign purposes."[53]

In our own struggle, it is crucial to see the one who also walked the road of life, was tempted in all ways as we, and who lived without sin (Heb 4:15). Jesus embraced his Father's dark will of suffering in living and dying for the sake of others, and God raised him up and exalted him as Lord and Messiah. Tabb remarks, "This Jesus *rescues* his people, *responds* to prayer, and *empowers* and *identifies with* his suffering witnesses, who proclaim to the nations that salvation and forgiveness of sins are available in Jesus's name alone. For Christians, God . . . acts decisively *through suffering* to set the world of sin and suffering right again."[54] By God's grace, and in the power of the Spirit, we walk in faithfulness as we struggle and suffer in the war against sin. And we do this in community, knowing that the wounds and rebuke from a friend can be trusted (Prov 27:5–6), embracing the reminders and encouragements that God has won the victory, he has provided means for our perseverance (including discipline), and he who began a good work in us will bring it to completion at the day of Jesus Christ (Phil 1:6). And thus we end fittingly with this hymn from Martin Luther:

> A mighty Fortress is our God,
> A Bulwark never failing;
> Our Helper He amid the flood
> Of mortal ills prevailing:
> For still our ancient foe
> Doth seek to work us woe;

53. Tabb, *Suffering in Ancient Worldview*, 220, emphasis original.
54. Ibid., 221, italics original.

His craft and power are great,
And, armed with cruel hate,
On earth is not his equal.

Did we in our own strength confide,
Our striving would be losing;
Were not the right Man on our side,
The Man of God's own choosing:
Dost ask who that may be?
Christ Jesus, it is He;
Lord Sabaoth His Name,
From age to age the same,
And He must win the battle.

And though this world, with devils filled,
Should threaten to undo us,
We will not fear, for God hath willed
His truth to triumph through us:
The Prince of Darkness grim,
We tremble not for him;
His rage we can endure,
For lo! his doom is sure,
One little word shall fell him.

That word above all earthly powers,
No thanks to them, abideth;
The Spirit and the gifts are ours
Through Him who with us sideth:
Let goods and kindred go,
This mortal life also;
The body they may kill:
God's truth abideth still,
His Kingdom is forever.

# 8

# Suffering and Discipline in the Overlap of the Ages

—Guy Waters

## Introduction

In confessional Reformed theology, suffering is not a mark of the church.[1] Neither is suffering an attribute of the church.[2] One may better characterize suffering as the present mode of the church's existence. In

---

1. At first glance, Reformed confessional documents seem to disagree when it comes to the marks of the church. The Westminster Confession of Faith identifies a single mark—profession of the true religion (25.2). The Belgic Confession identifies three marks, the preaching of "the pure doctrine of the Gospel"; the "pure administration of the sacraments as instituted by Christ"; and the administration of "church discipline" (Art. 29). The disagreement is more apparent than real. As Francis Turretin observed in the seventeenth century, "For whether [the church's mark(s)] is called one alone (to wit, the truth of doctrine and conformity with the word of God) or many (to wit, the pure preaching of the word with the lawful administration of the sacraments, to which some add the exercise of discipline and holiness of life and obedience given to the word), it is all the same thing" (Turretin, *Institutes of Elenctic Theology*, 3:87). This is so because, Turretin continues, the sacraments and discipline "flow from the word of God and are appendages of it." Compare the concurring assessments of Bannerman, *The Church of Christ*, 1:62; and Berkhof, *Systematic Theology*, 576–77.

2. In distinction from a mark, which serves to identify the church *qua* church, attributes are characteristics of the church that are "not peculiar to [the church]" and do "not distinguish it from all other bodies" (Bannerman, *The Church of Christ*, 1:64). Historically, these attributes include unity, holiness, catholicity, and apostolicity. The church's attributes have also been termed "properties" (ibid.). It is important to note that Roman Catholics and Protestants have fundamental disagreements concerning the definition of each of these four attributes, on which see Bannerman, *The Church of Christ*, 1:64; and Berkhof, *Systematic Theology*, 572–76.

union with Christ, believers now "suffer with [Christ] in order that we also may be glorified with [Christ]" (Rom 8:17; cf. Phil 3:10).[3] The fact that we now "share Christ's sufferings" indicates that we shall "rejoice and be glad when his glory is revealed" (1 Pet 4:13).[4] As Christ has suffered and then entered into glory, so the body of Christ must suffer and then enter into glory.[5] It is by this means that God progressively conforms believers to the Christ to whom they have been united. In this respect, then, suffering is not an occasional aspect of the church's life. Suffering qualifies or colors the entirety of the church's existence in the overlap of the ages.[6]

In light of the pervasiveness of suffering in the church's present existence, we expect to find and do in fact find some point of contact between suffering and formal, corrective discipline in the church.[7] Such an intersection between suffering and discipline, however, raises several questions. Should discipline involve the intentional infliction of temporal pains, whether physical or psychological, upon the offender? Should the offender receive and experience discipline along these lines? Protestant Christians have typically and correctly answered these questions in the negative.[8] We

---

3. Douglas J. Moo helpfully observes that such suffering "is not identical to that 'dying with Christ' which takes place at conversion. Rather, the suffering Paul speaks of here refers to the daily anxieties, tensions, and persecutions that are the lot of those who follow the one who was 'reckoned with the transgressors' (Luke 22:37)" (Moo, *The Epistle to the Romans*, 506).

4. Peter's reasoning underscores the necessity and indispensability of suffering to the Christian in the present time. As Thomas R. Schreiner notes, "Rejoicing in their present suffering is mandated, precisely so that believers will have joy in God's presence at the day of judgment. How believers respond to suffering, in other words, is an indication of whether they truly belong to God at all" (Schreiner, *1–2 Peter, Jude*, 220).

5. "Suffering and then glory was the order appointed for Christ himself . . . The same order applies to those who are heirs with him . . . It is [however] more than a parallelism of order. It needs to be noted that they suffer *with* him and this *joint* participation is emphasized in the case of suffering as it is in the case of glorification" (Murray, *The Epistle to the Romans*, 1:299, emphasis original).

6. That is to say, the church lives within the overlap of two ages or space-time orders, the eschatological "age to come" that has broken into history in the resurrection of Christ, and the "present age" characterized by sin, suffering, shame, and death. See further Vos, *The Pauline Eschatology*, 1–41; and Ridderbos, *When The Time Had Fully Come*, 44–60.

7. We may simply register here a distinction, to which we will return below, between formal, corrective discipline and discipline in the broader sense of the totality of the church's oversight over itself.

8. One of the "Preliminary Principles" of the Book of Church Order of the Presbyterian Church in America (PCA) is, "since ecclesiastical discipline must be purely

are still bound to answer how the church's discipline rightly reflects the mode of suffering that characterizes the church's life in this age.

Paul's counsel to the Corinthians in 1 Corinthians 5:1–13 helps us to see how suffering and formal, corrective discipline rightly relate. At first glance, it may seem that Paul is counseling a fairly severe discipline, one that involves the infliction of temporal pains and penalties upon an unnamed offender in the church. Paul instructs the Corinthians to "deliver this man to Satan" and to do so "for the destruction of the flesh," presumably the "flesh" of this individual (1 Cor 5:5). At the end of his instructions, he quotes from the Pentateuch, "Purge the evil person from among you" (1 Cor 5:13b). This command, in its original Old Testament context, may involve capital punishment and certainly involves physical and forced removal of "the evil person" from the community of Israel. Paul's citation of this text at least raises the question whether Paul is directing the Corinthians to inflict the same kind of discipline upon the offender in its midst.

What kind of discipline, then, is Paul imposing upon the church, and how does this method of discipline intersect with the church's suffering? Does it have any affinities with the form of discipline practiced in ancient Israel? How does it reflect the fact that the church is the community upon whom "the end of the ages has come" (1 Cor 10:11)?

In 1 Corinthians 5:1–13, Paul shows the church that discipline and suffering should be understood in fundamentally eschatological terms. Once discipline and suffering are properly understood along these lines, the church will be well positioned to exercise formal, corrective discipline in a manner consistent with and reflective of her identity and calling as the body of Christ. To that end, we will offer some reflections on the implications of Paul's argument in 1 Corinthians 5 for the nature and exercise of church discipline today.

---

moral or spiritual in its object, and not attended with any civil effects, it can derive no force whatever, but from its own justice, the approbation of an impartial public, and the countenance and blessing of the great Head of the Church" (*The Book of Church Order of the Presbyterian Church in America*, "Preliminary Principles" §8). This Preliminary Principle dates to the formation of the Presbyterian Church in the United States of America (PCUSA) in 1789.

PART 3: DISCIPLINE

## Suffering and Discipline in 1 Corinthians 5

In 1 Corinthians 5:1–13, Paul addresses the church in Corinth for their mishandling of a case of scandal in their midst.[9] The offender is likely guilty of gross sexual immorality ("for a man has his father's wife," 5:1). Paul's indignation stems in part from the fact that even the gentile world knew that such behavior was wrong ("of a kind that is not tolerated even among pagans," 5:1). But Paul also knew that the Pentateuch had pronounced the offender's action to be sin (Lev 18:8; Lev 20:11; Deut 22:20 [=LXX Deut 23:1]; Deut 27:20).[10]

It would be a mistake to conclude that Paul's sole concern is with this individual and his admittedly scandalous action. Paul broadens his sphere of concern as his argument progresses. He begins with the offender himself, "a man" (5:1); "him who has done this deed" (5:2); "the one who did such a thing" (5:3). He then extends his concern to address the category of persons of whom this individual is representative, "such a one" (5:5, AT; ESV, "this man"); "sexually immoral people" (5:9). Paul further extends his concern to encompass other classes of offenders, "but now I am writing to you not to associate with anyone who bears the name of brother if he is guilty of sexual immorality or greed, or is an idolater, reviler, drunkard, or swindler—not even to eat with such a one" (5:11), "the evil person" (5:13).

It is fair to say, then, that Paul's interest in 1 Corinthians 5 is not exclusively with this particular offender, nor even sexual offenders within the church, but with a whole range of offenders within the church. Furthermore, Paul's leading concern, strictly speaking, is not with the offender himself, but with the church's response to the offense, "and of a kind that is not tolerated even among pagans" (5:1); "And you are arrogant! Ought you not rather to mourn?" (5:2). The church in Corinth has failed to take the action that Paul expects of it. Or, we may say, the action that the church has taken, namely its tolerance of the offender and its arrogance in so doing, is utterly unbecoming of the church.

If Paul faults the Corinthian church for its responses to the offender's actions, he also prescribes the way in which he expects the church properly to handle the matter. As Paul knew from the Pentateuch the man's behavior was sinful, so he identifies the expected response from the Pentateuch at

9. What follows summarizes and is dependent upon Waters, "1 Corinthians 5:13."

10. Schrage, *Der Erste Brief An Die Korinther*, 269, 370; Thiselton, *The First Epistle to the Corinthians*, 386.

the end of 1 Corinthians 5, "Purge the evil person from among you" (v. 13). Although Paul does not use an introductory formula to indicate that these words come from the Old Testament, they are verbally identical with at least five texts from LXX Deuteronomy (17:7; 19:9; 21:21; 22:21; 24:7).[11] Paul therefore intends his statement in 1 Corinthians 5:13 to be a citation of one or more of these Deuteronomic texts.[12]

Paul's statements in 1 Corinthians 5:1 and 5:11 suggest that all of these Deuteronomic texts are in view in 1 Corinthians 5:13.[13] In 5:1, Paul identifies the offender's sin in terms that verbally approximate LXX Deut 23:1 and 27:20. Of the vices that Paul mentions in 5:11, five appear in Deuteronomy and these vices, according to Deuteronomy, "warrant exclusion" from the covenant community.[14] Paul's argument in 1 Corinthians 5, then, is thick with references to the text of Deuteronomy.

We have, then, in 1 Corinthians 5:1, 11, 13 a sustained engagement with the text of Deuteronomy. The significance of this engagement emerges by appreciating how, for Paul, the church is in the place of Israel (cf. 1 Cor 10:1–13).[15] The church, for Paul, is God's covenant community, called to pursue and to uphold holiness, and to expel notorious violators of the standards of God's holiness.

With these parameters in mind, we may reflect on the character of the offender's expulsion from the church. To appreciate the character of that expulsion, we also need to understand the character of the community from which he is to be expelled. Both the community and the expulsion in view in 5:13 are eschatological in nature.

In 1 Corinthians 5:5, Paul juxtaposes two terms that are familiar to students of Paul—"flesh" and "Spirit" (ESV, "spirit").[16] The goal of the discipline

---

11. On the form of the text of 1 Cor 5:13 and its similarity to these texts from Deuteronomy, see, for example, Zaas, "'Cast Out the Evil Man from Your Midst,'" 259 n. 2. The only difference between 1 Cor 5:13 and these five texts from Deuteronomy is the number of the main verb ἐξαίρω. Compare as well the similar, but not identical, phrase in LXX Deut 13:6.

12. Rosner, *Paul, Scripture, and Ethics*, 61–64.

13. For a fuller statement of the argument that follows, see further Waters, "Curse Redux?," 239–41.

14. Rosner, *Paul, Scripture, and Ethics*, 70; cf. Garland, *1 Corinthians*, 189; Hays, *First Corinthians*, 88.

15. Rosner, *Paul, Scripture, and Ethics*, 68–81; Hays, *The Conversion of the Imagination*, 23.

16. We take here the Greek term πνεῦμα to denote the person and ministry of the Holy Spirit, on which see Ridderbos, *Paul*, 64–68.

that the apostle enjoins upon the church is two-fold. First, Paul desires that the offender's "flesh" be "destroyed." Second, Paul desires that "Spirit may be saved in the day of the Lord" (AT).[17] There have been three basic attempts to explain Paul's statement in this verse, particularly with reference to the juxtaposition of "flesh" and "Spirit."[18] The first sees Paul speaking anthropologically. That is, "flesh" and "spirit" reflect the two aspects or dimensions of the human person, the body and the soul, respectively. One problem with this interpretation is that there is no possessive pronoun ("his") in the Greek text associated with the Greek word πνεῦμα. Another problem is that it suggests Paul's understanding of an immaterial or non-material salvation on the Day of the Lord. The implausibility of such a suggestion becomes evident from Paul's argument in 1 Corinthians 15, where it is the whole person of the believer, body and soul, that will experience, on the Last Day, the fullness of the salvation that Christ has won for his people.

The second understanding of "flesh" and "Spirit" is ecclesiological. The term "flesh" is said to denote the church's fleshly arrogance and boasting; the term "Spirit" is said to refer to the presence of the Spirit in the church. While this view does account for the absence of any explicit personal pronoun after either noun, it encounters at least two problems. First, it fails to explain how it is that the expulsion of the offender will cure the church of her boasting. Second, it involves Paul declaring that the Spirit himself will be "saved" on the "day of the Lord," an otherwise unattested declaration in Paul's writings.

The third and best understanding of these two terms is eschatological. "Flesh" refers, as it often does in Paul, to the present, Adamic order, characterized by sin, curse, death, and shame. "Spirit" denotes the age to come, inaugurated by Christ in his death and resurrection, and characterized by righteousness, blessing, life, and glory.[19] Paul, therefore, speaks of the offender as a "whole person viewed from different angles. 'Spirit' means the whole person as oriented towards God. 'Flesh' means the whole person as oriented away from God."[20]

---

17. The ESV renders the latter clause of 5:5, "so that his spirit may be saved in the day of the Lord." This translation likely reflects the view that Paul is speaking anthropologically in this verse. We will note the problems with this line of interpretation momentarily.

18. For a fuller discussion, see Waters, "Curse Redux?," 245–47.

19. On which, see now Thiselton, *First Epistle to the Corinthians*, 390–400.

20. Murphy-O'Connor, *1 Corinthians*, 42. Compare Grosheide, *De eerste Brief*, 143.

One confirmation that Paul is thinking in fundamentally eschatological terms emerges in 1 Corinthians 5:7, "Cleanse out the old leaven that you may be a new lump, as you really are unleavened. For Christ, our Passover lamb, has been sacrificed." This command evokes the Feast of Unleavened Bread, which in turn evokes the Feast of Passover (Exod 12:18–20; 13:7). Paul here is relating the Passover sacrifice to Christ, as type to antitype. Paul sets Christ, and particularly Christ in his sacrificial death for sin, before the Corinthians in pointedly eschatological terms. This reality of Christ's death in 1 Corinthians 5:7b grounds the imperative in 5:7a, "cleanse out the old leaven that you may be a new lump, as you really are unleavened."[21] Paul tells the church that the "old" must give way to the "new." It is the eschatological community, in Christ, that is "new." The man's sin that has become the occasion of the Corinthians' "boasting" (5:6a) is the "old" that must be put away.[22] It is this boasting that Paul has, in 1 Corinthians 1–4, identified with the "flesh" (1 Cor 1:29; 3:21). The Corinthian church, Paul insists, must live in light of the eschatologically new community that they really are.

Paul, then, understands both the Corinthian church and the discipline of the offender in fundamentally eschatological terms. The church is the eschatological community, the people of God upon whom the end of the ages has come (1 Cor 10:11). She is the eschatological community by virtue of the finished work of Christ. Christ has come and has undergone the unique and unrepeatable death to which the repeated Passover sacrifices pointed and anticipated (1 Cor 5:7a). As such, the church has corresponding obligations that rest upon it (1 Cor 5:7b). Similarly, Paul understands the discipline of the offender in eschatological terms in 1 Corinthians 5:5. He expresses an eschatological optimism that the Day of the Lord will prove this individual to be a saved person. Not only does Paul understand the church and the offender in eschatological terms, but he does so in similar ways. Each has fallen short of the privileges and obligations that are incumbent upon professed participants in the eschatological age to come.

We may now turn to give closer attention to the discipline of the offender. We will first explore what this discipline's significance is for the church. We will then reflect on this discipline's significance for the offender.

---

21. Grosheide, *De eerste Brief*, 146.

22. Fee, *First Epistle to the Corinthians*, 235–36; Hodge, *Exposition of the First Epistle to the Corinthians*, 86.

PART 3: DISCIPLINE

The church, for Paul, is the eschatological community (1 Cor 10:11). She is so in light of the Christ's Passover sacrifice, which inaugurated the new covenant (11:25). The threat to her integrity as the church is what Paul terms "leaven" (5:6). This leaven, which represents the offender's sin, must be removed from the church. In so doing, the church will "celebrate the festival, not with the old leaven, the leaven of malice and evil, but with the unleavened bread of sincerity and truth" (5:8). It is in connection with the offender's removal that the church will give expression to her putting off boasting and putting on sincerity and truth. The church, Paul stresses, should express her new life in Christ by committing to the work of formal, corrective discipline.

The offender is to be removed from one realm or domain (the eschatological community) to another. Paul denominates this act and the sphere to which the offender is to be removed as a "deliver[ance] to Satan" (5:5). Satan is in view here as "the god of this world" (2 Cor 4:4).[23] The effect of the offender's removal from the church is that he will be returned, as it were, to the world, the Adamic order or realm characterized by sin. This handing over is a formal act of the assembled church in the "power" of the risen Lord Jesus (5:4).[24] In this act, the church judicially and declaratively commits the offender to the realm of sin and, thus, to this realm's head, Satan.[25]

The aim of this removal and handing over to Satan is "the destruction of the flesh" and salvation of the offender's "Spirit . . . in the day of the Lord" (5:5).[26] The purpose of this removal, then, is remedial, not punitive, as the verbal parallel at 1 Timothy 1:20 suggests.[27] The goal of this act is, according to Paul, the eschatological salvation of the offender, that he will be among those who will be presented "guiltless" on the Day of the Lord

---

23. Significantly, Paul has earlier in this letter associated boasting with the values of the "world" (1 Cor 1:26–29), over which Satan presides.

24. Taking the "power of the Lord Jesus" to refer to the ministry of the Spirit of Christ in the assembled church, on which see Waters, "Curse Redux?," 244–45, cf. Fee, *First Epistle to the Corinthians*, 206.

25. Paul uses the Greek verb παραδίδωμι elsewhere to denote such a judicial action of God towards sinners (Rom 1:24, 26, 28) and towards his Son on the cross (1 Cor 11:23; Rom 4:25; Rom 8:32), cf. LXX Job 2:6.

26. See Fee, *First Epistle to the Corinthians*, 204–5.

27. Ὑμέναιος καὶ Ἀλέξανδρος, οὓς παρέδωκα τῷ σατανᾷ, ἵνα παιδευθῶσιν μὴ βλασφημεῖν (1 Tim 1:20). Note the descriptive phrase of Calovius, *medicinale remedium*, cited in Meyer, *Critical and Exegetical Handbook*, 114.

(1 Cor 1:8).[28] The means to that end is what Paul calls "the destruction of the flesh" (5:5). To be sure, some commentators understand the relegation of this offender to the realm of Satan necessarily to entail the offender's physical suffering and even his death.[29] But this interpretation is impossible in light of Paul's injunction to the church "not even to eat with such a one" (5:11).[30] The view that the church's discipline designedly leads to the offender's temporal harm rests on a misinterpretation of Paul's word "flesh." What Paul seeks is not the offender's temporal harm or death so much as his cessation from participation and involvement in sin.[31] To this end, the offender is consigned to a realm "outside the edifying and caring environment of the church where God is at work."[32] The offender will be at Satan's disposal. To be sure, Satan, in God's hands, may effect the "destruction of the flesh" through physical suffering (cf. 2 Cor 12:7). But here it is important to remember the character of this severe discipline. This committal to Satan is, as we have seen, remedial in nature. Paul's hope is that the offender would undergo experiences that would, by God's grace, occasion his ultimate, eschatological salvation. The goal of this committal is that the offender would, on the Day of Judgment, be counted among the saved. This act of the church's discipline, then, is not final, eschatological judgment (as 1 Cor 4:5; cf. Rom 2:5, 8). It is a pointer to or sign of that day. The offender is to be committed to the realm of curse and death in order that he may be freed from the captive influences of flesh and in this way be found to be saved on the Day of Judgment.

Does Paul, then, understand the church's disciplinary removal of an offender from her number to involve the infliction of temporal penalties, even death? This scenario may but need not be the outcome for this individual. But if it is, it will not be the church that will serve as the instrument of infliction. It will be Satan, under the government of God. God's declared will, through his servant Paul, is that the offender not be eternally destroyed but ultimately saved. From the church's perspective

---

28. And yet, "Paul does not intend that he must wait until the final Day to be saved" (Fee, *First Epistle to the Corinthians*, 213).

29. Havener, "A Curse for Salvation," 341. See also the literature cited at Ridderbos, *Paul*, 471 n. 128.

30. So rightly Fee, *First Epistle to the Corinthians*, 212.

31. Thiselton, *First Epistle to the Corinthians*, 396.

32. Ciampa and Rosner, *The First Letter to the Corinthians*, 208.

then, this act of discipline is in itself and as to its purpose and its goal entirely remedial in nature.[33]

## Suffering and Discipline in the Church Today

We are now in a position to reflect on the implications of Paul's teaching in 1 Corinthians 5 for suffering and formal discipline in the context of the church. In the first place, Paul emphasizes the importance and priority of identity to the church's practice of discipline. Specifically, Paul urges the church to see herself as the eschatological community of God in Christ (1 Cor 5:7b). To that end, Paul's argument in 1 Corinthians 5 is thick with references to Deuteronomy (e.g., 1 Cor 5:1, 11, 13). These references serve to reinforce Paul's basic message that the church is eschatological Israel. The church's unique identity sets upon the church the necessity and urgency of holiness (1 Cor 5:7a). It is in light of this identity that formal discipline is required of the church. The church may not tolerate "leaven" in her midst (5:7). In fact, the very tolerance of leaven is itself symptomatic of the community's fleshly attitude and is corrupting of the holiness of the body (5:6b). When the Corinthian church removes the offender, it will evidence and prove the presence of a demeanor that befits the eschatological community of God. The fact that they have not yet done so indicates an intolerable gap between her eschatological identity and her appropriation of that identity in her attitudes and practices. To redress that problem, Paul argues, the Corinthians must first regain a practical understanding of who they are in Christ.

Second, formal discipline concerns the church as much as it does the offender. To be sure, the occasion of the discipline that Paul counsels in 1 Corinthians 5 is the notorious sin of a member of the Corinthian congregation. Paul's deepest concern, however, is the church's failure to understand who she is in Christ, and to take the actions that are therefore required of her. Discipline, then, is integral to the life and well-being of the church, even as it is integral to the spiritual well-being of the offender. A church that steadfastly refuses to engage in formal discipline when she is called upon to do so is a sick church, not a healthy church, and may even prove to be no true church at all.

---

33. Even as this discipline equally promotes the holiness of the community (5:6–8), and the reputation and glory of God in the world (cf. 5:1).

Third, Paul's argument has shown us how to think and how not to think about suffering in relation to the church's practice of discipline. Negatively, Paul makes no provision for the church to inflict temporal harms or penalties upon the offender. To say this, however, is not to say that the church's discipline is a meaningless and impotent gesture. The church's disciplinary action, Paul insists, is a formal act of the church and is undertaken in the "power of our Lord Jesus," that is, the ministry of the Holy Spirit. The church's role is to render a judgment, in concurrence with the apostle's declaration (1 Cor 5:3), and then formally to pronounce that judgment in the context of her gathered assembly (5:4). The effect of that judgment is the removal of the offender from the recognized bounds of the eschatological community (5:13). While that action is not definitive, eschatological judgment, it is a pointer to that judgment.

These parameters to the church's engagement in formal discipline help us to appreciate the degree to which discipline entails suffering for the church and for the offender. For the church, the appropriate response to the offender's action is to "mourn" (1 Cor 5:2a). It is in a posture of mourning, not arrogance, that the Corinthians are to excommunicate the offender (5:2b). The church is to mourn the presence and influence of such a scandalous offender in their midst. Paul would certainly expect the church to mourn the dire spiritual implications of this grievous sin for an individual who has yet to repent of it.

Paul's argument gives indication that this posture of mourning should extend beyond the act of excision from membership. Paul commands the church "not to associate . . . not even to eat with such a one," that is, one "who bears the name of brother" but is known for living in some open sin (5:11). Obedience to this command required the radical modification of the church members' relationships with this offender or with any other notorious offender. The absence of the disciplined person not only from the Lord's Supper but also from common meals with members of the church in Corinth could not but have been but an occasion for grief and sorrow on the part of the church.[34]

---

34. While the command "not to eat" undoubtedly involves common, everyday meals, it surely has particular reference to the Lord's Supper. Paul will address, later in this letter, the qualifications that are necessary for an individual to partake of the Supper (1 Cor 10:14–22; 11:17–34). It is fitting that an individual, removed from the fellowship of the church, should be barred from an ordinance that expresses the fellowship of the communing individual not only with Christ but also with his body (1 Cor 10:16–17).

The church's discipline was the occasion of suffering for the offender as well. He is removed from the church and committed to a realm where Satan presides (1 Cor 5:5). The outcome of this deliverance is what Paul calls the "destruction" of "flesh," that is, the prevalence of sin in this individual's life. Although Paul does not specify details, one presumes that committal to Satan would have resulted in some degree of suffering for the offender. Furthermore, the individual was formally excluded from the communion of the church. While the act of exclusion, we have seen, is not punitive in its intention or design, it is not difficult to imagine this act occasioning some degree of psychological suffering in the life of the offender. Such suffering would have played a wholesome role in prompting him to be restored to the church through public confession and repentance.[35]

Fourth, the church's discipline is remedial in nature. It is not an act of final-eschatological judgment. It is, rather, an anticipation of or pointer to eschatological judgment. Paul was instructing the church to tell the offender, in excluding him from their communion, that if he persisted in his sin, all that awaited him was final judgment. Paul's hope was that the individual would find himself "saved" on the Last Day (1 Cor 5:5) and that this disciplinary act would be a means to that end. The remedial character of church discipline, then, was to dictate the tone and demeanor of formal church discipline, as well as the disposition of the church towards the offender, both during and subsequent to the infliction of the prescribed censure.

Finally, the necessity of formal church discipline highlights something important about the church in her present state in redemptive history. The church, as Paul reminds the Corinthians throughout this first letter, is a people on the way. They have yet to arrive at eschatological glory. As Israel in the wilderness, she is beset with temptations and threats on her pilgrimage to heavenly Canaan (1 Cor 10:1–13). It is in this condition of suffering that she is being gradually conformed to Christ and prepared to share in consummate glory with him (cf. Rom 8:17).

The church's present eschatological condition, then, is one of suffering. It is this condition that mandates discipline. Here it is important to remember that formal, corrective discipline is of a piece of a broader discipline that the whole church undergoes, all the time, in her present eschatological condition. As one manual of church order puts it,

---

35. Whether or not Paul's words in 2 Corinthians 2:5–12 describe the recovery of this particular offender, on which see Kruse, "The Offender and the Offense in 2 Corinthians 2:5 and 7:12."

> Discipline is the exercise of authority given the Church by the Lord Jesus Christ to instruct and guide its members and to promote its purity and welfare. The term has two senses: (a) the one referring to the whole government, inspection, training, guardianship and control which the church maintains over its members, its officers and its courts; (b) the other a restricted and technical sense, signifying judicial process.[36]

So long as the church, whether corporately or individually, remains incompletely conformed to Christ, discipline in the broadest sense of the term is necessary. Formal, corrective discipline is simply one way in which the suffering church submits herself to the tutelage and direction of her Glorified Head, Jesus Christ.

What Paul is saying to the church is very much countercultural. American Christians may well find themselves tempted to ask, Does discipline inflict unwanted and undeserved suffering on the Christian and on the church? Our culture prizes the individual, particularly the individual's rights and prerogatives as an autonomous, voluntary agent. In such a setting, discipline may seem to be a fundamental abridgment of those rights, an encroachment upon the prerogatives of the sovereign individual.

Paul thinks about discipline in an entirely different way. Because the church now suffers in Christ and is not yet glorified in Christ, discipline is a standing necessity and good for the church and for the Christian. The apostle does not question that the individual has certain inalienable rights in this world. But he thinks of the individual, endowed with those rights, in eschatological terms. Paul's desire is that professing Christians find themselves among the number of the "saved" on the Last Day (1 Cor 5:5). Paul, furthermore, does not think of individuals in isolation but as they stand in relation to the people of God. The church, the eschatological people of God, is called to holiness (5:7). This calling requires, at times, the severe mercy of the formal, corrective discipline of some of her members.

The Corinthian Christians needed to be weaned from worldly ways of thinking of themselves and of the church. This is a task that lies upon the church in every age. Thankfully, the apostle Paul, writing by inspiration of the Holy Spirit, has supplied the church with the categories and perspective that we need to think and live as God would have us. Since "Christ, our Passover lamb, has been sacrificed," we can do no less. It is in this way that we "glorify" the "God" who "bought" us with such a price (1 Cor 5:7; 6:20).

---

36. *The Book of Church Order of the Presbyterian Church in America*, §27–31.

# 9

# Redemptive Church Discipline and the Lord's Supper
*Lessons from Herman Bavinck*

—Justin L. McLendon

## Introduction

Dutch Reformed theologian Herman Bavinck (1854–1921) insisted the Lord's Supper evidences Christ's ongoing ministry within the local gatherings of his people. This fellowship meal serves as a means of grace for the church's life whereby believers in union with Christ exercise communion with their Lord and one another. Bavinck believed the Lord's Supper encompasses a time when "we lift up our hearts spiritually to heaven, where Jesus Christ, our advocate, is at the right hand of his heavenly father."[1] The church's appointed leaders are entrusted with administering church discipline for the protection of this meal's testimony, and to guard the sacred experiential celebration evidenced when the gathered body meets at the Lord's table.[2]

An exploration into Bavinck's doctrine of redemptive church discipline and its relationship to the Lord's Supper follows. Specifically, we will see how church discipline exists not merely as an exercise in the exclusion of an individual from the church's fellowship, but as a means of protecting the purity of the body's feasting on the risen Christ whose presence in the table meal nourishes his needy people unto holiness. Because Scripture prescribes a redemptive hope within administered discipline, churches

---

1. Bavinck, *Reformed Dogmatics*, 4:576. Henceforth, Bavinck, *RD*.
2. See Bavinck's description of the church's officers in Bavinck, *RD*, 4:340–47.

carefully reestablish table fellowship when their members are restored in repentance. On the other hand, unrepentant believers who have been removed from the Lord's Supper suffer a void of Christ's presence and nourishment, but this exclusion protects the body's purity within and its catholic witness without.

## Herman Bavinck and the Lord's Supper

Bavinck's understanding of church discipline and the Lord's Supper closely relates to his overall understanding of the *unio mystica*, or the believers' union with Christ. We must first acknowledge his robust treatment of the Lord's Supper and its relationship to this union to understand rightly how church discipline is employed for its protection.

Bavinck formed his views on the Lord's Supper early in his career where, in 1887, he published his essay evaluating John Calvin's view of the Lord's Supper through Scripture and history.[3] Bavinck closely aligned his own views with Calvin's, but he also sought to clarify aspects of Calvin's view he considered unclear. Bavinck later admitted, "Calvin's representation is not clear in every respect, especially not as it concerns communion with the true flesh and blood of Christ and the life that flows from them."[4] Bavinck's emphasis on the "life that flows" from communing with the living Christ will be examined later, but at this point, we can acknowledge how Bavinck's desire to clarify and build upon Calvin exposes his own allegiance to Calvin's theological formulation.[5] The first volume of Bavinck's *Reformed Dogmatics* (*Gereformeerde Dogmatiek*) first appeared in 1895, and the fourth and final volume appeared in 1901. As Ron Gleason notes, the four volumes went through customary editorial changes throughout the published editions, but Bavinck's view on the Lord's Supper remained unchanged throughout these publications.[6] Within a Reformed conception

---

3. Bavinck, "Calvin's Doctrine of the Lord's Supper."

4. Bavinck, *RD*, 4:558.

5. It is worth noting that Bavinck wrote his doctoral dissertation on the ethics of Ulrich Zwingli (Bavinck, *De Ethiek van Ulrich Zwingli*), and Bavinck believed Zwingli's memorial view of the Lord's Supper to possess a strong spiritual presence component. See Bavinck, *RD*, 4:556–61.

6. Gleason, "Calvin and Bavinck on the Lord's Supper," 275. Gleason claims the changes were negligible and mostly footnoting and minor wording alterations.

of the means of grace, one can sense in Bavinck's formulation a remarkable consistency throughout his theological pilgrimage.

Gleason suggests seven theses emerge from Bavinck's critique and embrace of Calvin's Lord's Supper view.[7] Considerable overlap exists in each thesis, but all form Bavinck's view: the Lord's Supper is a visible act where the gathered body experiences and receives nourishment by its union with Christ. Summarizing Bavinck's observations serves us well when discerning the responsibility of church discipline within and the projections of holiness it produces without.

First, God has brought believers into the Church by means of baptism, and this baptism serves as an initiation into the Father's household of love. In this sense, Bavinck relies upon Calvin's depiction of the covenant of grace which showcases God's fatherly love supplying every need. God is a faithful, covenant keeping God who brings his people into his church, and their response to him is genuine faith and thanksgiving, for his covenant love causes expressions of intimate worship and joyful obedience. Bavinck links the Lord's Supper to this act by connecting the corporate spiritual meal that is the Lord's Supper to Christ who is the life-giving bread, feeding our souls in salvation.

Second, for Bavinck, Christ is the substance and material of the Lord's Supper and this defines how Christ is for us, the crucified one, willingly given over in death, whose sacrifice feeds his people unto eternal life through his humanity and his deity. As Gleason notes, in this thesis, Bavinck is "not only concerned with the objective life of the believer, but also the subjective appropriation of Christ's person and work in our lives."[8] We have everything in Christ; he is not solely a person whose life is propped up in the abstract as a model for hopeful imitation among his most devoted followers. Instead, he is, in Pauline language, the very *life* of his people, the one from whom we live and exist because he eternally provides rich treasures of sustenance for our benefit. The meal that is Christ, in the substance and material of his work as our prophet, priest, and king is an eternal supply of spiritual nourishment. Our Christ gives living water to our thirsty and needy souls because He is the well that does not run dry.

The third thesis relates directly to the believers' mystical union with Christ, but we will return to this crucial formulation for further treatment in the following section. In the fourth thesis, the relationship between the

---

7. Gleason, "Herman Bavinck's Understanding," 5.
8. Ibid., 8.

fellowship with Christ's person and his benefits is inseparable. The gospel is an offering of Christ to the needy, and those believing in Christ receive Him and every benefit he offers in himself. One benefit, according to Bavinck, is our participation in Christ. He states, "By virtue of the eating of the bread and drinking from the cup, we not only obtain the Spirit of Christ and his benefits, which he secured through his death. Specifically, we become participants in the one flesh and blood of the crucified and now glorified Savior."[9] Here Bavinck underscores what sometimes lacks in Western individualistic conceptions of salvation, and the Lord's Supper exposes this tendency. If we are not careful, we can unintentionally portray salvation's work in our individual lives to the neglect of magnifying God's saving of individuals to make them into a people, corporately participating in and united with the living Christ.

In the fifth thesis, Bavinck expands upon Calvin's defense of Christ's real presence in the Lord's Supper. In distributing his grace with the supper, Christ manifests his role as prophet, priest, and king. As prophet, he proclaims and interprets his own death. As priest, he gives himself as an atoning sacrifice on the cross for his people. Finally, as king, he "freely makes available the grace secured and gives it to his disciples to enjoy under the signs of bread and wine."[10] This meal is the *Lord's* gift, and Christ not only secures by his person and work all that this gift includes, but he shares these provisions with its recipient. Thus, as Bavinck further states, "In the Lord's supper, Christ comes together with his church, and the church comes together with Christ, thereby testifying to their spiritual communion."[11]

Out of divine love, God has brought us into his house by grace, and we live on the nourishment the Lord Christ provides as we gather at his table. In our feeding on him, we expose our need, and in his gracious provision, we are participants in Christ's life and ministry. And the reason all of this is our reality is because Christ is truly present at the table. Bavinck explains:

> This fellowship with Christ is not exhausted in a participation in his benefits and is also not merely a harmony in thinking, feeling and willing, a unanimity, a harmony, but it is, indeed, the most intimate binding of person with person, of the total Christ according to his divine and human nature, according to both soul and

---

9. Cited in ibid., 14.
10. Bavinck, *RD*, 4:562.
11. Ibid.

body with the person of the believer equally according to both soul and body.[12]

In this statement, Bavinck expands upon remembering Christ in the fellowship meal to an abiding in Christ which produces fellowship with Christ, availing his benefits to his people through our union to him.

Sixth, the fellowship enjoyed in the Lord's Supper is brought about through the ministry and work of the Holy Spirit. Thus, our fellowship with the living Christ is a spiritual one, and the Spirit's role proves integral to the Lord's Supper because it provides the Trinitarian scope to the nature of our fellowship with the living Christ. Christ's ascended body is not present, for it is in Heaven, but the power, work, and ministry of the Holy Spirit in our lives so works in us at the Lord's table that we are spiritually present with Christ corporately, away from ourselves, united to one another in love, devotion, and mystery. Bavinck writes,

> It is precisely this working of the Holy Spirit that effects and maintains this communion with Christ, both apart from and in the Lord's Supper . . . When Christ himself, acting through the minister, gives them, with the signs of bread and wine, his body to eat and his blood to drink, they are strengthened and confirmed in that communion by the Holy Spirit and ever more intimately united in soul and body with the whole Christ.[13]

There is an appropriation by the Holy Spirit of the *unio mystica* in the holy meal, which increases and strengthens the communion of the believer with Christ. The actions of ministerial administration and the taking of the recipient, and the subsequent eating and communal fellowship all serve as visible evidences of the Holy Spirit's inner work and ministry.

Seventh, the promise and the seals of the covenant are inseparably bound together. Bavinck's usage of the language of seals speaks to the permanence of the Lord's Supper for those who believe. Unbelievers taking the Lord's Supper receive the signs of the meal (the bread and wine), but they do not receive what benefits these signs represent. Believers, however, receive the signs and the benefits which speak to the eschatological seal represented in Christ's meal. Bavinck notes, "Christ instituted the Supper as a permanent 'good' for his church. It is a benefit added to all the other benefits to signify the seal of the latter. And it will endure until the time of

---

12. Cited in Gleason, "Herman Bavinck's Understanding," 14.
13. Bavinck, *RD*, 4:578.

Christ's return. His death must be proclaimed until he comes . . . and only when he returns and has taken his disciples to himself will he sit down with all the disciples at the wedding supper of the Lamb."[14] Thus, current celebrations of the Lord's Supper remain one of the church's primary eschatological reminders of the future unmasking of the body of Christ's inseparable union with the Redeemer.

## Bavinck and Union with Christ

Each thesis forms a key component to Bavinck's overall understanding of the *unio mystica* and how the Lord's Supper gives this union its visibility. Bavinck scholars sense a heightened importance of this doctrine to his overall thought. Gleason suggests the *unio mystica* is the "golden thread that runs through the entire Reformed Dogmatics."[15] John Bolt suggests Bavinck has a "broader understanding of union with Christ than only the redemptive [work of Christ]."[16] Bavinck's view is all encompassing, bringing creation, redemption, and eschatology together in his formulation of union with Christ.

Within the *Reformed Dogmatics*, believers' union with Christ is so intimate and inseparable from the Lord's Supper that we are left to admit, at least from Bavinck's perspective, that this mystical union cannot be fully comprehended or expressed adequately in words. He admits, "As a matter of fact we cannot understand this unity in its depth and intimacy. It far transcends our thought."[17] Bavinck presents a robust expansion of our union with Christ by noting and avoiding the errors of pantheism, carefully showing our union with Christ is not a marrying together of our substance with Christ where we in some way become Christ. Instead, we enjoy a union whereby Christ lives and dwells in believers, and we exist in him. Bavinck also notes and avoids the errors of deism because in our mystical union, we reject the notion that God is remote and removed from us.[18] Bavinck contrasts his understanding of the believer's union with Christ against the

---

14. Ibid., 4:549.

15. Gleason, "A Short Sketch," 13. See also Gleason's unpublished dissertation where he argues the *unio mystica* is the "true hub" of Bavinck's theology: Gleason, "The Doctrine of the *Unio Mystica*," 1.

16. Bolt, *Bavinck on the Christian Life*, 71.

17. Bavinck, *Our Reasonable Faith*, 398.

18. Ibid., 399–401.

transubstantiation of Rome or the consubstantiation of Lutheran Christians, arguing both miss the point of Scripture for "only the Holy Spirit, who is the Spirit of God and the Spirit of Christ, can so unite people with Christ that they share in his person and benefits and cannot be separated from him by death or the grave, by the world or by Satan."[19] As a result, the mystical union is spiritual in nature, and as such, is of greater value and benefit to the believer than if it were only a physical union.

Thus, in the Lord's Supper, the mystical union with Christ, experienced in corporate gathering and partaking, develops through the Word as a means of grace. In Reformed theology, "means of grace" terminology coincides with what Richard Barcellos refers to as "delivery systems" from God. In this sense, God bestows to his people their needed "spiritual power, spiritual change, spiritual help, spiritual fortitude, [and] spiritual blessings."[20] Christ alone is the source and supply, as Bavinck states, for "Christ is and remains the acquisitor as well as the distributor of grace."[21]

Christ is the beginning and the end of this grace, for his provision awakens and protects those who abide in him. Bavinck comments, "In exactly the same manner in which a person is incorporated by faith into Christ, so that person is also strengthened and confirmed in that communion by the Lord's Supper. There simply is no other or higher communion."[22] Bavinck carefully observes that the Lord's Supper does not add any additional grace, for it provides the identical grace we received in the Word. Christ is truly present with his divine and human nature in the same way he is present in the gospel. Christ is no more physically located in the bread and the wine than he is in the Word proclaimed. These benefits are received by faith, which is requisite for the sacrament since God has obligated himself to bestow his benefits on all those who believe. The Lord's table exposes the believer's maturity in and with the living Christ. There is a comprehensibility of our blessings experienced in the supper as the work of the Holy Spirit is nothing less than the *unio mystica*.

When Paul rebukes the Corinthians, as a result of unrepentant incestuous sin, he reminds them that "you are not your own" (1 Cor 6:19), and in doing so, Paul joins together the disciplinary consequences when believers fail to protect the purity of our union. As Todd Billings helpfully notes,

---

19. Bavinck, *RD*, 4:577.
20. Barcellos, *The Lord's Supper as a Means of Grace*, 23.
21. Bavinck, *RD*, 4:448.
22. Ibid.

"because of their union with Christ, believers are to separate themselves from those living in unrepentant immorality," and this is Paul's response to the church at Corinth.[23] Bavinck's work in this regard manifests biblical fidelity and ecclesial assistance to contemporary churches.

## Church Discipline and The Lord's Supper

What role then does church discipline have in this meal? The Lord's Supper serves as ground zero for individual Christians gathered corporately to fellowship with Christ in their mystical union with Him by the power of the Spirit. Thus, forbidding someone from the Lord's Supper deals with a serious matter because it has individual and corporate ramifications. But discipline is required because, as Bavinck suggests,

> [The church] experiences conflict from within and without, is prey to all sorts of attacks by sin and deception, and at all times runs the danger of straying to the left or to the right. The church is a field that needs to be constantly weeded, a tree that must be pruned at the proper time, a flock that must also be led and pastured, a house that requires constant renovation, a bride who must be prepared to be presented as a pure virgin to her husband. There are the sick, the dying, the tested, the grieving; those who are under attack, conflicted, in doubt, fallen, imprisoned, and so forth, who need teaching and instruction, admonition and consolation. And even apart from these things, the church must increase in the knowledge and grace of the Lord Jesus Christ.[24]

Church discipline functions to give visibility, as a sign of Christ's ongoing rule of the church from heaven. Bavinck argues Christ's rule is administered through the elders whose primary function in church discipline is to resist the cry of Cain. We are our brother's keeper because we are members of one another, united in Christ, and together we suffer and rejoice with one another. Through the administration of church discipline, these benefits are maintained, and their purity preserved.

This suffering and rejoicing with one another proves critical in Bavinck's view. Removing a believer from this experience through discipline, then, is no small matter for it removes not only the individual from the supper, it removes the corporate nourishment one experiences with

---

23. Billings, *Remembrance, Communion, and Hope*, 142.
24. Bavinck, *RD*, 4:422.

the body from the individual. Intentionally, this restriction shows a Christian life void of abiding with Christ surely results in a life of misery and suffering. If the Lord's table is where God's people spiritually experience his presence in union with Him, then the removal of a Christian from this fellowship certainly intends to manifest misery in this one who should yearn for what he now cannot experience apart from the gathered body around the Lord's table.

Bavinck distinguished two types of discipline. First, there is a discipline that can only be called God's discipline. This kind is where "God himself, Christ, and sometimes also the apostles practice in his name and power. God may visit sins in the church, such as the unworthy use of the Lord's Supper with sickness and death."[25] Not surprisingly, Bavinck notes the cases of Ananias and Sapphira of Acts 5, Paul's striking Elymas with blindness in Acts 13, and the case in 1 Corinthians 5 where Paul in his absence pronounced judgment on the incestuous person and urged the church to banish the unrepentant sinner to Satan.

Second, there is a common sort of discipline Bavinck called the "ordinary practice of discipline enjoined upon the congregation."[26] Bavinck summarizes the various texts dealing with the causes leading to this form of discipline: from those whose doctrine breeds division, to those whose words and deeds harm the church's unity. In these circumstances, Bavinck provides a sequence of events for how discipline is initiated all the way through to the excommunication process. His instruction is the perfect blend of systematic formulation and practical application. In all cases of discipline, Bavinck first urges us to remember that churches are not disciplining "impersonal things, writings, buildings, lands, but always persons, and not those who are outside the church, for God judges those who are outside . . . and not the deceased, not a group or a class of people, but always specific individual persons who are members of the church."[27] What a helpful reminder that the church deals with the messy lives of real people, weak and helpless, totally dependent upon Christ for life. A return to this redemptive tone and strategy to this approach would certainly benefit elders and churches inwardly and provide a more robust witness to the unbelieving world.

---

25. Ibid., 4:424.
26. Ibid.
27. Ibid., 4:425.

Further, church discipline is not levied against an assortment of weaknesses that may exist within the body. As Michael Horton has said, "The supper is a means of grace for the weak, not a reward for the strong."[28] Instead of shaming the weak, redemptive church discipline focuses on the sins that cause offense among the members of the congregation. Of these sins, Bavinck urges a careful distinction between private sins and public sins. Private sins are dealt with through the prescriptive text of Matthew 18, and those private sins only "assume the character of public sins when private admonitions go unheeded" which leads to the eventual involvement of the congregation.[29] Most church discipline happens here, when believers are confronted with sin as prescribed through Matthew 18, and godly confrontation leads to full sorrow and repentance. In this sense, this discipline remains private because it is never brought to the congregation.

Regardless of how the sin became public, whether it is by nature a public sin or when the steps of Matthew 18 have proven to be unsuccessful leading to responsible congregational intervention, Bavinck proposes the following. The first step serves as one of reassurance and aims for repentance and restoration. Bavinck suggests, "The moment the transgressor shows sincere repentance, all church discipline in the narrow sense stops."[30] Regarding the Lord's Supper, successful discipline leads one to full restoration to table fellowship. In those cases where one has been removed from the Lord's table, discipline proves to be our prayerful hope to see a brother or sister reunited with the corporate body to celebrate our union with Christ.

God uses discipline to correct our defective behavior and bring us to obedience. This is not only God's desire, for he is determined to have holy children (Heb. 12:6), but it is the church's hope and ambition. But Bavinck's redemptive church discipline carefully allows for a waiting period before the repentant believer is permitted to return to the Lord's Supper. He explains,

> The moment the transgressor shows sincere repentance, all church discipline in the narrow sense stops. The Lord's Supper may still be denied in order that the scandal may be removed from the congregation and the sincerity of the confession may become more evident, but this is, strictly speaking, no longer discipline. Those who confess their sin find mercy with God and therefore also with his church.[31]

---

28. Horton, *The Christian Faith*, 819.
29. Bavinck, *RD*, 4:426. Also, see especially Kimble, *40 Questions*, 161–66.
30. Ibid.
31. Ibid.

A two-fold justification exists in delaying reentry to the Lord's table. One, as previously noted, in Bavinck's judgment, the Lord's table is one of corporate feast where our spiritual communion increases and strengthens. If a scandalous sin has so corrupted the body's fellowship, the cloud of scandal may have to dissipate so that the formerly unrepentant sinner's return does not harm the body's fellowship, unity, or corporate growth. The purity of the table is paramount, and the level of purity directly relates to the congregational vitality. For example, when surveying the Lord's Supper debate within the Reformation, Bavinck believed the bifurcation of discipline from the Lord's Supper resulted in the loss of inward spiritual significance. He claimed, the "relaxation of discipline further contributed to [the] externalization of the Lord's Supper and prompted people to view the sacraments as being merely signs of an external covenant, to which everyone who lived a decent life was entitled."[32] Without discipline, the Lord's Supper is outsourced to a mere duty or activity, losing its spiritual sustenance. In Bavinck's view, discipline rightly applied works as a buttress against this tendency. To be clear, the Lord's Supper serves not for those winning at living a decent life, but when an unrepentant believer requires discipline, its administration protects the church's celebration and proclamation of Christ.

Two, an external reason the church is justified in delaying readmission to the table exists. For Bavinck, this reason addresses the catholicity of the church. On December 18, 1888, one year after publishing his article evaluating Calvin's Lord's Supper views, Bavinck delivered his inaugural Kampen Rectoral Address, entitled: "The Catholicity of Christianity and the Church."[33] The historical backdrop of this address provides clarity regarding Bavinck's emphases and how he used this academic address to confront the ecclesial unity of the Dutch Reformed Churches.[34]

At this point, Bavinck had been the theology professor at Kampen for five years. The church supporting the school, the Christian Reformed Church, experienced a rebirth in the immediate period preceding Bavinck's remarks on catholicity. According to Barend Kamphuis, two years prior, in

32. Ibid., 559.

33. Bavinck, "The Catholicity of Christianity and the Church."

34. On this point, Bavinck's own historical survey of Dutch theology is noteworthy. See Bavinck, "Recent Dogmatic Thought in the Netherlands." In his closing sentence, while stating his hope for unity within the Dutch Reformed groups, Bavinck admits, "a great deal depends on the success of this union." For a substantive summary of Bavinck's separatist roots, see Eglinton, *Trinity and Organism*, 4–50.

1886, Abraham Kuyper spearheaded a different group to leave the National Dutch Reformed Church.[35] Kuyper and Bavinck desired for their two churches to combine and unite with each leader leveraging their popularity to bring about this harmony. Though both were united in their hopes for unification, there was significant resistance to this desired merger, most especially from those aligned with Bavinck's church.[36]

Bavinck's address on catholicity is a reaction to his own denomination and exposes his concern for two critical issues. One, the increasing sectarianism within the academic and theological communities and, secondly, a lingering dualism, which distinguished the life of the church from its responsibilities to the redemption of the world. The commonality between both of Bavinck's concerns, the concern of sectarianism and what one might call a sacred/secular dualism, was what Bavinck believed to be an oversight of genuine catholicity. He argued the sectarianism of his day failed to respect the catholicity of the church, and the dualism failed to honor the catholicity of the Christian faith undergirding the church.

Biblically speaking, Bavinck believed the prophets promised catholicity by declaring that religion would not be limited to ethnic Israel forever because all peoples will be blessed through Abraham's seed. This promise is fulfilled in the catholicity of the church throughout the New Testament where God further expresses his desire to save the cosmos through the provision of His Son, the One through whom the world was made, by Jesus' reconciling work on the cross. Christ's work is the backbone of the church's catholicity. Bavinck adds, "This catholicity of the church . . . presupposes the catholicity of the Christian religion. It is based on the idea that Christianity is a world religion that should govern all people and sanctify all creatures irrespective of geography, nationality, place and time."[37]

The responsibility of protecting this cosmic view of catholicity rests within the church, and Bavinck understood church discipline to be the church's greatest tool to guard the purity of the global witness of the church. Simply put, the depth and breadth of the church's catholicity is inextricably tied to the church's dedication to redemptive church discipline. Practically, this view allows the church to withhold the Lord's Supper from a repentant sinner until the cloud of scandal is removed or at least until it can be made public repentance has occurred. The church bears

---

35. Kamphuis, "Herman Bavinck on Catholicity."
36. Ibid., 97.
37. Bavinck, "The Catholicity of Christianity and the Church," 21.

the awesome responsibility to address everything disturbing the unity of the Lord's fellowship meal and the witness that meal projects through the lives of those participating.

Church discipline is a serious, strategic, and prayerful effort on behalf of the church to bring the sinner back into the community of faith and to save its catholicity. Bavinck states it this way:

> It is not simply a right but a solemn duty to exercise church discipline against those who disturb the unity of doctrine teaching and the church. The church is admonished to distance herself from such, to let them go, in order that repentance might take place. Seen in this way the exercise of church discipline is not in tension or conflict with the church's catholicity—on the contrary! It is precisely because church discipline may never become or lead to a καθαίρεσις [tearing down or destroying] but rather to οἰκοδομή [build and edify] (II Cor. 13:10) and thus may never be applied in order to get rid of someone, it remains the earnest prayer of the church, throughout the process of discipline, that this last extreme measure commanded by the Lord might bring the stubborn and recalcitrant sinner back to the loving care of the Savior. In discipline the holiness of the church is revealed but no less its catholicity.[38]

Sin rarely restricts itself to an individual issue or circumstance; in fact, sin nearly always has corporate ramifications for the whole body, who is affected by the misdeeds and sins of one member. One of Bavinck's best insights regarding catholicity is his insight into the very catholic practice of church discipline.

## Applications for Local Church Ministry

Several applications emerge for ministers involved in the weekly leadership of local church ministry. First, ministers must take heed to the spiritual weightiness of administering church discipline. In Bavinck's scheme, a genuine believer, under discipline and thus removed from participating in the Lord's Supper, genuinely suffers from the lack of spiritual abiding with Christ enjoyed and experienced at the Lord's table. In Bavinck's formulation, the suffering experienced from removal occurs because of the believer's union with Christ. When the church removes an unrepentant member, the church is in some way causing the one under discipline to

---

38. Ibid., 227–28.

relive the absence of Christ's presence in his or her life that existed prior to conversion, at least in its corporate sharing with the gathered body at the Lord's Supper. This point does not mean that an individual, a genuine believer, under discipline, lacks a real union with Christ, but it seems Bavinck's scheme suggests that one under discipline will not know and experience fully the spiritual blessings within this mystical union absent of the corporate table fellowship. When ministers, following the traditions and prescribed practices of their local church, seek to exclude a believer from the Lord's table in a case of discipline, the ministers must recognize the spiritual deprivation which will ensue.

While this emphasis is a strength to the real presence view, one need not hold a Reformed or real presence view of the Lord's Supper to appreciate the spiritual significance of church discipline's effect on both the body and the individual under discipline. For example, as John Hammett has urged, those affirming a memorial view must not be so concerned to deny Christ's presence that they end up teaching a "doctrine of real absence."[39] Hammett rightly notes the significance of the Lord's Supper is renewal, and regardless of one's view regarding Christ's presence, the body of Christ seeks renewal through the fellowship meal. Through his robust theology of believers' mystical union and its realization through the Lord's Supper, Bavinck reveals how excluding an unrepentant sinner affects the fellowship of the whole.

Second, believers are called upon to watch over one another with care and provide the necessary accountability leading to individual and corporate holiness. Those in church leadership are given clear calls for the "watch care" provided to those under their care (Heb 13:17), and this ministry of intentional care extends throughout the whole body, as the author of Hebrews plainly states: "See to it that no one misses the grace of God and that no bitter root grows up to cause trouble and defile the many" (Heb 12:15, author's translation). The phrase "see to it" is plural, indicating a corporate responsibility which cannot be neglected due to the complexity of dealing with the assortment of issues in discipline cases.

It is not just the unrepentant believer under discipline who feels the impact of non-participation, for the unrepentant sinner's absence necessarily impacts the participatory nature of the gathered body. The body suffers with their brother or sister who is removed from fellowship as this absence disrupts the congregational ethos. Brian Vickers rightly notes, the "very

---

39. Hammett, *Biblical Foundations for Baptist Churches*, 281.

nature of the Supper, being a corporate experience, should focus attention on the community of believers. It is not a time only for individual contemplation and personal communion with Christ; the communion is between Christ and His body with individuals as members of that body."[40] The Lord's Supper proves to be the communal experience where one's absence is most concretely experienced. Among other things, the visual absence of one under discipline encourages repentance among the body (1 Cor 5:5).

Third, redemptive church discipline exposes the spiritual detriment evident in one's isolation, and this void will lead to further spiritual calamity until restoration is complete. Unrepentant Christians isolated from the confines of corporate blessings and protection certainly tread a perilous path. As Bavinck notes,

> Whoever isolates himself from the church, i.e., from Christianity as a whole, from the history of dogma in its entirety, loses the truth of the Christian faith. That person becomes a branch that is torn from the tree and shrivels, an organ that is separated from the body and therefore doomed to die. Only within the communion of the saints can the length and the breadth, the depth and the height, of the love of Christ be comprehended.[41]

Thus, any action on the part of the church to discipline a member will bring about not only visual isolation (for the one is visibly barred from the Lord's table) but, in profound theological and practical ways, the one disciplined will experience a spiritual isolation which will inevitably require sensitive pastoral wisdom and care.

Fourth, Bavinck's connection of church discipline to catholicity serves as a welcomed and needed perspective within contemporary ministry. For Bavinck, catholicity exists not as a reductionistic attempt to bring Christian theology down to its lowest common denominator in hopes of having the most people pledge affiliation. Instead, a proper view of catholicity ensures a broad Christian worldview and eschatological hope the church itself enjoys. Bavinck claims,

> This catholicity of the church, as the Scriptures portray it for us and the early churches exemplify it for us is breathtaking in its beauty. Whoever becomes enclosed in the narrow circle of a small church (*kerkje*) or conventicle, does not know it and has never experienced its power and comfort. Such a person shortchanges

---

40. Vickers, "Celebrating," 337.
41. Bavinck, *RD*, 1:83.

> the love of the Father, the grace of the Son, and the fellowship of the Spirit and incurs a loss of spiritual treasures that cannot be made good by meditation and devotion. Such a person will have an impoverished soul. By contrast, whoever is able to see beyond this to the countless multitudes who have been purchased by the blood of Christ from every nation and people and age, whoever experiences the powerful strengthening of faith, the wondrous comfort in times of suffering to know that unity with the whole church militant that has been gathered out of the whole human race from the beginning to the end of the world, such a person can never be narrow-minded and narrow-hearted.[42]

For believers, catholicity's beauty remains in the Lord's Supper, and church discipline protects it. Christians must make every effort to keep inseparable discipline and discipleship, for the New Testament, the early church, the Reformers, and believers since have advocated church discipline as a distinguishing aspect of true Christianity. Billings rightly states that "discipline relates to the healthy functioning of the covenant community and its distinctive witness in a world of moral confusion."[43]

Fifth, ministers should use teaching opportunities and intentional conversations to refresh the minds of believers in their posture towards the Lord's table. Because church discipline juxtaposes uniquely with the Lord's Supper (1 Cor 10–11), ministers ought to remind believers that partaking of the Lord's Supper is not to be merely observed with a posture of passivity; rather, partaking of the Lord's Supper proclaims, heralds, and visually demonstrates the way things are about God's people.

Ministers are called upon to watch over one another's pastoral care and provide the necessary accountability leading to individual and corporate holiness. Ministers can assist the church through formative discipline in hopes of avoiding corrective discipline. Formative discipline occurs frequently through the ordinary means of grace as God's Word is preached and the Spirit purifies hearts and minds through humble submission. United to Christ through the Spirit's power, believers encourage one another, suffer with one another, and live with a cruciform love which prevents the corrective discipline which excludes part of the body from corporate communion. But sometimes corrective discipline is necessary. It is for the good of the person involved; it is good for the church; and it is good for the global witness of Christ.

42. Bavinck, *RD*, 4:227.
43. Billings, *Remembrance, Communion, and Hope*, 143.

## Conclusion

The gospels indicate how Jesus corrected his disciples (Matt 8:26; Mark 10:14, 16:14; Luke 9:54–55). In the life of the local church, ministers possess the weighty responsibility of protecting the purity of the body and their celebration at the Lord's Supper. Church discipline serves as the means ministers use to guard against the internal and external devastation unrepentant sin can bring among the body. In Bavinck's view, church discipline exists not merely as an exercise in the exclusion of an individual from the church's fellowship, but as a protection to the purity of the body's feasting on the risen Christ whose presence in the table meal nourishes his needy people unto further holiness. When church discipline removes an unrepentant believer, a real spiritual void is experienced for the one excluded, but this void remains necessary because the Lord's Supper protects the body's purity within and its catholic witness without.

Local church ministry provides frequent opportunities for ministers to put theology to the test. Ministers cannot avoid the practical situations calling for the careful work of shepherding with theological precision and heartfelt concern. In fact, one's theology often shows its depth and a minister his mettle when situations call for theological responses. But this testing is expected, and it is good. For, as Bavinck states, "A theology must demonstrate its right and truth, not only in the area of science, but also and more powerfully amidst the awful realities of life—at the sickbed and deathbed, in suffering and want, in distress and death, to the guilt-laden conscience and to the heart thirsting for reconciliation and peace."[44] One's theology of redemptive church discipline and its correlation to the Lord's Supper is such a place for theological demonstration. Bavinck's careful work gives ministers ample opportunities to explore how individual and corporate union with Christ visibly demonstrates itself in the Lord's Supper.

---

44. Bavinck, *The Certainty of Faith*, 17.

# Bibliography

Adams, Jay E. *Handbook of Church Discipline: A Right and Privilege of Every Church Member*. Grand Rapids: Zondervan, 1974.
Ames, William. *The Marrow of Theology*. Translated by John Dykstra Eusden. Grand Rapids: Baker, 1997.
———. "To the Reader." In *Conscience with the Power and Cases Thereof*. London, 1643.
Aquinas, Thomas. *The Aquinas Catechism: A Simple Explanation of the Catholic Faith by the Church's Greatest Theologian*. Manchester, NH: Sophia Institute, 2000.
———. *Commentary on the Gospel of John*. Translated by Fabian Larcher and James A. Weisheipl. 3 vols. Washington, DC: Catholic University of America Press, 2010.
———. *Summa Contra Gentiles*. Translated by Anton C. Pegis et al. 5 vols. Notre Dame: University of Notre Dame Press, 1975.
Augustine. "Homilies on the Gospel of St. John." In *Homilies on the Gospel of John; Homilies on the First Epistle of John; Soliloquies*, edited by Alexander Roberts et al. Nicene and Post-Nicene Fathers, First Series 7. Buffalo, NY: Christian Literature, 1888.
———. "Letter 185." In *The Confessions and Letters of St. Augustine, with a Sketch of his Life and Work*, edited by Philip Schaff. Nicene and Post Nicene Fathers, First Series 1. Buffalo, NY: Christian Literature, 1887.
———. *Teaching Christianity*. Edited by John E. Rotelle. Translated by Edmund Hill. Hyde Park, NY: New City, 1996.
Bannerman, James. *The Church of Christ*. 2 vols. Edinburgh: T. & T. Clark, 1868.
*Baptism, Eucharist and Ministry*. Faith and Order Paper No. 111. Geneva: World Council of Churches, 1982.
Barcellos, Richard C. *The Lord's Supper as a Means of Grace: More than a Memory*. Fearn, Scotland: Christian Focus, 2013.
Bargerhuff, Eric J. *Love that Rescues: God's Fatherly Love in the Practice of Church Discipline*. Eugene, OR: Wipf & Stock, 2010.
Barrett, C. K. "Proclamation and Response." In *Tradition and Interpretation in the New Testament: Essays in Honor of E. Earle Ellis*, edited by Gerald F. Hawthorne and Otto Betz, 3–15. Grand Rapids: Eerdmans, 1987.
Bavinck, Herman. "Calvin's Doctrine of the Lord's Supper." Translated by Nelson D. Kloosterman. *Mid-America Journal of Theology* 19 (2008) 127–42.
———. "The Catholicity of Christianity and the Church." Translated by John Bolt. *Calvin Journal of Theology* 27 (1992) 220–51.

———. *The Certainty of Faith*. Translated by Harry der Nederlande. St. Catharines, ON: Paideia, 1980.

———. *De Ethiek van Ulrich Zwingli*. Kampen: Zalsman, 1880.

———. "Recent Dogmatic Thought in the Netherlands." Translated by Geerhardus Vos. *The Presbyterian and Reformed Review* 10 (April 1892) 209–28.

———. *Reformed Dogmatics*. Edited by John Bolt. Translated by John Vriend. 4 vols. Grand Rapids: Baker Academic, 2008.

———. *Our Reasonable Faith*. Grand Rapids: Eerdmans, 1956.

Beasley-Murray, G. R. *Baptism in the New Testament*. Grand Rapids: Eerdmans, 1994.

Beeke, Joel R. "Laurence Chaderton: An Early Puritan Vision for Church and School." In *Church and School in Early Modern Protestantism: Studies in Honor of Richard A. Muller on the Maturation of a Theological Tradition*, edited by Jordan J. Ballor, David S. Sytsma, and Jason Zuidema, 321–37. Studies in the History of Christian Traditions 170. Leiden: Brill, 2013.

———. *Puritan Reformed Spirituality*. Grand Rapids: Reformation Heritage, 2004.

Beeke, Joel R., and Randall Pederson. *Meet the Puritans*. Grand Rapids: Reformation Heritage, 2006.

Beeke, Joel R., and J. Stephen Yuille. "Biographical Preface." In *The Works of William Perkins*, edited by J. Stephen Yuille, 1:ix–xxxii. Grand Rapids: Reformation Heritage, 2014.

———. *William Perkins*. Welwyn Garden City, UK: EP, 2015.

Beilby James K., and Paul Rhodes Eddy, eds. *Understanding Spiritual Warfare: Four Views*. Grand Rapids: Baker Academic 2012.

Berkhof, Louis. *Systematic Theology*. Grand Rapids: Eerdmans, 1938.

Bernard of Clairvaux. *On the Song of Songs*. Translated by Kilian Walsh and Irene Edmonds. 4 vols. Kalamazoo, MI: Cistercian, 1971–80.

Beza, Theodore. *Master Bezaes Sermons Upon the Three First Chapters of the Canticle of Canticles*. Oxford: Barnes, 1587.

———. *A System of Doctrine on the Sacramental Substance*. In *A Clear and Simple Treatise on the Lord's Supper*, translated by David C. Noe and Christopher M. Sanicola. Grand Rapids: Reformation Heritage, 2016.

*The Bible and Holy Scriptures Conteyned in the Olde and Newe Testament*. Geneva: Hali, 1560.

Bierma, Lyle D. *The Theology of the Heidelberg Catechism: A Reformation Synthesis*. Louisville: Westminster John Knox, 2013.

Billings, J. Todd. *Remembrance, Communion, and Hope: Rediscovering the Gospel at the Lord's Table*. Grand Rapids: Eerdmans, 2018.

———. *The Word of God for the People of God: An Entryway to the Theological Interpretation of Scripture*. Grand Rapids: Eerdmans, 2010.

Blench, J. W. *Preaching in England in the Late Fifteenth and Sixteenth Centuries*. New York: Barnes & Noble, 1964.

Blue, Ken, and John White. *Church Discipline that Heals*. Downers Grove, IL: InterVarsity, 1985.

Bolt, John. *Bavinck on the Christian Life: Following Jesus in Faithful Service*. Wheaton, IL: Crossway, 2015.

Bonaevallis, Ernaldus. *De Cardinalibus Christi Operibus*. In *Patrologia Latina*, vol. 189, edited by J-P. Migne, cols. 1690–78. Paris: Migne, 1854.

Bonhoeffer, Dietrich. *Discipleship*. Translated by Barbara Green and Reinhard Krauss. Dietrich Bonhoeffer Works 4. Minneapolis: Fortress, 2001.

*The Book of Church Order of the Presbyterian Church in America*. 6th ed. Lawrenceville, GA: Office of the Stated Clerk of the General Assembly of the Presbyterian Church in America, 2017.

Brett, Murray G. *Growing Up in Grace: The Use of Means for Communion with God*. Grand Rapids: Reformation Heritage, 2009.

Breward, Ian. "Introduction." In *The Works of William Perkins*, vol. 3, edited by Ian Breward, 3–131. The Courtenay Library of Reformation Classics. Appleford, UK: Sutton Courtenay, 1970.

———. "William Perkins and the Origins of Puritan Casuistry." *The Evangelist Quarterly* 40 (1968) 16–22.

Bridges, Jerry. *The Discipline of Grace: God's Role and Our Role in the Pursuit of Holiness*. Colorado Springs: NavPress, 1994.

Brook, Benjamin. *The Lives of the Puritans*. Morgan, PA: Soli Deo Gloria, 1996.

Bunyan, John. *The Holy War*. Grand Rapids: Baker, 1992.

———. *The Pilgrim's Progress*. Carlisle, UK: Banner of Truth, 1977.

Byars, Ronald P. *The Sacraments in Biblical Perspective*. Louisville: Westminster John Knox, 2011.

Calvin, John. *Commentaries on the Epistle of the Apostle Paul to the Romans*. Translated by John Owen. Calvin's Commentaries 19. Grand Rapids: Baker, 2003.

———. *The Gospel according to St. John 1–10*. Edited by David W. Torrance and Thomas F. Torrance. Translated by T. H. L. Parker. Calvin's New Testament Commentaries 4. Grand Rapids: Eerdmans, 1995.

———. *Institutes of the Christian Religion*. Translated by Ford Lewis Battles. The Library of Christian Classics 20–21. Philadelphia: Westminster, 1960.

*Catechism of the Catholic Church*. Ligouri, MO: Ligouri, 1994.

Ciampa, Roy E., and Brian S. Rosner. *The First Letter to the Corinthians*. The Pillar New Testament Commentary. Grand Rapids: Eerdmans, 2010.

Clark, Samuel. *The Marrow of Ecclesiastical History, Contained in the Lives of one hundred forty eight Fathers, Schoolmen, First Reformers, and Modern Divines*. London, 1654.

Cochran, Gregory C. *Christians in the Crosshairs: Persecution in the Bible and around the World Today*. Bellingham, WA: Lexham, 2018.

———. "Diokology and the Inception of the Regnal Righteousness Dynamic in Christian Persecution." PhD diss., Southern Baptist Theological Seminary, 2010.

Cooper, Charles Henry, and T. Cooper. *Athenae Cantabrigiensis, Volume 2: 1586–1609*. Cambridge: Deighton, Bell, 1861.

Cox, Don. "The Forgotten Side of Church Discipline." *Southern Baptist Journal of Theology* 4 (2000) 44–58.

Croy, N. Clayton. *Endurance in Suffering: Hebrews 12.1–13 in Its Rhetorical, Religious, and Philosophical Context*. Society for New Testament Studies Monograph Series 98. Cambridge: Cambridge University Press, 1998.

Curtis, Mark. *Oxford and Cambridge in Transition, 1558–1642*. Oxford: Oxford University Press, 1965.

Davies, Horton. *The Worship of English Puritans*. Morgan, PA: Soli Deo Gloria, 1997.

Davis, George B. "Whatever Happened to Church Discipline?" *Criswell Theological Review* 1 (1987) 345–61.

Dempster, Stephen G. *Dominion and Dynasty: A Theology of the Hebrew Bible*. Edited by D. A. Carson. New Studies in Biblical Theology. Downers Grove, IL: InterVarsity, 2003.

Dennison, James T., ed. *Reformed Confessions of the 16th and 17th Centuries in English Translation: Volume 4, 1600–1693*. Grand Rapids: Reformation Heritage, 2014.

Dever, Mark E., ed. *Polity: Biblical Arguments on How to Conduct Church Life (A Collection of Historic Baptist Documents)*. Washington, DC: Nine Marks Ministries, 2001.

Dever, Mark, and Paul Alexander. *The Deliberate Church: Building Your Ministry on the Gospel*. Wheaton, IL: Crossway, 2005.

Disley, Emma. "Degrees of Glory: Protestant Doctrine and the Concept of Rewards Hereafter." *Journal of Theological Studies* 42 (1991) 77–105.

Eglinton, James. *Trinity and Organism: Towards a New Reading of Harman Bavinck's Organic Motif*. London: Bloomsbury, 2012.

Erickson, Millard. *Christian Theology*. Grand Rapids: Baker, 1985.

Eusden, John. *Puritans, Lawyers, and Politics*. New Haven: Yale University Press, 1958.

Falls, Thomas B., trans. *Saint Justin Martyr: The First Apology, The Second Apology, Dialogue with Trypho, Exhortation to the Greeks, Discourse to the Greeks, The Monarchy; or the Rule of God*. New York: Christian Heritage, 1948.

Farrow, Douglas. *Ascension and Ecclesia: On the Significance of the Doctrine of the Ascension for Ecclesiology and Christian Cosmology*. Edinburgh: T. & T. Clark, 1999.

Fee, Gordon D. *The First Epistle to the Corinthians*. Rev. ed. The New International Commentary on the New Testament. Grand Rapids, Eerdmans, 2014.

Ferguson, Everett. *Baptism in the Early Church: History, Theology, and Liturgy in the First Five Centuries*. Grand Rapids: Eerdmans, 2009.

Fesko, J. V. *The Trinity and the Covenant of Redemption*. Fearn, UK: Mentor, 2016.

———. *Word, Water, and Spirit: A Reformed Perspective on Baptism*. Grand Rapids: Reformation Heritage, 2010.

Finney, Charles G. *Lectures on Revivals of Religion*. 2nd ed. New York: Leavitt, Lord, 1835.

———. *Memoirs of Rev. Charles G. Finney Written by Himself*. New York: Revell, 1876.

Frei, Hans W. *The Eclipse of Biblical Narrative: A Study in Eighteenth and Nineteenth Century Hermeneutics*. New Haven: Yale University Press, 1974.

Friedrich, Gerhard. "κῆρυξ, κηρύσσω, κήρυγμα." In *Theological Dictionary of the New Testament*, edited by Gerhard Kittel and Gerhard Friedrich, 3:687–88. Translated by Geoffrey W. Bromiley Grand Rapids: Eerdmans, 1965.

Fuller, Thomas. *Abel Redevivus: or, The Dead Yet Speaking. The Lives and Deaths of the Modern Divines*. London, 1651.

———. *The Holy State*. Cambridge, 1642.

Garland, David E. *1 Corinthians*. Baker Exegetical Commentary on the New Testament. Grand Rapids: Baker, 2003.

Garrett, James Leo. *Baptist Church Discipline*. Nashville: Broadman & Holman, 1962.

George, Timothy. "Theology Worth Smuggling." *First Things* (September 21, 2015). http://www.firstthings.com/web-exclusives/2015/09/theology-worth-smuggling.

Gilhooly, John R. *40 Questions About Spiritual Warfare*. Grand Rapids: Kregel Academic, 2018.

Gleason, R. N. "Calvin and Bavinck on the Lord's Supper." *Westminster Theological Journal* 45 (1983) 273–303.

———. "The Doctrine of the *Unio Mystica* in the Theology of Dr. Herman Bavinck." PhD diss., Westminster Theological Seminary, 2001.

# BIBLIOGRAPHY

———. "Herman Bavinck's Understanding of John Calvin on the Lord's Supper." http://www.richardsibbes.com/_hermanbavinck/hermanbavinck.org-Gleason2.pdf.

———. "A Short Sketch." http://www.richardsibbes.com/_hermanbavinck/hermanbavinck.org-Gleason1.pdf.

Godet, F. L. *Commentary on St. Paul's First Epistle to the Corinthians*. Translated by A. Cusin. Clark's Foreign Theological Library, n.s. 27, 30. Edinburgh: T. & T. Clark. 1886.

Godsey, John D. *The Theology of Dietrich Bonhoeffer*. 1960. Reprint, Eugene, OR: Wipf & Stock, 2015.

Grassi, Ernesto. *Rhetoric as Philosophy: The Humanist Tradition*. Translated by John Michael Krois and Azizeh Azodi. Carbondale: Southern Illinois University Press, 1980.

Grosheide, F. W. *De eerste Brief Aan de Kerk te Korinthe*. 2nd ed. Commentaar op het Nieuwe Testament. Kampen: Kok, 1957.

Grudem, Wayne. *Systematic Theology*. Grand Rapids: Zondervan, 1994.

Gurnall, William. *The Christian in Complete Armor*. Peabody, MA: Hendrickson, 2010.

Hammett, John S. *Biblical Foundations for Baptist Churches: A Contemporary Ecclesiology*. Grand Rapids: Kregel, 2005.

Havener, Ivan. "A Curse for Salvation—1 Corinthians 5:1–15." In *Sin, Salvation, and the Spirit: Commemorating the Fiftieth Year of the Liturgical Press*, edited by Daniel Durken, 334–44. Collegeville, MN: Liturgical, 1979.

Hays, Richard B. *The Conversion of the Imagination: Paul as Interpreter of Israel's Scripture*. Grand Rapids: Eerdmans, 2005.

———. *First Corinthians*. Interpretation. Louisville: John Knox, 1997.

Hein, Kenneth. *Eucharist and Excommunication: A Study in Early Christian Doctrine and Discipline*. Bern: Herbert Lang, 1975.

Heppe, Heinrich. *Reformed Dogmatics: Set Out and Illustrated from the Sources*. Edited by Ernst Bizer. Translated by G. T. Thomson. London: George Allen & Unwin, 1950.

Hicks, John Mark. "Stone-Campbell Sacramental Theology." *Restoration Quarterly* 50 (2008) 35–48.

Hill, Christopher. *God's Englishman: Oliver Cromwell and the English Revolution*. New York: Harper & Row, 1970.

Hodge, Charles. *An Exposition of the First Epistle to the Corinthians*. New York: Carter & Brothers, 1866.

Holmes, Michael W., ed. and trans. *The Apostolic Fathers: Greek Texts and English Translations*. 3rd ed. Grand Rapids: Baker Academic, 2007.

Horton, Michael. *The Christian Faith: A Systematic Theology for Pilgrims on the Way*. Grand Rapids: Zondervan, 2011.

———. *People and Place: A Covenant Ecclesiology*. Louisville: Westminster John Knox, 2008.

Hoskyns, Edwyn Clement. *The Fourth Gospel*. Edited by Francis Noel Davey. 2nd ed. London: Faber and Faber, 1947.

House, Paul. *Bonhoeffer's Seminary Vision: A Case for Costly Discipleship and Life Together*. Wheaton, IL: Crossway, 2015.

Hovey, Craig. *To Share in the Body: A Theology of Martyrdom for Today's Church*. Grand Rapids: Brazos, 2008.

# BIBLIOGRAPHY

Hulse, Erroll. "William Perkins: Application in Preaching." In *The Pure Flame of Devotion: The History of Christian Spirituality*, edited by G. Stephen Weaver and Ian Hugh Clary, 177–94. Kitchener, ON: Joshua, 2013.

Jeschke, Marlin. *Discipling in the Church: Recovering a Ministry of the Gospel*. 3rd ed. Scottdale, PA: Herald, 1988.

———. *Discipling the Brother*. Scottdale, PA: Herald, 1979.

Johnstone, Henry W., Jr. *Philosophy and Argument*. University Park: Pennsylvania State University Press, 1959.

Jordan, Mark. "Theology and Philosophy." In *The Cambridge Companion to Aquinas*, edited by Norman Kretzman and Eleanor Stump, 232–51. Cambridge Companions to Philosophy. Cambridge: Cambridge University Press, 1993.

Kamphuis, Barend. "Herman Bavinck on Catholicity." *Mid-America Journal of Theology* 24 (2013) 97–104.

Kimble, Jeremy. *40 Questions about Church Membership and Discipline*. Grand Rapids: Kregel, 2017.

———. *That His Spirit May Be Saved: Church Discipline as a Means to Repentance and Perseverance*. Eugene, OR: Wipf & Stock, 2013.

Kingdon, D. P. "Discipline." In *New Dictionary of Biblical Theology: Exploring the Unity Diversity of Scripture*, edited by T. Desmond Alexander et al., 448–50. Downers Grove, IL: InterVarsity, 2000.

Klink, Edward W., III. *John*. Zondervan Exegetical Commentary on the New Testament 4. Grand Rapids: Zondervan, 2016.

———. *The Sheep of the Fold: The Audience and Origin of the Gospel of John*. Society for New Testament Studies Monograph Series 141. Cambridge: Cambridge University Press, 2007.

Kolb, Robert, and Timothy J. Wengert, eds. *The Book of Concord: The Confessions of the Evangelical Lutheran Church*. Minneapolis: Fortress, 2000.

Knuteson, Roy. *Calling the Church to Discipline: A Scriptural Guide for the Church that Dares to Discipline*. Nashville: Thomas Nelson, 1977.

Kreider, A. E. "Standards with Love." In *Studies in Church Discipline*, edited by Maynard Shelly, 105–12. Newton, KS: Mennonite Publication Office, 1958.

Kruse, Colin G. "The Offender and the Offense in 2 Corinthians 2:5 and 7:12." *Evangelical Quarterly* 60 (1988) 129–39.

Kuivenhoven, Maarten. "Condemning Coldness and Sleepy Dullness: The Concept of Urgency in the Preaching Models of Richard Baxter and William Perkins." *Puritan Reformed Journal* 4 (2012) 180–200.

Labberton, Mark. *Called: The Crisis and Promise of Following Jesus Today*. Downers Grove, IL: InterVarsity, 2014.

Laney, J. Carl. *A Guide to Church Discipline*. Minneapolis: Bethany, 1985.

Latimer, Hugh. "The Second Sermon of Master Hugh Latimer on the Beatitudes." In *The Sermons of the Right Reverend Father in God, and Constant Martyr of Jesus Christ, Hugh Latimer, Some Time Bishop of Worcester*. London: Paternoster-Row, 1824.

Lauterbach, Mark. *The Transforming Community: The Practice of the Gospel in Church Discipline*. Carol Stream, IL: Christian Focus, 2003.

Leclerq, Jean. "Influence and Noninfluence of Dionysius in the Western Middle Ages." In *Pseudo-Dionysius: The Complete Works*, edited by Paul Rorem, 25–32. New York: Paulist, 1987.

Lee, Sidney, ed. *The Dictionary of National Biography*. London: Smith, Elder, 1909.

# BIBLIOGRAPHY

Leeman, Jonathan. *Church Discipline: How the Church Protects the Name of Jesus.* Wheaton, IL: Crossway, 2012.

Litfin, Duane. *Paul's Theology of Preaching: The Apostle's Challenge to the Art of Persuasion in Ancient Corinth.* Downers Grove, IL: IVP Academic, 2015.

———. *St. Paul's Theology of Proclamation: 1 Corinthians 1–4 and Greco-Roman Rhetoric.* Society for the New Testament Studies Monograph Series 79. Cambridge: Cambridge University Press, 1994.

Lombard, Peter. *The Sentences.* Translated by Giulio Silano. 4 vols. Toronto: Pontifical Institute of Mediaeval Studies, 2007–10.

Lovelace, Richard C. "The Anatomy of Puritan Piety: English Puritan Devotional Literature, 1600–1640." In *Christian Spirituality III*, edited by Louis Dupré and Don E. Saliers, 294–323. New York: Crossroad, 1989.

Luther, Martin. "The Babylonian Captivity of the Church, 1520." In *Word and Sacrament II*, edited by Abdel Ross Wentz, 11–126. Luther's Works 36. Philadelphia: Muhlenberg, 1959.

———. "The Blessed Sacrament of the Holy and True Body of Christ, and the Brotherhoods." In *Word and Sacrament I*, edited by E. Theodore Bachmann, 49–73. Luther's Works 35. Philadelphia: Muhlenberg, 1960.

———. "First Lectures on the Psalms." In *First Lectures on the Psalms II—Psalms 76–126*, edited by Hilton C. Oswald. Luther's Works 11. St. Louis: Concordia, 1976.

———. "The Holy and Blessed Sacrament of Baptism, 1519." In *Word and Sacrament I*, edited by E. Theodore Bachmann, 29–43. Luther's Works 35. Philadelphia: Muhlenberg, 1960.

———. "On the Councils and the Church, 1539." In *Church and Ministry III—Liturgy and Hymns*, edited by Eric W. Gritsch, 9–178. Luther's Works 41. Philadelphia: Fortress, 1966.

———. "Preface to the Wittenberg Edition of Luther's Writings: Dr. Martin Luther's Preface." In *Career of the Reformer IV*, edited by Lewis William Spitz, 283–88. Luther's Works 34. Philadelphia: Fortress, 1960.

———. *Sermons on the Gospel of St. John: Chapters 1–4.* Edited by Jaroslav Pelikan. Luther's Works 22. St. Louis: Concordia, 1957.

Manton, Thomas. "To the Reader." In *Several Sermons Upon the Twenty-Fifth Chapter of Matthew.* 22 vols. The Works of Thomas Manton. Birmingham: Solid Ground Christian, 2008.

Marcus, Joel. *Mark 1–8: A New Translation with Introduction and Commentary.* Anchor Bible. New York: Doubleday, 2000.

Marion, Jean-Luc. *Being Given: Toward a Phenomenology of Givenness.* Translated by Jeffrey L. Kosky. Stanford: Stanford University Press, 2013.

———. *The Visible and the Revealed.* Translated by Christina M. Gschwandtner et al. New York: Fordham University Press, 2008.

Marshall, I. Howard. "Congregation and Ministry in the Pastoral Epistles." In *Community Formation in the Early Church and the Church Today*, edited by Richard Longenecker, 105–25. Peabody, MA: Hendrickson, 2002.

Martyn, J. Louis. *Galatians: A New Translation with Introduction and Commentary.* The Anchor Yale Bible. New Haven: Yale University Press, 1997.

McKim, Donald Keith. *Ramism in William Perkins' Theology.* New York: Lang, 1987.

Meyer, H. A. W. *Critical and Exegetical Handbook to the Epistles to the Corinthians.* Translated by D. Douglas Bannerman. New York: Funk & Wagnalls, 1890.

Miller, Perry. *Errand into the Wilderness*. Cambridge, MA: Belknap, 1956.
———. *The New England Mind*. New York: MacMillan, 1939.
Moo, Douglas J. *The Epistle to the Romans*. New International Commentary on the New Testament. Grand Rapids: Eerdmans, 1996.
Morison, Samuel. *The Intellectual Life of Colonial New England*. 2nd ed. New York: New York University Press, 1956.
Moss, Candida. *The Myth of Persecution: How Early Christians Invented a Story of Martyrdom*. New York: HarperOne, 2013.
Mosse, George L. *The Holy Pretence: A Study in Christianity and Reason of State from William Perkins to John Winthrop*. Oxford: Blackwell, 1957.
Muller, Richard. "William Perkins and the Protestant Exegetical Tradition: Interpretation, Style and Method." In *A Commentary on Hebrews 11 (1609 Edition)*, edited by John H. Augustine, 71–94. New York: Pilgrim, 1991.
Murphy-O'Connor, Jerome. *1 Corinthians*. New Testament Message. Wilmington, DE: Michael Glazier, 1979.
Murray, John. *The Epistle to the Romans*. 2 vols. New International Commentary on the New Testament. Grand Rapids: Eerdmans, 1959, 1965.
Myers, Jeremy. "Clarifying the Confusion of the Sinner's Prayer." https://faithalone.org/magazine/y2005/ 05_12_2. html.
Oden, Thomas C. *Corrective Love: The Power of Communion Discipline*. St. Louis: Concordia, 1995.
Orsi, Robert A. *History and Presence*. Cambridge, MA: Belknap, 2016.
Osborne, Grant. *Revelation*. Baker Exegetical Commentary on the New Testament. Grand Rapids: Baker Academic, 2002.
Owen, John. *Of Communion with God the Father, Son, and Holy Ghost*. In *The Works of John Owen* 2. Edinburgh: Banner of Truth, 1997.
———. "Of the Mortification of Sin in Believers." In *Overcoming Sin and Temptation*, edited by Kelly M. Kapic and Justin Taylor, 41–140. Wheaton, IL: Crossway, 2006.
Packer, James I. *An Anglican to Remember—William Perkins: Puritan Popularizer*. St. Antholin's Lectureship Charity Lecture. London, 1996.
———. *Evangelism and the Sovereignty of God*. London: InterVarsity, 1961.
———. *A Quest for Godliness: The Puritan Vision of the Christian Life*. Wheaton, IL: Crossway, 1990.
Papadopolos, Styulianos G. "Prologue." In *Saint Paul and Corinth: 150 Years Since the Writing of the Epistles to the Corinthians*, edited by Constantine J. Belezos, 19–23. International Scholarly Conference Proceedings 1. Athens: Psichogios, 2009.
Patterson, W. B. *William Perkins and the Making of Protestant England*. Oxford: Oxford University Press, 2014.
Peeler, Amy L. B. *You Are My Son: The Family of God in the Epistle of Hebrews*. Library of New Testament Studies 486. New York: Bloomsbury, 2014.
Pelikan, Jaroslav. *The Christian Tradition*. 5 vols. Chicago: University of Chicago Press, 1971–89.
Pelikan, Jaroslav, and Valerie Hotchkiss, eds. *Creeds and Confessions of Faith in the Christian Tradition*. 3 vols. New Haven: Yale University Press, 2003.
Perelman, Chaim. "Philosophy and Rhetoric." In *Advances in Argumentation Theory and Research*, edited by J. Robert Cox and Charles Arthur Willard, 287–97. Carbondale, IL: Southern Illinois University Press, 1982.

Perelman, Chaim, and Luci Olbrechts-Tyteca. *The New Rhetoric: A Treatise on Argumentation*. Translated by John Wilkinson and Purcell Weaver. Notre Dame: University of Notre Dame Press, 1969.
Perkins, William. *The Art of Prophesying; or, A treatise concerning the sacred and only true manner and method of preaching*. In *The Works of William Perkins* 2. London, 1631.
———. *An Exposition of the Lord's Prayer in the Way of Catechising, Serving for Ignorant People*. In *The Works of William Perkins* 1. London, 1626.
———. *A Faithful and Plain Exposition Upon the Two First Verses of the Second Chapter of Zephaniah*. In *The Works of William Perkins* 3. London, 1631.
———. *A Godly and Learned Exposition upon Christ's Sermon in the Mount*. In *The Works of William Perkins* 3. London, 1631.
———. *Of the Calling of the Ministry, Two Treatises, Describing the Duties and Dignities of that Calling*. In *The Works of William Perkins* 3. London, 1631.
———. *A Reformed Catholic; or, A declaration showing how near we may come to the present Church of Rome in sundry points of religion, and wherein we must forever depart from them*. In *The Works of William Perkins* 1. London, 1626.
———. *A Treatise Tending unto a Declaration, whether a man be in the estate of damnation, or in the estate of grace*; OR *A Treatise Tending Unto a Declaration, whether a man be in the estate of damnation, or in the estate of grace: and if he be in the first, how he may in time come out of it: if in the second, how he may discern it, and preserve in the same to the end*. In *The Works of William Perkins* 1. London, 1626.
———. *Two Treatises. I. Of the nature and practice of repentance. II. Of the combat of the flesh and spirit*. In *The Works of William Perkins* 1. London, 1626.
Piggin, F. S. "Excommunication." In *Evangelical Dictionary of Theology*, edited by Walter A. Elwell, 422–3. 2nd ed. Grand Rapids: Baker Academic, 2001.
Pipa, Joseph A. "William Perkins and the Development of Puritan Preaching." PhD diss., Westminster Theological Seminary, 1985.
Piper, John. *Brothers, We Are not Professionals: A Plea to Pastors for Radical Ministry*. Nashville: Broadman & Holman, 2002.
Plantinga, Alvin. *Knowledge and Christian Belief*. Grand Rapids: Eerdmans, 2015.
Poettecker, Henry. "The New Testament Community." In *Studies in Church Discipline*, edited by Jacob T. Friesen et al. Newton, KS: Mennonite Publication Office, 1958.
Powlison, David. "The Classical Model." In *Understanding Spiritual Warfare: Four Views*, edited by James K. Beilby and Paul Rhodes Eddy, 89–111. Grand Rapids: Baker Academic 2012.
Rack, Henry D. *Reasonable Enthusiast: John Wesley and the Rise of Methodism*. 3rd ed. London: Epworth, 2002.
Rae, Murray A. *History and Hermeneutics*. London: T. & T. Clark, 2005.
Rainer, Thom. "We Are First Baptist Church Sutherland Springs, TX." https://thomrainer.com/ 2017/11/first-baptist-church-sutherland-springs-texas/.
Rescher, Nicholas. *Philosophical Reasoning: A Study in the Methodology of Philosophizing*. Oxford: Blackwell, 2001.
Ridderbos, Herman. *Paul: An Outline of His Theology*. Translated by J. R. DeWitt. Grand Rapids: Eerdmans, 1975.
———. *When The Time Had Fully Come: Studies in New Testament Theology*. Grand Rapids: Eerdmans, 1957.
Rorem, Paul, ed. *Pseudo-Dionysius: The Complete Works*. Classics of Western Spirituality. New York: Paulist, 1987.

Rosner, Brian S. *Paul, Scripture, and Ethics: A Study of 1 Corinthians 5–7*. AGJU 22. Grand Rapids: Baker, 1999.

Schouls, Peter A. "Communication, Argumentation, and Presupposition in Philosophy." *Philosophy and Rhetoric* 2 (1968) 183–99.

Schrage, Wolfgang. *Der Erste Brief An Die Korinther*, vol. 1. Evangelisch-katholischer Kommentar zum Neuen Testament 7:1. 3 vols. Neukirchener-Vluyn: Neukirchener, 1991.

Schreiner, Thomas R. *1–2 Peter, Jude*. NAC 37. Nashville: B&H, 2003.

———. "The Biblical Basis for Church Discipline." In *Those Who Must Give an Account: A Study of Church Membership and Church Discipline*, edited by John S. Hammett and Benjamin L. Merkle, 105–30. Nashville: B&H, 2012.

———. *Romans*. Baker Exegetical Commentary on the New Testament. Grand Rapids: Baker, 1998.

———. *Run to Win the Prize: Perseverance in the New Testament*. Wheaton, IL: Crossway, 2010.

Seaver, Paul. *The Puritan Lectureships: The Politics of Religious Dissent, 1560–1662*. Palo Alto, CA: Stanford University Press, 1970.

Scott, Ian W. *Implicit Epistemology in the Letters of Paul: Story, Experience and the Spirit*. Tubingen: Mohr/Siebeck, 2006. Reprinted as *Paul's Way of Knowing: Story, Experience, and the Spirit*. Grand Rapids: Baker Academic, 2009.

Simons, Menno. *Christian Baptism*. In *The Complete Writings of Menno Simons*, edited by J. C. Wenger, 231–87. Translated by Leonard Verduin. Scottdale, PA: Mennonite, 1984.

Smith, D. Moody. "When Did the Gospels Become Scripture?" *Journal of Biblical Literature* 119 (2000) 3–20.

South, James T. *Disciplinary Practices in Pauline Texts*. Lewistown, NY: Mellen, 1992.

Spellman, Ched. "The Drama of Discipline: Toward an Intertextual Profile of *Paideia* in Hebrews 12." *Journal of the Evangelical Theological Society* 59 (2016) 487–506.

Stanton, Norman, R. "The Reestablishment of Proper Church Discipline." In *Restoring Integrity in Baptist Churches*, edited by Thomas White, Jason G. Duesing and Malcolm B. Yarnell, 199–220. Grand Rapids: Kregel, 2008.

Stein, Robert H. *A Basic Guide to Interpreting the Bible: Playing by the Rules*. Grand Rapids: Baker, 1994.

Tabb, Brian J. *Suffering in Ancient Worldview: Luke, Seneca, and 4 Maccabees in Dialogue*. Library of New Testament Studies 569. New York: Bloomsbury, 2016.

Tanner, Norman P. *Decrees of the Ecumenical Councils*. 2 vols. Washington, DC: Georgetown University Press, 1990.

Taylor, Charles. *The Language Animal: The Full Shape of the Human Linguistic Capacity*. Cambridge, MA: Belknap, 2016.

Te Velde, Rudi. *Aquinas on God: The "Divine Science" of the Summa Theologiae*. Ashgate Studies in the History of Philosophical Theology. Burlington, VT: Ashgate, 2006.

Thiselton, Anthony C. *The First Epistle to the Corinthians*. New International Greek Testament Commentary. Grand Rapids: Eerdmans, 2000.

Thompson, James W. *Moral Formation according to Paul: The Context and Coherence of Pauline Ethics*. Grand Rapids: Baker Academic, 2011.

———. *Pastoral Ministry according to Paul: A Biblical Vision*. Grand Rapids: Baker Academic, 2006.

Thompson, Nicholas. *Eucharistic Sacrifice and Patristic Tradition in the Theology of Martin Bucer 1534–46*. Studies in the History of Christian Traditions 119. Leiden: Brill, 2005.
Ton, Josef. *Suffering, Martyrdom, and Rewards in Heaven*. Lanham, MD: University Press of America, 2000.
Trueman, Carl R. *The Creedal Imperative*. Wheaton, IL: Crossway, 2012.
———. *Luther on the Christian Life: Cross and Freedom*. Wheaton, IL: Crossway, 2015.
Turretin, Francis. *Institutes of Elenctic Theology*. Translated by James T. Dennison Jr. 3 vols. Phillipsburg, NJ: P&R, 1992–1997.
Tyacke, Nicholas. *Anti-Calvinists: The Rise of English Puritanism, c. 1590–1640*. Oxford: Clarendon, 1987.
Ursinus, Zacharias. *The Commentary of Dr. Zacharias Ursinus on the Heidelberg Catechism*. Translated by G. W. Williard. 1852. Reprint, Phillipsburg: P&R, n.d.
Vander Broek, Lyle D. "Discipline and Community: Another Look at 1 Corinthians 5." *Reformed Review* 48 (1994) 5–13.
Vermigli, Peter Martyr. "Address to the Strasbourg Senate." In *The Peter Martyr Reader*, edited by John Patrick Donnelly, Frank A. James III and Joseph C. McLelland, 160–64. Kirksville, MO: Truman State University Press, 1999.
———. "Epitome of the Book Against Gardiner." In *The Peter Martyr Reader*, edited by John Patrick Donnelly, Frank A. James III and Joseph C. McLelland, 153–60. Kirksville, MO: Truman State University Press, 1999.
———. "Vermigli to Beza." In *Life, Letters, and Sermons*, edited by John Patrick Donnelly, 134–47. The Peter Martyr Library 5. Kirksville, MO: Thomas Jefferson University Press, 1999.
Vickers, Brian. "Celebrating the Past and Future in the Present." In *The Lord's Supper: Remembering and Proclaiming Christ Until He Comes*, edited by Thomas R. Schreiner and Matthew R. Crawford, 313–40. Nashville: B&H, 2010.
Vos, Geerhardus. *The Pauline Eschatology*. 1930. Reprint, Phillipsburg, NJ: P&R, 1994.
Waters, Guy. "Curse Redux? 1 Corinthians 5:13, Deuteronomy, and Identity in Corinth." *Westminster Theological Journal* 77 (2015) 237–50.
Watson, Francis. *Text, Church and World: Biblical Interpretation in Theological Perspective*. Edinburgh: T. & T. Clark, 1994.
Webster, John. "Biblical Reasoning." *Anglican Theological Review* 90 (2008) 733–51.
———. *Holy Scripture: A Dogmatic Sketch*. Current Issues in Theology 1. Cambridge: Cambridge University Press, 2003.
———. "On Evangelical Ecclesiology." In *Confessing God: Essays in Christian Dogmatics II*, 153–94. London: Bloomsbury T. & T. Clark, 2016.
———. *Word and Church: Essays in Christian Dogmatics*. Edinburgh: T. & T. Clark, 2011.
Wray, Daniel E. *Biblical Church Discipline*. Carlisle, PA: Banner of Truth, 1978.
Wright, Louis B. "William Perkins: Elizabethan Apostle of 'Practical Divinity.'" *Huntington Library Quarterly* 3 (1940) 171–96.
Yeago, David S. "The New Testament and the Nicene Dogma: A Contribution to the Recovery of Theological Exegesis." *Pro Ecclesia* 3 (1994) 152–64.
Yocum, John. "Scripture, Clarity of." In *Dictionary for Theological Interpretation of the Bible*, edited by Kevin J. Vanhoozer, 727–30. Grand Rapids: Baker Academic, 2005.
Yuille, J. Stephen. "Ready to Receive: Humbling and Softening in William Perkins's Preparation of the Heart." *Puritan Reformed Journal* 5 (2013) 91–106.
Zaas, Peter S. "'Cast Out the Evil Man from Your Midst' (1 Cor 5:13b)." *Journal of Biblical Literature* 103 (1984) 259–61.

Zanchi, Girolamo. *De Religione Christiana Fides—Confession of Christian Religion*. Edited by Luca Baschera and Christian Moser. 2 vols. Studies in the History of Christian Traditions 135. Leiden: Brill, 2007.

Zwingli, Ulrich. *An Exposition of the Faith*. In *Zwingli and Bullinger*, edited by Geoffrey W. Bromiley, 245–79. Philadelphia: Westminster, 1953.

———. *Of Baptism*. In *Zwingli and Bullinger*, edited by Geoffrey W. Bromiley, 129–75. Philadelphia: Westminster, 1953.

# Name Index

Ames, William, 38, 57
Aquinas, Thomas, 35–36, 54
Augustine of Hippo, 12–14, 35, 60, 71, 97–98, 108

Barcellos, Richard, 144
Bargerhuff, Eric, 122n49
Barrett, C. K., 22
Bates, William, 35
Bavinck, Herman, 138–54
Beasley-Murray, G. R., 69–70
Bernard of Clairvaux, 55
Beveridge, Henry, 84n48
Beza, Theodore, 36–37, 55, 65
Billings, J. Todd, 6, 144, 153
Bolt, John, 143
Bonaevallis, Ernaldus, 54
Bonhoeffer, Dietrich, 96, 100n19, 111–12
Bunyan, John, 112
Byars, Ronald, 74

Calvin, John, xiv, 14, 36–37, 43–44, 64, 71, 81, 84, 102, 120n42, 139–41, 148
Chaderton, Laurence, 37, 41n26
Chilton, David, 106n36
Chrysostom, John, 35
Cocceius, Johannes, 57
Collinges, John, 35
Cotton, John, 38
Cox, Don, 116
Croy, N. Clayton, 118
Cyprian of Carthage, 54

Davis, George, 119n40
Diocletian, 97
Disley, Emma, 102

Elam, E. A., 82n42
Elizabeth I, Queen, 39
Erickson, Millard, 74–75, 81–82, 85, 89, 107

Farel, William, 36
Finney, Charles, 77–78
Friedrich, Gerhard, 20
Fuller, Thomas, 37–38

Galerius, 97
Garrett, James Leo, 121n47
George, Timothy, 28
Gilhooly, John, 114
Gleason, Ron, 139–40, 143
Godet, F. L., 26
Goodwin, Thomas, 48
Graham, Billy, 78
Grassi, Ernesto, 23–24
Grudem, Wayne, 75, 81–82, 85, 120
Grünewald, Matthias, 28
Gurnall, William, 112–13

Hammett, John, 151
Harvey, Gabriel, 41n26
Hein, Kenneth, 122n50
Hemer, Colin, 106n36
Horton, Michael, 147
Hovey, Craig, 98–100, 108
Howe, John, 35

# NAME INDEX

Jeschke, Marlin, 117n33
Johnstone, Henry, 23n6
John the Baptist, 14, 28

Kamphuis, Barend, 148
Kingdon, D. P., 119
Kreider, A. E., 121n45
Kuyper, Abraham, 149

Latimer, Hugh, 102
Leeman, Jonathan, 116
Lenin, Vladimir, 104
Lewis, C. S., 99n13
Lombard, Peter, 71
Lovelace, R. C., 39n23
Luther, Martin, xiv, 13, 36, 59, 64, 71, 73, 75, 81, 102, 110–11, 123

Manton, Thomas, 35
Martyn, J. Louis, 25n10
Maximian, 97
Miller, Perry, 39n22
Moo, Douglas J., 126n3
Morison, Samuel, 39n22
Morris, Leon, 107
Moses, 26–27, 66, 88
Moss, Candida, 95, 97
Mounce, Robert H., 106n36
Muller, Richard, 44n49, 45n49

Nehemiah, 32–33

Oden, Thomas, 120n41
Olbrechts-Tyteca, Luci, 22–23
Osborne, Grant, 106
Owen, John, 54–57, 59, 63, 66, 109

Packer, J. I., 28, 42n32, 44n47
Pelikan, Jaroslav, 80
Perelman, Chaim, 22–24
Perkins, Hannah, 37
Perkins, Thomas, 37
Perkins, William, 35–49
Piggin, F. S., 117n34
Pipa, Joseph, 41n26, 47n61

Plantinga, Alvin, 26n11
Poettecker, Henry, 121n45
Powlison, David, 114
Preston, John, 38
Pseudo-Dionysius, 58–59, 82, 88

Rack, Henry, 78
Rae, Murray A., 6
Rainer, Thom, 96
Ramus, Peter, 41n26
Rescher, Nicholas, 23n6

Schouls, Peter, 23n6
Schreiner, Thomas, 121, 126n4
Scott, Ian, 24–25
Scotus, Duns, 35
Sewell, E. G., 82n42
Sibbes, Richard, 38
Simons, Menno, 76
Slane, Craig, 100n19
Spellman, Ched, 118
Stalin, Joseph, 104
Sunday, Billy, 78
Swete, Henry Barclay, 106n36

Tabb, Brian, 123
Thompson, James, 122
Ton, Josef, 98, 100–108
Tyndale, William, 102

Ursinus, Zacharias, 57, 60

Vander Broek, Lyle, 120
Vermigli, Peter Martyr, 55, 65
Vickers, Brian, 151
Viret, Pierre, 36

Walvoord, John, 106n36
Webster, John, 7, 10–11, 74
Wesley, John, 77–79

Yeago, David S., 9

Zanchi, Girolamo, 55

# Subject Index

American Restoration Movement, 69–70, 78, 88
*Anfechtung*, 110–11
ascension, Jesus', 64, 66

*Babylonian Captivity of the Church*, 73
baptism, 12–14, 59, 62–63, 69–80, 86–87, 90–92, 97, 140
*Baptism, Eucharist and Ministry*, 70, 79
Belgic Confession, 60, 125n1
Book of Church Order of the Presbyterian Church in America, 126n8

calling, 21, 25, 27, 29–34, 113, 127, 137
canon, biblical, 5, 8–9, 12, 44
catholicity, xv, 125n2, 148–50, 152–53
Christian Reformed Church, 148
Christ's College, Cambridge, 37–38
Church of England, 37n9, 39–40, 47
*communio*, 53–68
communion, xiii, 53–68, 70, 72–74, 81–84, 86–89, 117n34, 136, 138–39, 141–42, 144, 148, 152–53
condign merit, 103, 105
*Consensus Tigurinus*, 81n36
consubstantiation, 64, 144
Council of Constance, 84n46
Council of Trent, 63–64

Day of Judgment, 126n4, 133
Day of the Lord, 130–32
Deuteronomy, 118–19, 129, 134
*Didache*, 83

discipline, church, 95, 97–103, 108, 110, 115–17, 119–23, 125n1, 127, 136, 138–40, 145–54
discipline, corrective, 109–10, 115–18, 120n42, 126–27, 132, 136–37
discipline, divine, 110, 118–19
discipline, formative, 110, 115–16, 153
diokological, 100, 108
Donatism, 98
Dutch Reformed Church, 148–49

evangelism, 18, 27–28, 74, 78
excommunication, xiv, 110, 117–18, 121–22, 146
exegesis, ecclesial, 4, 10–15
exegesis, historical-critical, 9, 14
*exitus-reditus*, 54, 58

Faith and Order Commission, 70, 79
Feast of Passover, 131–32, 137
Feast of Unleavened Bread, 131–32
flesh, 4, 8, 41, 61–62, 65, 72, 86–88, 105, 109–15, 121–23, 127, 129–34, 136, 139, 141
French Confession, 60

Geneva Bible, 55
good works, 102–3
grace, means of, 43, 74–75, 82, 90, 122n51, 138, 140, 144, 147, 153
Great St. Andrew's Church, 38

Heidelberg Catechism, 57

## SUBJECT INDEX

herald, 19–23, 25, 27, 29–31, 53, 58, 63, 67, 153
Holy Spirit, 10, 18, 23n6, 26n11, 43–44, 46–48, 56, 61–63, 76–80, 91, 102, 114, 129n16, 135, 137, 142, 144
hypostatic union, 54–55, 61

incarnation, 53–55, 61, 68, 72
International Day of Prayer for the Persecuted Church, 95
Israel, 6, 66, 86, 88, 127, 129, 134, 136, 149

knowledge, inclinational, 43
knowledge, notional, 43

Lateran Council IV, 83

Mark, Gospel of, 98–100
martyr-church, 98–100
martyrdom, 98–101, 103, 106, 108
Martyr, Justin, 83
Matthew, Gospel of, 100
ministry model, natural, 16–17, 29–31, 34
ministry model, Pauline, 17, 29–32, 34

Nicene Creed, 90, 96
Noble Death, 100n19

pacifism, 100
Pentecost, 63, 77, 80
persecution, xiv, 95–104, 106, 108–9, 111, 113, 119n37, 126n3
perseverance of the saints, 113, 118–23
perspicuity of Scripture, 10
persuader, 19–23, 26–27, 29, 31
persuasion, 19, 22, 24–25, 29
proclamation, 18–19, 23–29, 40n26, 63, 67, 85, 148

Quakers, 73, 76

Ramism, 40n26
*res significata*, 72
rewards, heavenly, 95, 98, 100–108
rhetoric, Greco-Roman, 19–25, 29

sacraments, xiv–xv, 14, 43, 53–92, 98, 125n1, 144, 148
sacred language, 23
Salvation Army, 73, 76
Satan, 112–14, 122n49, 127, 132–33, 136, 144, 146
Scripture, doctrine of, 4–11
Second Great Awakening, 78
Second Helvetic Confession, 61
self-denial, 99, 111
Song of Songs, 55
spiritual warfare, 110, 114–15
Stone-Campbell Movement, 69
suffering, xiv–xv, 55, 57, 96, 101, 103–6, 108–13, 115, 118–19, 122–23, 125–37, 145–46, 150, 153–54

*tentatio*, see *Anfechtung*
Tetrapolitan Confession, 60
*traditores*, 97
transubstantiation, 63–64, 81, 144
Turretin, Francis, 125n1

*unio mystica*, 139, 142–44
union, 43, 53–68, 80, 82, 88, 96, 126, 138, 139–40, 142–48, 150–51, 154

vocation, *see* calling
Vatican Council II, 92n54

Westminster Confession of Faith, 57, 60, 125n1
Westminster Shorter Catechism, 61
World Council of Churches, 70, 79

Zwingli, Ulrich, 36, 61, 64, 70, 72–73, 76, 81–82, 87, 139n5

# Scripture Index

## Old Testament

### Genesis
| | |
|---|---|
| 1:3 | 62 |

### Exodus
| | |
|---|---|
| 12:18–20 | 131 |
| 13:7 | 131 |
| 24:9–11 | 88 |
| 24:11 | 66 |

### Leviticus
| | |
|---|---|
| 18:8 | 128 |
| 20:11 | 128 |

### Numbers
| | |
|---|---|
| 21:8–9 | 26 |

### Deuteronomy
| | |
|---|---|
| 8 | 118 |
| 8:5–6 | 118 |
| 12:23 | 67 |
| 13:6 | 129n11 |
| 17:7 | 129 |
| 17:8–11 | 119n40 |
| 19:9 | 129 |
| 19:19–20 | 119n40 |
| 21:21 | 129 |
| 22:20 | 128 |
| 22:21 | 129 |
| 23:1 | 128, 129 |
| 24:7 | 129 |
| 27:20 | 128 |

### Nehemiah
| | |
|---|---|
| 3 | 33 |
| 6:15 | 33 |

### Job
| | |
|---|---|
| 2:6 | 132n25 |

### Psalms
| | |
|---|---|
| 23 | 112 |
| 68 | 63 |
| 119 | 111 |
| 119:22 | 111 |
| 119:23 | 111 |
| 119:28 | 111 |
| 119:50 | 111 |
| 119:53 | 111 |
| 119:71 | 111 |
| 119:84 | 111 |
| 119:115 | 111 |
| 119:136 | 111 |
| 119:153 | 111 |
| 119:157 | 111 |
| 119:161 | 111 |
| 119:176 | 111 |
| 133:2 | 56 |

# SCRIPTURE INDEX

## Proverbs

| | |
|---|---|
| 3 | 118n37 |
| 3:11–12 | 118 |
| 27:5–6 | 123 |

## Isaiah

| | |
|---|---|
| 6 | 88 |
| 9:6 | 55 |
| 42:1–3 | 63 |

## Jeremiah

| | |
|---|---|
| 3:16–17 | 105 |

## Daniel

| | |
|---|---|
| 12:3 | 103 |
| 12:13 | 103 |

# New Testament

## Matthew

| | |
|---|---|
| 3:17 | 79 |
| 5:13–16 | 41 |
| 8:26 | 154 |
| 18 | 117n32, 117n33, 147 |
| 18:15–20 | 110 |
| 18:17 | 118 |
| 19:28 | 108 |
| 20:24 | 108 |
| 25 | 35 |
| 25:21 | 32 |
| 25:23 | 32 |
| 26:40 | 108 |
| 28:19 | 14 |
| 28:20 | 65 |

## Mark

| | |
|---|---|
| 8:31–38 | 111 |
| 10:14 | 154 |
| 10:29–30 | 100 |
| 13:13 | 100 |
| 16:14 | 154 |

## Luke

| | |
|---|---|
| 1:35 | 55 |
| 3:16 | 62 |
| 3:22 | 63 |
| 9:54–55 | 154 |
| 10:38 | 63 |
| 19:17 | 32 |
| 22:16–8 | 67 |
| 22:37 | 126 |
| 24 | 85 |
| 24:1 | 83 |
| 24:13 | 83 |
| 24:30–35 | 83 |
| 24:45 | 26 |

## John

| | |
|---|---|
| 1:1 | 14 |
| 1:6 | 14 |
| 1:12 | 22 |
| 1:14 | 55, 72 |
| 1:16 | 56 |
| 1:33 | 13 |
| 3:3 | 79 |
| 3:5 | 79 |
| 3:14–15 | 26 |
| 3:22 | 12 |
| 3:22–26 | 12 |
| 3:30 | 28 |
| 4:2 | 12–14 |
| 6 | 88 |
| 6:40 | 27 |
| 6:54 | 67, 88 |
| 8:28 | 27 |
| 11:43 | 62 |
| 12:23 | 27 |
| 12:32 | 27 |
| 12:33 | 27 |
| 14:15 | 32 |
| 17:5 | 27 |

## Acts

| | |
|---|---|
| 2:33 | 63 |
| 2:38 | 63, 79, 90, 92 |
| 5 | 146 |
| 8:39 | 79 |
| 10:48 | 14 |
| 13 | 146 |
| 13:48 | 26 |
| 16:14 | 26 |
| 18:1–17 | 34n15 |
| 20:7 | 83 |
| 22:16 | 79 |

## Romans

| | |
|---|---|
| 1:1 | 21 |
| 1:3 | 55 |
| 1:6 | 22 |
| 1:24 | 132 |
| 1:26 | 132 |
| 1:28 | 132 |
| 2:5 | 133 |
| 2:8 | 133 |
| 4:25 | 132 |
| 5:1 | 115 |
| 5:5 | 91 |
| 6:1–14 | 112 |
| 6:1–11 | 79 |
| 6:12 | 109 |
| 6:13 | 109 |
| 7:7–25 | 114 |
| 8:1–5 | 111 |
| 8:13 | 109 |
| 8:17 | 126, 136 |
| 8:28–30 | 109 |
| 8:28–29 | 111 |
| 8:32 | 132 |
| 9:5 | 55 |
| 10 | 21–22 |
| 10:1 | 21 |
| 10:9 | 21 |
| 10:12–17 | 21 |
| 10:13 | 21 |
| 10:17 | 22, 43 |
| 12:4 | 115 |
| 13:12 | 121n47 |
| 16:25–26 | 66 |

## 1 Corinthians

| | |
|---|---|
| 1–4 | 17–19, 25n10, 30, 34, 131 |
| 1:1 | 21 |
| 1:2 | 109 |
| 1:17 | 135n34 |
| 1:23–24 | 31 |
| 1:17 | 21, 31 |
| 1:18 | 22, 23, 133 |
| 1:20 | 19 |
| 1:21 | 21 |
| 1:23 | 29 |
| 1:24 | 22, 23, 29 |
| 1:26 | 31 |
| 1:26–29 | 132n23 |
| 1:29 | 131 |
| 2:4 | 26 |
| 2:12 | 25 |
| 2:13 | 21 |
| 2:14 | 18 |
| 2:15 | 18 |
| 3:10–15 | 101 |
| 3:21 | 131 |
| 4:1 | 66 |
| 4:1–5 | 30 |
| 4:2 | 32 |
| 4:3 | 31 |
| 4:5 | 133 |
| 4:17 | 18 |
| 5 | 117n32, 120, 127–129, 134, 146 |
| 5:1–13 | 110, 127–128 |
| 5:1 | 129, 134 |
| 5:2 | 135 |
| 5:3 | 135 |
| 5:2–7 | 120 |
| 5:4 | 132, 135 |
| 5:5 | 110, 122n49, 127, 129, 131, 132, 136, 137, 152 |
| 5:6 | 132 |
| 5:6–8 | 120, 120n42 |
| 5:6–7 | 120 |
| 5:7 | 131, 134, 137 |
| 5:8 | 132 |
| 5:9 | 128 |

## 1 Corinthians (continued)

| | |
|---|---|
| 5:11 | 129, 134, 135 |
| 5:13 | 127, 129, 129n11, 134, 135 |
| 6:9–11 | 121 |
| 6:11 | 79, 121 |
| 6:18–20 | 121 |
| 6:19 | 144 |
| 6:20 | 137 |
| 10–11 | 153 |
| 10:1–13 | 129, 136 |
| 10:3–4 | 86 |
| 10:11 | 127, 131, 132 |
| 10:14–22 | 135n34 |
| 10:16–17 | 135n34 |
| 10:16–20 | 86 |
| 10:17 | 62 |
| 11:17–34 | 135n34 |
| 11:20 | 83 |
| 11:23 | 132n25 |
| 11:25 | 67, 132 |
| 11:27 | 67 |
| 11:33 | 83 |
| 12:12 | 32 |
| 12:13 | 79 |
| 12:27 | 115 |
| 15 | 130 |
| 16:2 | 83 |

## 2 Corinthians

| | |
|---|---|
| 1:1 | 21 |
| 2:5–11 | 110 |
| 2:5–12 | 136n35 |
| 2:14 | 112 |
| 4:4 | 132 |
| 5:7 | 24 |
| 5:17 | 112, 121 |
| 10:1–6 | 113 |
| 10:3–5 | 114 |
| 10:4 | 110 |
| 12:7 | 133 |
| 12:8–10 | 111 |
| 13:10 | 150 |

## Galatians

| | |
|---|---|
| 1:1 | 21 |
| 3:1 | 27 |
| 3:26–27 | 79 |
| 5:6 | 119 |
| 5:11–22 | 114 |
| 6:1–2 | 110, 116 |

## Ephesians

| | |
|---|---|
| 1:3, 4 | 56 |
| 4:1 | 121 |
| 4:1–16 | 63 |
| 4:5 | 62 |
| 4:22–24 | 121n47 |
| 5:7–14 | 121n47 |
| 5:25–27 | 122 |
| 6:10–18 | 110, 113 |
| 6:10–20 | 114 |
| 6:12 | 114 |

## Philippians

| | |
|---|---|
| 1:6 | 122, 123 |
| 1:27 | 121n47 |
| 2:10–11 | 107 |
| 2:12–13 | 122 |
| 3:10 | 126 |
| 3:18 | 121n47 |

## Colossians

| | |
|---|---|
| 1:18 | 56 |
| 1:27 | 66 |
| 2:2 | 66 |
| 2:11–14 | 91 |
| 2:12 | 91 |
| 2:12–13 | 79 |
| 3:9 | 121n47 |
| 4:3 | 66 |

## 1 Thessalonians

| | |
|---|---|
| 4:1–8 | 121n47 |
| 5:4–8 | 121n47 |

## 1 Timothy

| | |
|---|---|
| 1:18 | 110 |
| 1:20 | 122n49, 132, 132n27 |
| 3:16 | 55 |
| 5:19–20 | 119n40 |
| 5:20 | 120 |

## 2 Timothy

| | |
|---|---|
| 2:15 | 3, 4 |

## Titus

| | |
|---|---|
| 3:5 | 79, 91 |
| 3:6 | 56 |

## Hebrews

| | |
|---|---|
| 1:1 | 62 |
| 3:12–13 | 110 |
| 4:15 | 123 |
| 9:14 | 63 |
| 10:23–25 | 110 |
| 10:24–25 | 83, 115 |
| 12 | 119 |
| 12:3–11 | 110, 118 |
| 12:3 | 119 |
| 12:5 | 119 |
| 12:6 | 147 |
| 12:8–10 | 119 |
| 12:11 | 119 |
| 12:15 | 120, 151 |
| 12:24 | 66 |
| 13:3 | 96 |
| 13:12–13 | 112 |
| 13:17 | 151 |

## James

| | |
|---|---|
| 1:3–5 | 111 |
| 1:13 | 114 |
| 2:14–26 | 119 |
| 4:7 | 114 |

## 1 Peter

| | |
|---|---|
| 2:11 | 113, 123 |
| 3:20–21 | 79 |
| 4:13 | 126 |
| 5:8–9 | 114 |

## 2 Peter

| | |
|---|---|
| 1:4 | 61 |

## 1 John

| | |
|---|---|
| 2:15–17 | 114 |
| 5:20 | 26 |

## Revelation

| | |
|---|---|
| 1:7 | 107 |
| 2:26 | 106 |
| 3:19 | 118 |
| 19:15 | 106 |
| 21 | 113n19 |
| 22:5 | 105 |
| 22:13 | 7 |

www.ingramcontent.com/pod-product-compliance
Lightning Source LLC
Chambersburg PA
CBHW062046220426
43662CB00010B/1671